I NEED THAT

I NEED THAT

CREATING AND MARKETING PRODUCTS PEOPLE ARE COMPELLED TO BUY

LAURIER MANDIN

graphos

Original Title: I Need That:
Creating and Marketing Products People Are Compelled to Buy
First edition: September, 2024

Published by Graphos Inc.

Hardcover ISBN: 9798335114066
Paperback ISBN: 9798339558163

To Tia.

I've always needed you.

Index

INTRODUCTION

Who Needs This Book?

WHEN I FIRST SET OUT to write this book, I was driven by frustration. Through my quarter century (at the time) of marketing products, I'd witnessed too many brilliant people bleed their retirement funds, exhaust investors, and focus many of the best years of their lives on products that were doomed from the very start.

The real tragedy? With the right knowledge, many of these visionaries could have been building and selling products people genuinely need. This realization led me to a crucial question: What exactly are those "certain things" that separate successful products from failures?

Five years and numerous iterations later (because books, like products, almost always take longer than expected), I'm thrilled to release *I Need That* — a one-of-a-kind guide to creating products that truly deserve a place in buyers' hearts.

This book is the result of extensive research and decades of real-world application. It's designed to be both informative and actionable, equipping you with the knowledge and tools to create and market products that people not only want, but need.

Each chapter delves into a crucial aspect of need-driven product development and marketing, from understanding the psychology of needs to validating your own product ideas with the right people. You'll find a mix of theory, real-world examples, and practical strategies throughout.

At the end of each chapter is a section called "Key Insights." These bullet-point summaries distill the most valuable lessons from the chapter, helping you review the most critical concepts and absorb them more deeply — or go back to at any time for a quick refresher.

Following the Key Insights, you'll see a section titled, "Do These Now for Quick Wins." Each contains bite-sized, actionable tasks designed to be completed in 10–30 minutes.

I strongly encourage you to tackle these items immediately, or schedule them for the very near future. The power of this book lies not just in reading it and remembering a few sparkly new ideas, but in applying its principles *directly* to your work. These quick wins will help you make tangible progress in refining your product strategy, enhancing your marketing approach, and strengthening your connection with customers.

Throughout the book, you'll also find "Innovation Interludes." These are mini case studies of impactful products that exemplify the principles discussed in the same chapter. They offer real-world context and inspiration for your own product development journey.

By the time you've read the final chapter, you'll have a deep understanding of how to identify and fulfill genuine consumer needs. You'll know how to validate your ideas, align your product with customer goals and beliefs, and navigate the challenges of scaling.

Most importantly, you'll have the knowledge and tools to avoid launching a product that fails to resonate with its intended audience.

Remember, this book is only partly for absorbing information

— it's mostly to get *you* taking action. Reading alone won't change how you do anything, or what you get back.

Use it as a workbook, a reference guide, and a source of inspiration. Highlight key passages, jot down your thoughts in the margins, and revisit chapters as you progress in your product development journey. Challenge the ways you think, and extract the best ways to improve what you're doing.

Then, when you adopt the insights and strategies you've learned, you'll have no excuse to launch a failed product.

You'll better understand *why* you're building your product, *who* you're building it for, and *how* to ensure it fulfills a genuine need.

So, let's jump into what it means to create products that people don't just want, but truly need!

CHAPTER 1

Decoding Consumer Needs

In This Chapter:

- *Common pitfalls in product development and marketing*
- *The dangers of underestimating buyer resistance*
- *Real-life examples of product successes and failures*
- *Identifying the true needs of your target audience*

WAY TO GO, product maker*!!!*

The pages that follow hold the proven secrets to selling literally anything to anyone.

Snowballs to Alaskans, steaks tartare to vegans, or Stairmasters to Sherpas! Whatever you are selling, I will teach you how to make masses of people desperately yearn for it.

Yecch.

Is *that* what you were hoping for?

If so, close this book now. Drop it and step away. Please do NOT under any circumstances buy it.

No book, no guru, no one can help you do those things. And if there's a wand or ring or enchanted trapezohedron that can, I hope you never find it.

Because it would be incredibly wrong. That's not how making and selling successful products is meant to work. The process of buying — and not buying — is tied to elaborate systems. And we should all be glad for that.

Since you're still with me, I'll explain.

You're a consumer yourself, a regular buyer of products, right?

Spend a little time walking through a shopping center, browsing Amazon or flipping through a magazine and you might see dozens of things you'd like to own. Flashy jewelry, cool tech gadgets, stylish clothes, trendy home décor items, and useful accessories.

Whatever you're into, every day you come across many products that are beautiful, sparkly, helpful and alluring. A smooth little voice in your head (that sounds exactly like your own) asks, "Hey, wouldn't it be nice?"

Yet usually, you'll buy exactly *none* of those things. Luckily, something intervenes to shut that voice down time after time, stopping it from turning you into a penniless hoarder.

So you carry on looking, touching, coveting — but for the most part not buying.

Until you encounter an item that triggers a completely different response. You find yourself no longer passively and objectively browsing, but willingly enchanted. Your mind begins freely projecting scenes in which a future version of yourself is enjoying the item, taking pride in it, feeling electrified about how this new possession has improved your life. Now the inner voice is screaming: "Hold everything. I NEED that!"

And this time there's no override. You won't accept one. You'll do whatever it takes to make this purchase.

Look around your home and you'll recall how you felt that kind of need for many of the objects you've acquired over the years. Even, and perhaps especially, the more expensive ones.

But why those relatively few things? What brought on the feeling of need that compelled you to buy those specific items and give them a place in your world? Why them and not the gazillion other products you briefly wanted — and then kept walking?

Part of the answer hinges on the millions of messages your brain has completely ignored, at a rate of over 10,000 per day. It's impossible to remember the vast majority of them, because they were immediately blocked, any trace erased forever. Certainly, some of those products could have provided you with great value, and a few might have even transformed the way you do important things.

Sadly, you'll never know for sure.

Most of the objects you've bought are likely commercially successful products. Masses of other people own an exact replica. At some point, a visionary individual (or teams of smart folks) conceived each one, thoughtfully designed it, had it engineered and manufactured to a high level of quality — and somehow succeeded in getting it on your radar. A staggering amount of thought, effort and investment went into the success of every manufactured product you own.

I've been privileged to be part of many product success stories like these over the past three decades, along with, of course, a few that *didn't* make it. Both kinds of experiences have shaped and deepened my understanding of why products do — and don't — catch on.

I'm fairly observant, pretty good at understanding data and recognizing patterns. I am also what psychologists refer to as an empath, meaning I'm both blessed and cursed with an ability to emotionally experience what others are feeling.

While this helps me put on other people's shoes to understand how different buyer types might feel about a new product, it also means I viscerally feel people's pain when things aren't going well.

Like in the case of one entrepreneur I'll call Ken.*

* Client's name and the product description have been changed

KEN'S STORY

A FEW YEARS AGO, Ken glided into my office, the scent of his expensive cologne filling the room. With a fresh barbershop fade in his hair, a chiseled jaw and the frame of a linebacker wrapped in a wrinkle-free suit, his presence was commanding. He looked sort of like a *Wrestlemania* version of Michael Scott from *The Office*.

Ken was carrying the kind of robust aluminum briefcase you'd expect to be stuffed with hundred-dollar bills or high-tech explosives.

He crunched my hand and *very* delicately set his briefcase on the boardroom table. The second option now seemed most likely.

Then he flipped up two clasps and dramatically opened the case to reveal a black foam interior, with custom-cut niches containing several shiny metallic devices.

He wiggled each one free and spaced them evenly across the middle of the table.

Together the devices made up a suite of smartphone accessories, he explained, swappable through a special quick connector. It all seemed somewhat elaborate to me, but the components were aesthetically quite nice, and the build quality looked decent.

As you'd probably guess, the presentation to which I was being treated was far from what any actual customer would likely experience. Ken next pulled out his phone and flipped through photos of the clamshell packaging in which the components were sold, the clear plastic kind that has to be cut open with sharp scissors.

He wrapped up his spiel, and finally began to open up about the predicament that had brought him here. The high-octane pitchman revved down as he shared the product's backstory.

At this point, Ken began to shift uncomfortably in his chair and tugged repeatedly at his necktie like it was trying to choke him. He was struggling to say something.

I felt unsettled too. Ken had been sent to me by an acquaintance whose successful product relaunch I had led — a rescue job after a generalist agency had botched pretty much everything. The trust and expectations set by that referral only made this harder for me.

Ken rubbed his temples and leaned forward, a plea crystallizing in his blue-gray eyes as they locked on mine.

"All right, here it is," he said, his voice hardly a whisper: "I just gotta know, do I pack it in, or take another run at this?"

I didn't have to answer. He read my expression and turned his gaze downward. His full voice came back.

"Yeah. So, I'm screwed, right?"

Right. He would be fine. Ken was clearly a survivor. But the product was hopeless.

Ken still had a solid day job, leading alongside his younger brother a mid-sized electrical engineering firm their father had founded decades ago. While the business was humming along as usual, Ken had never loved the work. This side project was a refreshing escape, and he'd devoted every available moment to it for years.

It was his baby. The dream of massive success had ignited an excitement he'd never felt at the family business. The adventure, the new experiences and the adrenaline rushes were addictive. People constantly asked him about his invention and his ego was as heavily invested as his wallet.

People he respected had swooned over the product, assuring him it was a billion-dollar idea. Ken's own estimation of the addressable market (meaning the specific portion of the *total* market a product can realistically target and serve) bore the kind of flaws I'd seen too many times.

And he'd enthusiastically held up those wild calculations as proof of his pals' accuracy. If just one in a thousand phone owners converted, the revenue would be astronomical.

He'd considered that to be his worst-case scenario, when in fact it was insanely optimistic.

Like many other product makers, he admitted to not having done any real validation. He'd leaned hard into the Steve Jobs quote about consumers never knowing what they want, until you show it to them.

Ken had drunk an ocean of his own Kool-Aid and steadfastly ignored any opposing signals.

He'd made three trips to China, eventually signing on with the manufacturer he distrusted least, and ordered an initial production run of fifty thousand units, which he was now selling on Amazon and through his own online store.

Make that *trying to sell.* An initial marketing-intensive growth trend had slowed to one or two orders a day as the budget ran out. Then one or two a week. Meanwhile, returns became frequent.

The product generally worked, but not as well as a lot of buyers expected. Reviews were mixed and enthusiasm was no longer the dominant theme.

Ken had poured a large chunk of his savings into the industrial designs, injection molds, manufacturing, patents and overseas freight.

He'd hired agencies to run a disappointing Kickstarter and a series of digital ad campaigns. A pricey PR partnership had failed to yield any real media coverage.

It was one disheartening result after another. Ken had burned through a small fortune, and couldn't even guess how many hours of his life he'd sunk into the dream.

All to find out people didn't need the darned thing.

And the friends who'd assured him it was a slam-dunk success? Only a handful of them eventually placed an order after being hounded by Ken and plied with discount codes. His brother dutifully displayed the set he'd bought on his desk at work. Ken had never seen the others use it.

He felt like he'd been duped by the world. People he trusted had lied to him about his idea being a game changer. They didn't even want the damn thing themselves!

It was technically a useful product, he believed.

Were the agencies targeting the wrong people, using the wrong messaging, or selling through the wrong channels?

And if so, what were the right people, messaging, and channels?

In other words, the things he should have known *before* designing or building the product — and definitely before going to market.

But I haven't even told you the worst part.

Ken's product was becoming obsolete. As a third-party accessory to other product makers' devices, the connectivity hardware he had used was being replaced by a faster, higher-bandwidth technology that was not backward compatible. It didn't directly connect with new phones or tablets.

That's known as a fragile dependency and Ken's had shattered.

So there he was, watching a garage full of accessories become less sellable by the day. It was devastating and humiliating.

Ken said he could create an adapter that worked with the new connection, but I reminded him that he would probably still face poor sales.

He shook his head, stood from his chair and demanded, "Then how can I make people *need* it?"

It seemed he was no longer hoping his problem might be solved by better positioning and marketing strategy — but for some form of mass mind manipulation. He wanted that enchanted trapezohedron!

This was far from the first time I'd been asked that kind of thing. Plenty of smart folks believe that marketing can be used to make people buy anything, whether they ought to or not. That a great marketer really *can* sell a Stairmaster to a Sherpa, and make the buyer delighted to have it.

It's not true, and it would be an evil thing to do.

The crater Ken had dug himself into was not one that could be marketed out of.

Why not? Because he had already exposed millions of people to the product. His positioning and branding weren't bad.

The dollar cost to consumers wasn't very high, but prospective buyers had shown that even at a deep discount, not enough were willing to buy. Those who did were often not delighted.

And when even friends or the early adopters on a crowdfunding platform aren't inclined to lay down their cash, the *product* is the problem. Aside from Ken himself, I wondered if a single human being had ever fantasized about his product.

None of this meant the product was terrible, because it wasn't.

What it meant was that few people did in fact need it.

And time had run out. Trying to help solve the problem through revamped marketing would only waste more of his money and almost certainly still end in failure.

The most realistic solution at this point was to liquidate Ken's inventory and carry the lessons forward.

With something people *do* need.

Need, you see, is a thing that has to come from the customer's side. As a marketer, you can tickle to create an itch, but you can't sell a lot of something that doesn't fill a meaningful void in many people's lives. We rarely buy what we simply like or want. Those things are everywhere.

We buy what we feel we *need*.

I only wish Ken's conundrum was less commonplace.

Even some of the world's largest brands have created, built and launched products that far too few people needed. Think of Google Glass, the Apple Newton, the Ford Edsel, the Microsoft Zune,

Facebook's Poke or Amazon's Fire Phone. These are just a handful of many mega-budget faceplants by some of the most successful brands in history.

No, you can't *make* people need your thing.

TWO FATAL MISTAKES

AS WITH KEN'S SITUATION, catastrophes often take root early on and tend to involve the same two mistakes:

1. **Failing to mentally connect your product** with a common and significant need; and
2. **Underestimating human resistance** to adopting it

Do one (or worse, both) and it doesn't matter how much you spend on industrial design, branding, marketing and media. If the product fails to connect with a need that is felt — if it doesn't spark true excitement and desire in a large audience of ideal buyers — it is doomed.

You can sell almost any product to a handful of outliers who are intrigued by the concept and would like to achieve what it promises to do. And you can unload a few more units through freak alignments of timing and unmanaged impulses.

But you'll soon learn that a *few* sales are innumerably too few and "meh" experiences never lead to sustained organic growth. To sell consistently, amass five-star reviews, build a following and achieve ongoing profitability, it takes a whole bunch more.

Your ideal buyer has to feel a powerful desire to own your product and excitedly say, "I need that."

In their head and even out loud.

And when they use the product, the experience has got to be exhilaratingly delightful — to the point they can't help but share it all over the place. Great products do that.

Note that I said "your ideal buyer," and not everyone. Not even

Nutella appeals to everyone. And not every customer who appreciates your product will be an ideal buyer. But those who are will feel like you created it just for them and they'll rave about it. Every highly successful consumer product has millions of ideal buyers — and wide-ranging ways to reach them. (By the way, having millions of ideal buyers in the world doesn't necessarily mean millions will buy the product. Only a fraction of any prospect pool will eventually convert to customers.)

So then, who is your ideal buyer and what does that person need from your product to send them running to the streets evangelizing it? (Or even just adding their contribution to a long list of rave reviews?)

How do you first find out if it's possible to get there with your product?

That's what this book is really about. I've enjoyed working with many entrepreneurs, product teams, innovators and global brands that brought amazing, super-innovative products to the world. Some of those products were Software as a Service (SaaS) applications and others were consumer products, packaged goods, foods or medical devices.

One thing the most successful ones had in common went back to their origin: a vision of helping people live fuller, healthier, happier, or more effective lives. They achieved success by identifying a common, deeply felt need, making an attractive, intuitive product to solve that need — and delighting customers beyond all expectations.

I love to work with clients right from the earliest days of the product development lifecycle, but sometimes that isn't possible. Further down the road, while most clients tend to be doing more things right than Ken was, many will have already made at least a few costly mistakes. Too often they will be deeply invested and too far along to course-correct without sizable new costs. And even at a later stage, a high percentage will still be clueless as to what it will take to achieve sustainable success in the marketplace.

Those are dangerous conditions that absolutely shouldn't be the norm.

Yet they are. Depending on the sector, between 70 and 95 percent of product commercialization efforts will end in failure.[1] I've found that no matter how experienced, schooled, or well-financed they are, the individuals and teams behind new products can seldom concisely articulate their audience's most powerful motivation to buy, let alone a concise strategy for turning their product into the one people will need.

And even if they could, they wouldn't likely understand the psychology behind that need. They'd be unlikely to trigger responses that leave large numbers of the right people fixated on the product. Meaning too few prospects will buy.

The job of this book is to help you understand customer needs as they relate to your product, so that you can recognize the most meaningful needs, make better products, market them effectively — and very intentionally exit that default trajectory to failure.

And while the stories and references I will use are mostly about physical products targeted to consumers, you'll find the principles apply equally to software apps, enterprise SaaS products and new business models. Because we're always marketing to human brains, adoption pulls the same levers of psychology and brain science, regardless of what your customers are buying, how it is sold, or the length of your sales cycle.

Success begins with understanding what it takes to conceive, design and manufacture a product with the rare intrinsic potential to be hugely successful.

Next is knowing how to grab attention and spark persistent desire, in ways you can scale to large audiences.

To create, position and sell products people truly *do need.*

KEY INSIGHTS FROM CHAPTER 1

- To understand true product need, recognize that successful products fulfill a genuine and significant need in the lives of consumers.
- To avoid misguided assumptions, acknowledge the fallacy of believing that marketing alone can create a need for a product where none exists.
- Consumer decision-making is influenced by psychological triggers and genuine desires.
- Two fatal mistakes are often made in product development: failing to connect with a real need and underestimating human resistance to adoption.
- Products that succeed tend to elicit genuine excitement and fulfill a meaningful void in consumers' lives.
- Define your ideal buyer persona and seek to understand what they truly need from your product to become enthusiastic advocates.
- Embrace a vision of creating products that genuinely improve people's lives, leading to sustained success in the marketplace.
- You can gain insights from past product failures, recognizing the importance of aligning product features with genuine consumer needs.

DO THESE NOW FOR QUICK WINS:

Here is where the real progress happens. At the end of each chapter, you'll find action items like these. Do them! They'll help you apply what you've learned, while moving your product forward. Hang on to your notes to refer to in later chapters and see how you progress.

This is an exciting part of your product journey. Have fun with it!

—

FLUSH OUT OBJECTIONS

Reflecting on the story of entrepreneur Ken, sanity-check your own expectations against the likely reality. Have objective people (not friends or family) provided feedback? What objections, concerns or hesitancy signals did these people raise that you may have brushed aside?

Spend 10 minutes thinking about these and write them out for reference as you continue to read this book.

Don't evaluate whether or not the objections are fair or likely to be widely held by prospective buyers — just start to keep track of them! For each objection, note possible ways to resolve it, disregarding for now the cost or effort the solution would take.

RESET YOUR MARKET EXPECTATIONS

Have you created projections for the size of your addressable market, whether in a notebook or in a formal plan? If so, put on the hat of a critical potential investor and look for potential flaws in how you arrived at your sales numbers.

No need to solve the flaws yet. Your job is to flush them out, and to create a reference to build on as you continue to explore.

If you haven't yet set expectations, do it now and put them in writing. You'll be glad you did.

CHAPTER 2

Birth of a Product Enthusiast

In This Chapter:

- *Personal stories of product obsession*
- *The power of emotional connections in driving product desire*
- *The role of innovation and iteration in successful product development*
- *Factors contributing to product-market fit and building a loyal following*

MANY OF US CAN REMEMBER the first time we were obsessed with a consumer product.

Can you? When you didn't just like or desire something being marketed to you, but felt a powerful and even enjoyable *need* to own it.

It usually starts out with a *wait, what?* moment and grows tentacles that dominate your thoughts and dreams, like the infatuation after a first kiss. (It's the same chemicals at work.)

The first time a product did that for me was in the spring of 1984. I was fifteen years old and my singular focus in life was competitive cycling. While my friends' bedrooms were decorated with posters of Indiana Jones, Rambo and bikini girls, I papered my walls with magazine clippings of pro bicycle racers.

Living in a small town, I trained mostly alone on my road bike, between the competitions I could finagle my father to drive me to. My obsession was largely his doing. Dad was a cycling aficionado before me, and for over a decade he organized (and usually won) an annual road race starting and ending in our hometown.

I logged every training ride in a paper journal, with the help of a terrible analog speedometer. It was a clunky contraption, driven by a plastic roller that spun against the sidewall of my bike's front tire. The data was imprecise and the speedometer's cable and mechanics created drag, making my rides less enjoyable and undoubtedly a little slower. The drive wheel had a tendency to misalign, wearing itself out and chewing up my tire's sidewall, so I constantly had to fiddle with it. It was infuriating and only moderately preferable to noodling out distances on a map. But I was a teenaged metrics junkie, and the data gave me a gauge of my progress as well as something to shoot for on the next ride. I liked to know how fast, not just how far I was going.

I eventually grew weary of fussing with it, at a time when cycling in general was losing its luster for me. The riding season was short where I lived, and roadsides were strewn with debris that punctured my tires. My performance had reached a plateau, and I wasn't winning any races. The cost-benefit balance had been trending negatively — as was my outlook. I found myself riding less and being distracted by new things.

One day, after a tough ride involving two flat tires, a bottle thrown from a passing truck, and a close race with a vicious farm dog, I finally decided I'd had enough. I was done with cycling.

I had thought about it a lot lately, and could hardly believe I'd wasted so much time on something completely pointless. Every ride, I'd end up right back where I'd started — except tired and hungry. You couldn't pay me to work that hard, and there I was doing it for free.

Amazing that I wasn't maimed or killed out there.

Dumbest sport on earth. Only possible thing dumber was doing it in my part of the world. I was voluntarily being the frog in a game of Frogger.

Well, this frog got wise.

It was time to move on to something more rewarding.

I flopped on the sofa and noticed a fresh copy of *Bicycling* magazine had just arrived in the mail.

I picked it off the end table, glanced at the cover — and despondently gave it a toss. I enjoyed a powerful chuckle at just how done I was with that. One hundred percent disinterested.

The magazine skittered on the floor, pages fluttering for a brief moment before it settled, open.

And something amazing caught my eye.

** Record scratch. Choir of angels.**

Whoa.

It was my first-ever look at the new Cateye Solar "cyclocomputer."

I swayed briefly to and fro, sucking in a cautious breath, like a mountaineer teetering on a precipice.

Then I snatched up the magazine and stared at the page.

SO. Not. Fair.

This sleek, wedge-shaped unit was a thing of beauty.

That photo had done something weird inside my brain, and I scanned the copy points to find out more about this sexy wonder of technology.

There was plenty to take in. To start with, the cyclocomputer's digital display could show my speed at a glance, in oversized digits. A few other bike computers existed, and they all had smallish displays. But this one's screen was huge, and made use of all that real estate to go big with the speed — and simultaneously provide a second metric. Stopwatch, trip distance, average speed, maximum speed, odometer — wondrously, even how many revolutions per minute my pedals were turning.

All with 99.9% accuracy. It achieved this voodoo magic through contactless magnetic sensors, meaning no roller drag would ever slow me down again.

But hold on. Had I not just decided, painfully and after plenty of deliberation, that I was *gonzo* from cycling? We'd broken up, and it was the smartest thing I'd ever done.

While that was technically true, it wasn't a fully informed decision. I had retired from the *old* way.

The judges went upstairs for review. It took 1.5 seconds before they presented their unanimous conclusion.

** 80s action movie music.**

I was back.

The Cateye Solar was expensive, and I didn't have much money. But man, I needed that thing.

So the price tag was just a speed bump.

For the next while, I trotted Dad's electric lawnmower door-to-door, mowing people's lawns for $10 each. (Not bad in those days, except that my offer included both front and back yards — and it seemed the takers were always folks with double lots and a jungle of grass.)

After school I would dash home, grab the mower and chop turf until it became too dark to tell the grass I'd cut from what I hadn't. It wasn't many days before I had what I needed and excitedly mailed off the order form with my bank draft.

While I waited for it to arrive, I flipped to that ad again and again, visualizing myself flying around corners and powering up hills, superhuman with that amazing Cateye Solar mounted at the center of my handlebars. The fantasies replayed constantly, and I thoroughly enjoyed each one.

And all these years later, I can still smell the exotic factory-fresh scent of the electronics when I opened the box and squeaked those shiny new components from their Styrofoam nests.

I was entirely crazy enough to believe an electronic device would make me a faster cyclist. Even crazier is that it did. I rode longer, harder and more frequently than I ever had, with all that 99.9% accurate data providing a host of personal targets to challenge on every ride. I started winning races again.

It was fun showing the thing off to curious friends and relatives — simultaneously flaunting the technology and my cycling stats on the biggest liquid crystal display anyone had ever seen. And, straight out of the future, it was solar powered.

Through long Canadian winters, to simulate riding on the road I used something else that was new at the time called a wind trainer: a heinously noisy contraption that clamped to the front fork of my bike while my rear tire spun four resistance turbines and a flywheel for inertia.

The front wheel with the main sensor magnet had to come off to use the trainer, but luckily Cateye had introduced a kit with longer wires to reach an additional magnet on the rear one. I sprang for it in a heartbeat.

And so, when the roads got seriously icy and it was too cold for even an irrational Canadian teenager to ride outside, I turned to grinding away on that rig indoors while my Walkman blasted Def Leppard and Guns N' Roses. I fixated on the Cateye Solar's display with eyes stinging from sweat, while those turbines roared like a 747 on takeoff. My family members couldn't have loved it when I trained, but they knew I was focused and keeping out of trouble.

The data continuously validated my effort, baiting me toward my next personal best. As helpful as the Cateye Solar had proven on the road, it was even more valuable in my basement self-torture chamber.

At the time, solar powered rechargeable batteries were in their infancy and when the winter sun became too weak to keep my cyclocomputer charged, I discovered the bathroom light could do the job.

Until the time I left it too close to a hundred-watt bulb.

I returned the next morning, pumped for my ride — to find my beloved Cateye Solar grotesquely disfigured. What was once a shimmering silvery display had turned a nightmarishly bubbled purple. I held it like an expired pet and convulsed in sobs.

I retreated to my bedroom and turned the lights off, hoping for a cataclysmic mass extinction event.

The next morning, having accepted that my Cateye Solar was still fatally warped and the world had failed to end, I went out and applied for an after-school job packing groceries at a local supermarket. (It was January, and there was no fresh snow to shovel, never mind grass to mow.) I took my dad's pre-interview advice and confidently told the store's manager I wasn't afraid of hard work. I was hired on the spot and immediately began persuading my new co-workers to let me take some of their shifts. I *really* needed the money, I said, letting them wonder if my family was short of food. They wouldn't have appreciated the real reason.

And as soon as I got my first paycheck, I sent away the mail order form that was waiting pre-completed in an addressed envelope.

I desperately needed that Cateye Solar.

Of course, in a literal sense, I did not. It served no essential purpose to me and I could have gone on to live a happy and complete life without it.

But I needed it to follow my dreams and to continue toward the fulfillment of a desired future state.

And eventually, to become who I am today. While that Cateye Solar helped me become a strong racer on the road and in the velodrome, that was temporary and much less important than I thought at the time. More meaningfully, it committed me to a path of lifelong fitness, boosted my confidence and cemented focus and consistency that would make me better at everything I do.

All from a little plastic product made in Japan.

I never did stop cycling, but the way I did it evolved. In the early 1990s I discovered indoor group classes using commercial stationary bikes. With great music, motivating instructors and a room filled with like-minded workout partners, it was vastly more enjoyable than grinding away alone all winter. I was hooked from the first ride. The only downsides were that I had to go to a fitness club several times a week to do it and there weren't any metrics to see if I was progressing.

ENTER THE IPHONE

MARKETERS LOVE overnight success stories. And we all want our next product's trajectory to be something like the iPhone's.

On January 9, 2007, I watched Steve Jobs introduce the iPhone, rekindling the very product-lust I'd felt nearly a quarter-century before over the Cateye Solar.

It felt as if Jobs was talking directly to me about the failings of my current smartphone, a Palm Treo, with its puny screen, horrendous web browsing and infuriating stylus. Nearly every iPhone feature Jobs demonstrated hit me right in the needs. Additional functions that were not mobile phone standards, like an integrated iPod and direct downloads from iTunes and the App Store were icing on the supreme deluxe cake. For my now grown-up mind (about as developed as it was likely to get), this was a new height in product obsession.

I turned to my wife, who was watching the live stream beside me and we said in unison, "I need one."

When the iPhone arrived in Canada, we sat together on a shopping mall floor, in a long line of people waiting for the shops to open, each of us fantasizing about how our lives would soon improve.

And in a multitude of ways, they all did. It's now hard to even remember how we did so many things before the iPhone. Anyone born later than 2002 or so will never know!

Suddenly, we could accomplish so much more away from our desks, perform tasks with greater ease — and literally achieve outcomes that were not even possible before.

The iPhone soon touched virtually every part of my own life, from tracking my wife's contractions before the births of our two daughters to controlling smart devices throughout our home and videoconferencing with teams around the world, all via a pocket-sized wireless device. Leaving home for the day without it now is more alarming than forgetting my wallet.

What irks Apple-haters about the iPhone is how much innovation credit it gets, despite not being the first smartphone, or even the first touchscreen smartphone. But that was never the point. In 2007 there were plenty of other smartphones, all racing to make better built-in keyboards and sell at a lower price.

Steve Jobs went the opposite way. He built his entry with no keyboard — and priced it at three times as much as competing phones. He made the technology work more intuitively, more reliably, with greater ease and vastly more pleasurably. And then he revealed it in such a way that millions of people immediately felt they needed it. Within a few years, every phone you saw looked and functioned very much like an iPhone.

That is the point.

"NEVER RIDE SOLO AGAIN"

AS A FORMER TRIATHLETE, John Foley was hooked on indoor cycling classes just like I was. But as president of bookseller Barnes & Noble's eCommerce department and the father of two young children, he was struggling to make it regularly to his workout sessions. He needed something better.

Foley was engaged in a losing battle to position Barnes & Noble's

Nook eReader against the Amazon Kindle. B&N was thought of as an old-school bookstore chain, while Amazon, having started out as an online discount bookseller, was now seen as the future of reading.

One day in a group cycling class, Foley contemplated how the Nook and Kindle were hardware and software platforms for consuming reading content at home. Why can't there be a platform to deliver motivational fitness content directly to workout equipment in your home?[1]

Through his work in the tech sector, Foley had observed that wireless streaming technology and internet bandwidth had become fast and accessible enough to provide quality live classes in any major city. The infrastructure had matured to a critical point.

Knowing this, he envisioned the product that would become Peloton (the French name for a group of bicycle racers) and pitched it to some prospective co-founders. He assembled a team who would build bike prototypes, develop the software and integrate music with the classes.

As with many new products, not much went smoothly or easily. After an early prototype was delivered from a service bureau 40 percent too big, Peloton bought a 3D printer and used it to prototype over 100 iterations of 20 different parts.[2]

Like Apple, Peloton would be vertically integrated; building the hardware, developing the software, and selling directly to consumers. The bike would use a belt drive instead of a chain, creating its resistance through contactless magnets that would render it nearly silent — perfect for people in apartments or needing to work out early without waking their household.

Foley knew a good product is one that improves many people's lives — not just the inventor's. Because he and his co-founders felt they needed Peloton so badly, he was certain others would too. He didn't need more evidence. But skipping marketplace validation created a worrisome credibility gap for other, very important people.

He expected raising money would be a walk in the park with such a great idea, backed by his Harvard degree and 20 years of leadership experience.

It turned out to be anything but. More than 400 institutional investors and thousands of angel investors gave his pitch a hard pass, seeing the concept as too complicated and, being completely unproven, much too risky. Many had been spooked away from connected tech combinations by Google's struggles with Nest — a much simpler product. Others were fearful of Foley's vertical integration plans, which would be highly ambitious for any company, much less a startup in a nonexistent space.[3]

Foley later admitted that he and his co-founders expected tens of thousands of people would throw money at Peloton. "Instead, it was crickets."[4]

After a year and a half, with a handful of angel investors on board, he went to Kickstarter — not to fund machining and manufacturing as the campaign claimed, but to finally validate the concept with consumers.

In 2014, Peloton began shipping its first at-home connected bikes for $2,245, plus $39 a month for the platform subscription. Foley's team had recruited ten of New York's top indoor cycling instructors to lead the classes and opened showrooms in major cities across the United States where people could experience the quality bikes, along with sexy clip-in shoes, the giant touchscreens — and the one-of-a-kind classes.

For Peloton, this hands-on, feet-in experience turned out to be the key to success. People had watched cinematic videos and read about the bike's high quality online, but that didn't generate enough sales. Only clipping in and experiencing a Peloton class could convey the entire concept — and solidify the need.

It certainly was not for everyone, though, and that's part of the magic. Whenever the right kind of person tried Peloton, they needed it immediately. And many did.

As you've probably guessed, I was one of them.

That kind of people were thrilled by the promise they'd "Never Ride Solo Again." Once they started buying, riding and sharing about it, Peloton went viral, attracting evangelistic fans that included Sir Richard Branson, Kate Hudson and the Obamas.[5]

Even if you're the diametric opposite of a Peloton fan (I've met many), you have to appreciate John Foley's vision and persistence. Although it took a long time, he kept trying new things until he found the right combination of buyer, positioning and conversion mechanisms.

Only then could Peloton kick into high gear.

What drives my own product obsessions is often technology. For others it may be a hobby, like fishing, crafting or cooking. Or a need to safeguard something precious.

But regardless of the use case, when you escalate desire for your product to the level of an obsessive need that sparks fantasy in the minds of right-fit buyers, success is nearly unstoppable.

The coming chapters are about that: how brands, inventors and product teams can harness the mechanisms that transform prospective buyers into obsessive product enthusiasts.

To do that, you must first understand what those mechanisms are.

KEY INSIGHTS FROM CHAPTER 2

- People often experience a powerful and intense desire, beyond mere liking or wanting, to own a product.
- An obsession with a product can develop from a small itch that grows to a dominating infatuation, sparking emotional connections and dreams associated with its ownership.
- Products that hold personal significance and align with a person's hobbies and interests, or improve personal performance, can trigger a strong need for ownership.
- Innovative product ideas often undergo numerous prototypes, iterations and adjustments before achieving the right fit for the market.
- Achieving the right combination of buyer, positioning and conversion mechanisms is crucial to reaching product-market fit.
- Products that fundamentally change how people live, work, or interact can trigger widespread adoption and obsession, even if the product isn't the first of its kind.
- Successful products prioritize intuitive, reliable and enjoyable experiences to drive obsession and widespread adoption.
- When a product addresses specific needs and desires effectively, it can generate evangelistic fans who share their positive experiences with others.
- This chapter introduces the concept of harnessing mechanisms that turn potential buyers into passionate enthusiasts for a product.

DO THESE NOW FOR QUICK WINS:

PERSONAL PRODUCT OBSESSION REFLECTION

Take 5 minutes to reflect on a personal experience where you felt an intense need for or obsession with a consumer product, similar to the author's experiences with the Cateye Solar cyclocomputer or the iPhone.

Write down the factors that contributed to your obsession, such as product features, design, functionality, or emotional resonance. What product fantasies did you have? How can your own product evoke similar desire and reveries in your audience?

NEED IDENTIFICATION SPRINT

Spend 15 minutes brainstorming potential product ideas or improvements based on unmet needs or frustrations you've experienced in your own life or observed in others.

Use the author's story as inspiration for identifying areas where innovative solutions could make a meaningful impact.

CUSTOMER EMPATHY MAPPING

Create a customer empathy map to better understand the thoughts, feelings, and motivations of your target audience, drawing insights from the author's description of his own journey as a consumer.

Include bullet lists of WHO we are empathizing with, that customer's GOALS, what they SEE in the marketplace, what we hear and imagine they SAY, what they DO now, what they HEAR others say, and what they THINK and FEEL (broken down to current pains and potential gains).

Identify key touchpoints and pain points in the customer journey where your product could address unmet needs or create moments of delight.

CATEGORY REDEFINITION EXERCISE

Look at a product category you're working on (e.g., smart-watches, home security, meal kits).

List the top 3–5 features that competitors focus on (e.g., for smartwatches: battery life, health data tracking, messaging).

Now, channel your inner Steve Jobs and spend 15 minutes imagining how you'd redefine this category:

1. What are customers really seeking but not getting? (For iPhone: intuitive touch, easy web browsing)
2. What new features could make old metrics less relevant? (iPhone: App Store, visual voicemail)
3. How can you shift from functional to emotional benefits? (iPhone: from "make calls" to "stay amazingly connected")
4. What's a totally new use case you could enable? (iPhone: "Your entire music library in your pocket")

After this exercise, you'll have a fresh perspective on product innovation — not just improving its standing within a category, but redefining it to align with unmet needs.

This is how you begin to turn "that'd be nice to have" into "I NEED that."

Harnessing mechanisms that lead to product obsession requires a deep understanding of user needs, innovative design and effective communication to create a product that not only fulfills a desire but becomes an integral part of users' lives.

CHAPTER 3

Why "Want" Isn't Good Enough

In This Chapter:

- *The limitations of relying on customer "wants" in product success*
- *The 10X Revelation and its implications for product development*
- *Overcoming friction and resistance in the buyer's journey*
- *Strategies for elevating product desire to the level of "need"*

YOU MIGHT REMEMBER THAT one of the two biggest mistakes innovators make in developing a new product is in underestimating buyer resistance.

And most of us could create a nearly endless list of products we like and desire but will probably never own. Some of those items would be intriguing but frivolous and others would be redundant to what we already use for the activities we do. You won't buy even the most mind-blowing new mattress if the one you sleep on is three months old and working fine.

Your list might include things that are impractical or extravagant, or that don't have a place in your life — like rare artwork, exotic cars, or a yacht. There are limits to how much stuff we have room to store and enough time to use. And every one of us has finite resources.

You can't possibly buy all the things you want, so you long ago learned to dismiss the vast majority of wants. It's incumbent on all of us to keep that dismissal threshold low, and we generally do.

When was the last time you saw a random new product advertised online, clicked through to the shop, pulled out your credit card — and made the purchase?

Like, maybe *never*.

As someone who has spent three decades studying behavioral economics, managing millions of dollars in ad spend and sifting through marketing analytics, I can tell you that the "see-click-buy" sequence I described there is a real but relatively infrequent scenario.

Yet it's what many product creators somehow expect will happen for their product — a high percentage of the time. When it doesn't, they're gobsmacked. *What went wrong?*

Some new products, when promoted enticingly to the right audience, do sell very easily. It's great fun to be part of. But those are the unicorns.

You're selling to humans, no matter what you're selling. Humans don't like gambling their hard-earned money on a purchase. We feel real pain when spending money (an effect proven by brain imaging) and become paralyzed by pressure or risk.

Studies show most people prefer a guaranteed $100 over a 50% chance at $300, even though the second option yields an average outcome of $150. And the lowest-risk competitor to your product is never a similar product: it is the painless, no-cost and entirely risk-free option of sticking with what they already have.

Impulse buys happen all the time, even for larger-ticket items. Most often they occur in environments like Costco or on Amazon, where product makers pay a premium to have their wares seen at exactly the right moment. They opt to take on most of the risk through those known, liked and trusted distributors' extremely liberal return policies. These are expensive trade-offs that without careful planning can gobble up a product's profit potential.

All buyers are invested in what they are currently using, through time and money they have already spent — two things consumers tend to overvalue for a long time afterwards. The money in buyers' pockets today is precious. Your new product is a risk — and your online store could be a scam. You are unknown, and stranger danger is even more terrifying online than in real life.

Forces of resistance like these are called "friction," and they don't just drag.

They push back hard, against every selling effort you make.

THE 10X REVELATION

IN ORDER TO OVERCOME all the friction and costs of abandoning existing solutions, your product has to be more than incrementally better than other options the buyer is considering.

How much better?

Most novice product makers (and even some pretty smart veterans I have known) would guess that twice as good ought to be plenty. I mean, that's 100 percent better than whatever the buyer has now!

But that's a major underestimation. More realistically, a product should be at least ten times better across key benchmarks than whatever buyers are currently using.

At first this might seem preposterous. And that sentiment is part of why so many new products fail — because their makers start out by arrogantly setting the bar much too low. (Underestimating human resistance to adoption is fatal mistake number two for a reason.)

But why is 10X the magical threshold?

Harvard Business School professor John T. Gourville developed a formula to explain why this factor (the genesis of which Gourville himself attributes to former Intel CEO Andrew Grove) applies in getting a customer to embrace a new product:

"Consumers overvalue the existing benefits of an entrenched product by a factor of three, while developers overvalue the new benefits of their innovation by a factor of three.

The result is a mismatch of nine to one, or 9X, between what innovators think consumers desire and what consumers really want."[1]

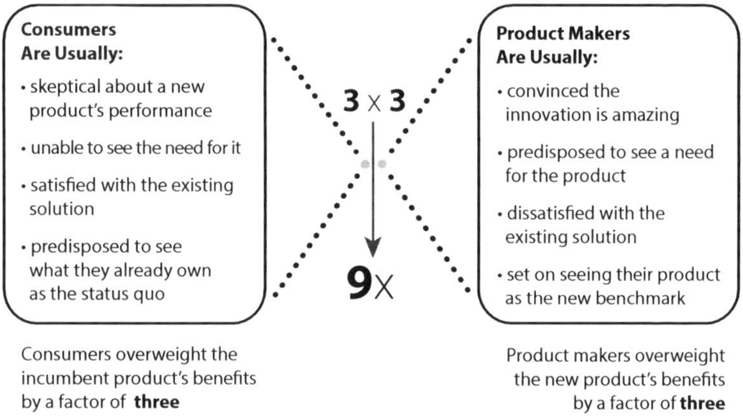

***Figure 3-1. The 10X Rule for Product Adoption:** Gourville's theory explains why new products need to be 10X better than existing solutions. Innovators tend to overvalue their product's benefits by 3X while consumers tend to overvalue their current solution by 3X, creating a 9X gap. To overcome this mismatch and drive adoption, a new product must offer at least a 10X improvement.*

If you've been involved in launching one or more products, you can surely give a nod to these assertions.

Inventors and product teams tend to overweight the new product's benefits by (at minimum) a factor of three across relevant benchmarks. Like our friend Ken, these people are blindingly close to the product and have consumed barrels of distortional Kool-Aid. In their minds, you'd be crazy not to buy it.

But back in the real world, call us crazy. Here, friction is again at least three times what seems reasonable to you well-intentioned but highly biased product makers.

Behavioral economics studies continuously reinforce that consumers are not predictable or even rational beings when it comes to purchasing decisions and that they tend to overvalue sunk costs, which is all money they've previously invested in solving a given problem.

They may experience "lock-in" with their existing ways, making it difficult, complicated or stressful to transition to something new.

So, their bank balance and the status quo are two things they're pained to part with — the same two things you're angling to take away.

What this means is that to reliably overcome these combined dynamics (going beyond a stalemate, which always ends in inaction) a product has to be at least ten times better, in ways that matter to the buyer, than whatever solution they currently use. I say "reliably" because you'll have to achieve this feat not once or twice, but many thousands of times to be successful.

My Cateye Solar wasn't just marginally better than the analog speedometer I was already using. It was much better looking and far more accurate, was more enjoyable to use, told me way more things, and didn't harm my bike tire or slow me down.

For me as a consumer, the status quo sucked. The Cateye Solar was way, *way* better.

On a scalable basis, in order to break through all the friction, resistance and fear of risking money to adopt something new, it's never been nearly enough for buyers to see the product as an interesting nice-to-have. Or even something they might briefly want.

They've got to feel they *need* it.

But what does "need" really mean?

KEY INSIGHTS FROM CHAPTER 3

- A common mistake in product development is underestimating the resistance buyers have towards adopting new products.
- People have limited resources, space and time to accommodate new products, so wants and nice-to-haves don't stand a chance.
- Impulse purchases are relatively rare and buyers are risk averse, preferring a guaranteed (or known) outcome over a gamble.
- New products are perceived as risks, especially when compared to existing solutions in which buyers have invested time and money.
- "Friction" refers to the resistance, challenges and uncertainties buyers face when considering a new product.
- A product must be at least 10X better than existing solutions to consistently motivate a scalable number of buyers.
- There is often a mismatch of perception between innovators (product developers) and consumers regarding the desirability and value of a new product. Inventors and product teams tend to overestimate the benefits of their new product due to their close involvement and biases. Consumers overvalue the money they have already spent (sunk costs) and are hesitant to part with their bank balance and the status quo.
- To succeed, a product must make buyers feel like they *need* it rather than merely want it.

DO THESE NOW FOR QUICK WINS:

FRICTION IDENTIFICATION

Spend 20 minutes identifying potential points of friction in your customer's journey, drawing insights from this chapter's discussion of buyer resistance.

Consider factors such as perceived risk, inertia, and the tendency to overvalue existing solutions, and brainstorm strategies for mitigating these sources of friction.

YOUR 10X BENCHMARKING ANALYSIS

Evaluate your product against key benchmarks and compare its performance to existing solutions in the market. To identify benchmarks, think about what can be measured, and compare your product with outcomes from other options. Do your best to be objective. Ideally, have an ideal user who is not a friend or relative do the measuring.

Use the 10X Revelation as a guiding principle to assess whether your offering provides at least ten times the value across relevant dimensions, such as efficiency, effectiveness, time spent or quality of user experience. If it does not, how can it be improved?

Chart out the ways, and estimate the cost and effort to achieve each one. Relative to these resources, how much is your product's success worth to you? Rank them based on the ratio of positive impact to what it would take to make such an improvement.

VALUE PROP REFINEMENT

Refine your value proposition to clearly communicate how your product or service addresses the unique challenges and aspirations of your target audience.

Emphasize the transformative impact of your offering and highlight its ability to deliver exponential value compared to existing solutions.

BEHAVIORAL ECONOMICS WORKSHOP

Organize a workshop with your team to collaboratively explore key principles of behavioral economics and their implications for your product development and marketing efforts. Share this chapter content in advance. (You might give each team member a copy of the book — or pass your own around. Just make sure everyone understands the concepts.)

Freely discuss concepts such as loss aversion, status quo bias and the endowment effect (how people place a higher value on an item that they own than they would give that same item if they did not own it), and brainstorm strategies for overcoming these cognitive biases in the context of your product. These are real barriers you will face, and solving them now will put you in a much better position out the gates.

Share with your team the total addressable market you noted after reading Chapter 1.

Discuss how your earlier calculations are affected based on the 10X Revelation, considering a realistic level of triple the expected customer resistance and the probability that you have also over-anticipated customer desire by a factor of three.

Harness teamwork to revise the size of this market and make your expectations for your potential share of it more realistic.

CHAPTER 4

The Most Powerful Word in Marketing

In This Chapter:

- *The significance and ubiquity of the word "need" in marketing*
- *The evolving perception of needs in modern society*
- *The power of "need" in driving consumer purchasing decisions*
- *The importance of customers expressing their need for a product*

NEED.

That fascinating monosyllabic word appears on the internet about 13.3 trillion times and over 500 times in this book. It's a word we all use daily, in a multitude of contexts:

"What do you **need** from me?"
"We're in **need** of money."
"I **need** sleep."
"Novelty is a fundamental **need**."
"You **need** to get this done today."
"I **need** to get one of those."

What does "need" really mean?

With such ubiquity and so many linguistic uses, you might suppose that, like similarly prevalent words in the English language, the meaning of "need" might be widely variable depending on the context. But it really isn't.

Let's look at the *Dictionary.com* definitions:

noun
a requirement, necessary duty, or obligation.
a lack of something wanted or deemed necessary.
urgent want, as of something requisite.

verb (used with object)
to have need of; require.

verb (used without object)
to be under an obligation
to be necessary

Through the various usages, all of those are pretty much the same thing. A must-have. A requirement. A necessity. A non-negotiable.

Seems any way you look at it, a need is just how you immediately think of it: a need.

And not only is it a word you've heard a lot, but you've been hearing it more and more often all your life. For real.

Based on a sample of one million books in English, the word "need" currently occurs about once every 2,500 words — about four times as frequently as it did two centuries ago — and nearly twice as often as it did in 1969 when I was born. If you include "needs," (with an "s") the frequency goes up to once every 1,600 words and the increase in usage since 1800 becomes six-fold.

By comparison, "want," and "desire," which were once both more popular in terms of literary usage, have each taken quite a different trajectory.[1]

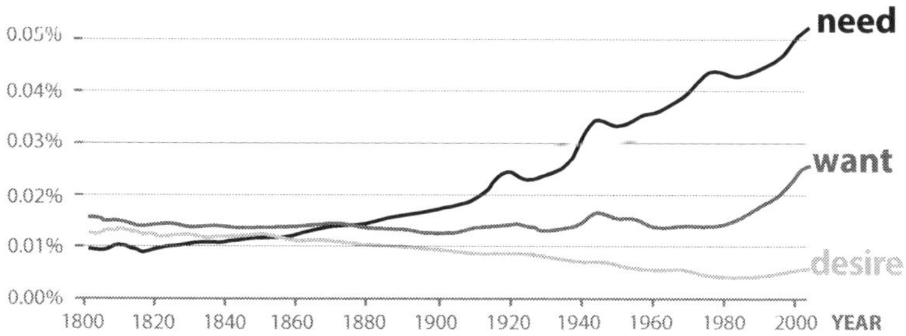

Figure 4.1. Word Frequency Trends 1800-2000: ***"Want," "need," and "desire" in literature. Initially similar, "need" surged 6X by 2000, overtaking the others. "Desire" declined, while "want" remained steady until 1980. These shifts reflect evolving consumer language and perceived necessities over two centuries.***

What's going on here? Do people genuinely *need* that many more things now than we have historically? Do we just imagine we do, or have we significantly altered our perception of what we need compared to what we merely want?

In reality, as we've become wealthier and less in truly dire need, we've continuously recalibrated our entire frame of reference for what it means to need something. And we think and talk about our needs much more frequently than ever before, especially in difficult times. (In Fig. 4.1, notice how the use of "need" surged during the two world wars and the 1973 oil crisis, all followed by a correction.)

Back In 1800, "need" primarily referred to basic survival requirements. Today, it often encompasses a much broader range of goods and services perceived as essential for modern life.[2]

In Samuel Johnson's 1755 *A Dictionary of the English Language*, which was widely used in 1800 (and language usage tends to lag behind dictionary definitions), "need" was defined as:

1. Exigency; pressing difficulty; necessity.
2. Want; distressful poverty.[3]

Kind of similar to how we define it today, but notably heavier on the urgency and typical Georgian-era bleakness.

The evolution of the word "need" through the last two centuries reflects major changes in society, economy, and consumer behavior. Indoor plumbing would be hard for us to live without, but was considered a luxury item a hundred years ago. My grandparents' farm had an outhouse and a well with a hand pump when I was a kid, and until quite a few years later, they didn't feel they needed anything else. In the 1970s, an air-conditioned vehicle was something to brag about. Today, even the most affordable vehicles include A/C as a standard feature. If it gets hot where you live, you need that.

A number of factors have affected how our perceptions and priories have changed. Marketing has continuously reshaped what consumers perceive as needs, contributing to a scarcity mindset, even in times of unprecedented abundance.[4]

More and better things are considered part of an "ordinary" life. At the same time, globalization has led to a more uniform, often elevated, standard of what constitutes a need across all the world's cultures.[5]

As a highly evolved species, we like to believe we know the difference between our needs, our wants and our nice-to-haves. What's interesting is that when we choose to say we "need" something, whether justified or not, we have already assigned that thing a heightened level of priority. And it tends to stick.

Even when we promote something quite frivolous to the level of "need," we elevate its importance, potentially even surpassing much more important things.

Sounds a little crazy, right?

But in behavioral economics, as in human interactions and politics, it is always a mistake to underestimate the power and impact of words. (I'll get to something else very interesting about this in a bit.)

The words we say, read and hear do matter, and they leave a mark.

All of us have had other people's words stick in our heads for years. I clearly remember specific words my parents, grandparents, teachers and other influential people — as well as a few minor figures — said when I was a child. You probably can too. Someone's word choices, whether motivating, inspirational, or even debilitating, altered the course of your life.

This one word — "need" — has become hard-coded into our individual drive for well-being: our competitiveness, happiness and ultimately our survival. Your mother and teachers used it when something was imperative. Believe me, it sank in. And it became tethered to critical needs in your real world.

Our brain recognizes critical needs in a nanosecond, and responds to them more rapidly than we can even comprehend. The instant we perceive that something is a need, we mentally authorize that thing to overcome virtually any amount of friction and will do literally whatever it takes to rationalize, action and ultimately fulfill that need.

In my teenaged mind, I genuinely needed that Cateye Solar, so I worked my tail off until I got it. (Twice.) As an adult, I willingly sat for hours on a cold tile floor waiting to buy an overpriced smartphone — with a perfectly functional one in my pocket. I had other, more necessary, things to do and buy that went on the back burner. My actions belie how badly I needed those objectively frivolous items.

And you can bet I defended those decisions.

Because once we've made a choice based on perceived need, we'll do that. Even when tests using transcranial magnetic stimulation manipulate volunteer subjects' choices, the same people will vigorously insist they consciously made those choices and stand behind them. This rationalize-and-defend behavior happens automatically and imperceptibly, regardless of whether or not an action was driven by our own decision-making processes.

And the most powerful driver of our actions is need.

Need is the magic elixir of marketing and is at the heart of every product success story.

You can't possibly buy all the things you want. Even if you had all the time and money in the world, you'd be silly to try.

But you'll always find a way to get the things you've come to feel you need.

And that's why "need" is the most powerful word in marketing.

But of course, like with all things powerful or magical, there is a catch.

The word's full power is not unleashed in keynotes, marketing copy, or messaging.

Its maximum impact does not come from how authoritatively you say it, how often, or how big a megaphone you use. In fact, doing so as a marketer will cause its power to melt away.

It only works when your buyers feel, think and say it *themselves*.

KEY INSIGHTS FROM CHAPTER 4

- The word "need" is used extensively in various contexts, but its core meaning remains consistent: a must-have, a necessity, a requirement.

- The word "need" is used more frequently now than in the past, reflecting changes in how we perceive and communicate our needs over time.

- As society becomes wealthier, the perception of what constitutes a need has evolved.

  Our frame of reference for needs has changed as we've become less focused on survival.

- When something is perceived as a "need," it gains heightened priority and importance in our minds, often leading us to rationalize and fulfill that need regardless of obstacles.

- Words, including "need," hold significant power and have a direct impact on behavior, both in marketing and human interactions.

  Saying "I need that" creates a psychological connection that solidifies a desire as a *de facto* need that people will rationalize and defend.

DO THESE NOW FOR QUICK WINS:

NEED DISCOVERY BRAINSTORMING SESSION

Organize a 30-minute brainstorming session with your team to identify unmet needs within your target market.

Encourage creative thinking and explore unconventional solutions to address these needs effectively.

NEED-ORIENTED CUSTOMER JOURNEY MAP

Set aside 25 minutes to develop a customer journey map that highlights key touchpoints where customers express or realize their needs, and in doing so are likely to look at your product and say (or post on a social media ad), "I need that."

Use this map to tailor your marketing efforts and product features to align with customer needs at each stage of their journey.

CHAPTER 5

The Psychology of Needs

In This Chapter:

- *Maslow's Hierarchy of Needs and its relevance to product marketing*
- *Addressing functional, safety, social, esteem, and self-actualization needs*
- *The impact of generational and cultural differences on need prioritization*
- *Strategies for aligning products with customers' psychological needs*

AN AMERICAN PSYCHOLOGIST named Abraham Maslow (1908–1970) is responsible for some of the most important knowledge to date about human needs and the way we prioritize them.

Recent innovations in brain imaging and behavioral psychology continue to validate Maslow's ideas. He remains the tenth most cited psychologist of the twentieth century and a principal contributor to the field of humanistic psychology.[1]

Of all his work, Maslow is best known for his "Hierarchy of Needs," a five-tier pyramid that ranks human needs in ascending order.

If you've ever taken a marketing course, you've probably come across this hierarchical schematic.

The most urgent and non-negotiable needs, physiological ones, appear at its base. Moving upward, the needs become less urgent and more subjective, relating increasingly to living a happy and fulfilled life rather than just staying alive, intact and out of imminent danger.

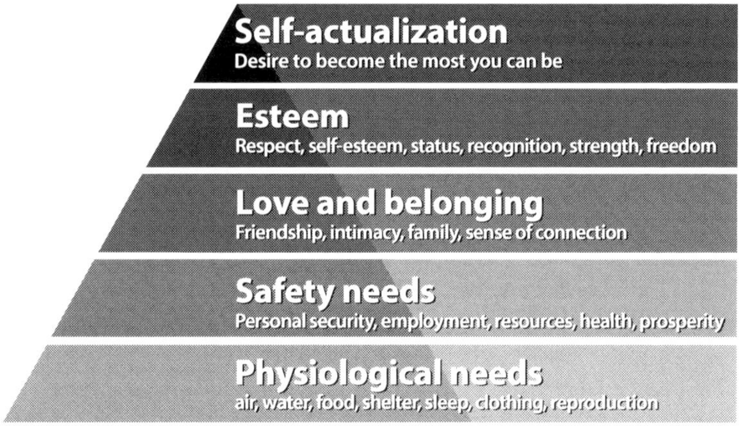

***Figure 5.1. Maslow's Hierarchy of Needs:** A pyramid illustrating human motivations, from basic physiological needs at the base to self-actualization at the peak. This model offers insights into consumer behavior and product development priorities.*

Understanding these needs and which ones relate to the product you are marketing is very important, yet I've seldom seen marketers and innovators intentionally make that kind of direct analysis.

Fewer still ever connect the dots in communicating the product's value as it relates to those needs for their customers.

It's a shame, because the framework is not very complicated and the connections are important.

After all, these needs are fundamental to our nature.

PHYSIOLOGICAL NEEDS

IF THERE'S ONE THING marketers know a ton about, it's pain.

We talk about pain points all the time, dissecting and analyzing which ones a product relieves in as many ways as we can add to a Miro board. Pain is a powerful driver of needs, and physiological needs, when recognized, can be irresistible motivators. But not necessarily to buy *our* product.

By default, a pain-driven motivation has consumers run to their most tried-and-true solution and apply it in the same way they always do. For humans as with other animals, our plainly obvious route is the lowest-risk approach. The last thing we want is for something untested to make a painful problem worse. We're wired and conditioned throughout our lives to think that way.

Each of us has a built-in scale prioritizing which type of pain we respond to with the greatest immediacy. If you are very tired, you become increasingly fixated on getting rest until you find a safe and decently comfortable place to lie down.

That is, unless you're also feeling hunger pains. Getting food automatically becomes a higher priority, and can make resting harder to do because your brain refuses to let you curl up and starve to death.

And thirst trumps hunger. So, on a hot day, the urgency to find water becomes even more intense than your drive to eat. Humans have survived for over a month without food, but with no water, you will die of dehydration in just a few days — much less if you're hot or doing work.

Finally, even if you are exhausted, starving and on the verge of death by dehydration, should something happen to remove your air supply (really sorry about your day!) getting oxygen instantly becomes the one and only thing on your mind.

No one needs to teach us this order of importance and there's nothing we can do to change it. It's deeply instinctive and common to all creatures.

With due respect to Maslow, I believe physiological needs often technically end with air, water, food and sleep. If you don't have all of those, you will soon die.

Shelter and clothing needs are environment-dependent. In a

Canadian winter, these are existential needs. But a few native tribes in Nigeria, New Guinea, Brazil and Venezuela go completely or mostly nude (belts, beads and creative piercings notwithstanding) and pretty much always have. They can sleep under the stars in their birthday suits and be just fine.

And while reproduction is essential to the survival of any species, all kinds of people live a full and happy life without doing it.

Aside from possibly splitting the first tier of Maslow's hierarchy into existential physiological needs and pretty-darned-essential physical ones, I am generally with him on the rest.

And so, if we have a hardwired order of priority for those key physiological needs, does the same order exist for the others?

Not exactly. There are multiple systems at play, altogether making us more … human. More on that soon.

Because physiological needs are handled basically on autopilot, marketing for them is done quite differently. While a great many products serve those needs, most consumers in wealthier developed countries shop for them from a low-pain to no-pain perspective.

Hydration is a primary physiological need, yet in any major city you can buy water shipped all the way from the Fijian rainforests. Or water that made a 30-year underground journey before being carbonated at the San Pellegrino source in Terme, Italy — and was then transported overseas in glass bottles to satisfy your discerning thirst. The water you buy to drink might also be sweetened, colored, flavored and supplemented with vitamins, electrolytes, alcohol, taurine and other ingredients.

The purpose of going to such trouble is literally *never* to prevent people dying of thirst and seldom even to enhance athletic performance. Too few consumers experience those needs at a sufficiently painful level to sustain a mass-marketed product, and much simpler, cheaper alternatives can do the same job. That fancy water aims to satisfy needs a full three tiers up Maslow's pyramid from thirst.

Similarly, we always market food on the basis of excitement, variety, flavor, nutrition, convenience and enjoyment rather than baseline survival. We sell homes based on luxury lifestyle amenities and location, not on their ability (however legitimate) to keep residents warm, dry and safe from pointy-toothed predators.

Staying alive, apart from in survivalist niches, is no longer a top-of-mind problem, nor is on the radar of most actual consumers.

With numerous product alternatives for nearly every category of physiological need (even canned fresh air and dizzying walls of energy drink brands), consumer buying decisions on these traditionally highest-need items are driven by brand status, manufactured differentiation and fairly trivial preferences instead of life-sustaining attributes.

If you market food and beverage products, you probably understand the reasons why consumers choose your offerings over others. In many cases, it's being in the right place, where hungry and thirsty people go for refreshment. Coca-Cola and Pepsi have spent a century jockeying to own exclusive rights to key locations for convenience, visibility and brand status.

Other times, it's about becoming the "it" product of the moment. White-collar boxers Logan Paul and KSI leveraged their combined 40 million social media followers to take on Pepsi's top energy drink Gatorade with their own Prime Hydration and became overnight market leaders.[2]

Sustaining popularity is a whole other challenge: it's not a sprint but an ultramarathon.

Most people reading this book — and nearly everyone you market to — should feel incredibly blessed to have never in their lives been painfully hungry. (Nearly a billion humans are starving right now, living incredibly different lives from your target audience members, but that's a whole other shelf of books.)

SAFETY NEEDS

AFTER PHYSIOLOGICAL NEEDS, Maslow's next tier is about safety. With basic survival under control, you seek to avoid being burned, bludgeoned, eaten or otherwise rendered dead before you can fulfill your purpose on this planet.

Safety needs extend from basic predator avoidance to shelter, job security, preventing illness and placing yourself and your family unit in a physically and emotionally safe environment.

Numerous products leverage safety as a selling point, from helmets and car seats to personal protective equipment (PPE) and home security systems.

Innovators in these spaces tend to sell by proclaiming whatever astonishing new level of protection the product provides. Then, as competition shows up and the market matures, they shift their focus to reputation, comfort, reliability, aesthetics, safety test ratings and ease of use. If you're shopping for a bike helmet, you probably think of comfort, airflow and aesthetics more than whether the product will protect your melon in a crash — functionality that safety standards systems like ANSI, Snell and ASTM have thankfully turned into table stakes.

I believe there is an unseen "flip" in Maslow's pyramid, at which point our needs become subjective; when our minds become empowered to rearrange the hierarchy to align with our likes and dislikes and values, to seek the experiences and rewards that have somehow crept into our fantasies.

And we're wired to make these choices nearly as urgently as with true physiological needs. Like characters in a story who finally accept their mission and become prepared to make any sacrifice to achieve it, we'll then focus our efforts and increase our risk tolerance to acquire what our mind tells us we need.

For the purpose of discussing needs as drivers of product sales,

I refer to all perceived needs as if they are *de facto* needs. Because as you're seeing, a need is any desire impulse (potentially including the silliest, most frivolous yearning) that gets granted non-negotiable status by the mind of a buyer.

That's the flip.

As marketers, we must recognize that above physiological needs, the line between want and need is always a construct of the consumer's mind. It is critical to our success that in the buyer's perception, the product *does* flip from a want to a need.

This happens most effectively when a fantasy centered on the product takes shape — one that proves enjoyable enough to be beckoned back again and again.

That fantasy, like nearly all fantasies, is usually better than the actual experience of owning the product. If you can remember looking forward to receiving a specific toy as a kid, that's the better-than-real-life experience I'm talking about. The real toy was probably fairly unspectacular, or even flawed, and didn't get nearly as much action in the real world as it enjoyed in your imagination.

That kind of fantasy is a powerful motivator, and while the subject matter and context evolves as we mature, we never grow out of it.

Daydreams or fantasies take up an enormous part of everyone's life. According to one large-scale study published in the journal *Science*, we spend an average of 46.9 percent of our waking hours daydreaming. That's nearly half of our available time.

And according to the same study, we're happier when we're daydreaming than we are when living in our actual life. Fully twice as much of our happiness is derived from our fantasy world than from our reality.[3]

As Maslow reminds us, need is always relative. In order to motivate someone to take action on a particular need, it has to outrank every other competing need at that time. That means as a buyer, I've got to fantasize about your solution substantially more than I feel I need the money it costs, the space it will take up in my home and the time I'll spend figuring out how to use it effectively. (It's likely I'll have to get rid of my old thing that still kind of works, which also pains me.)

Buyers' brains vigilantly make these evaluations to protect their hard-won resources and sunk costs, yet product makers, as we've seen, have a stubborn tendency to underestimate and even completely ignore this.

TRIGGERING THE FLIP

Marketers talk a lot about wants versus needs, as if they are entirely different, fixed categories for a given motivation. This line of thinking ignores the subjective, malleable nature of most first-world needs. A want is always weaker in terms of motivation — until it flips into a need.

And counter-intuitively, something that appears on the surface to be a want can flip into something stronger. The difference is purely in how one's brain frames the goal and its alternatives. While I may need to re-tile my bathroom floor to prevent my floorboards and joists from rotting away, I don't feel like doing the work or paying a contractor. So, I will put it off as long as possible.

At the same time, if I really want the new all-terrain toy of my dreams, I will subconsciously flip that fairly frivolous desire into a need. Re-framing of this kind often aligns with safety needs. I'll decide my existing ATV is unreliable, which is dangerous. I have to keep up with my friends' new rides or be left alone in the wild, which could be the end of me. *I need this safer ATV, see?*

Meanwhile, the bathroom floor collapses under my family's feet.

What you've got to do as a product maker, then, is to help prospective buyers elevate their desire to own your product to the level of fantasy. The combination of an enticing product daydream with a plausible safety need is marketing dynamite.

We'll get to how we (safely) formulate that soon. But first, let's talk about love, baby.

LOVE AND BELONGING

IN THE 2001 MOVIE *CAST AWAY*, in which Tom Hanks plays an executive marooned alone on an island in the Pacific, his character befriends a flotsam volleyball and humorously dubs it "Wilson" (the brand name printed on its surface). The movie is largely about loneliness and the profound importance of social connection.

Hanks later said that even the job of playing such an isolated character, with no one else in the cast, nearly drove him insane. By the end of filming, he believed he could hear what Wilson was saying to him.[4]

Social needs — the necessity of friendships, love and community — are deeply important to us humans. While hermits and real-life castaways have proven it is technically possible to survive with no external love or belonging, their lot has never been a trendy one — and studies have shown that prolonged solitude can be devastating to one's mental health.

Simply having human companionship is seldom enough: we want to belong. Many people feel miserably alone in a crowded seniors' facility or a school hallway full of peers.

Social belonging means unlocking a sense of acceptance with family, online communities, classmates, neighbors, co-workers, sports teams, religious organizations, gangs (judgment-free zone here) or any other people who matter to you.

Many brands have found their place as a substitute for traditional ways of connecting and fitting in with a group of peers. The majority of young people today do not attend church, belong to youth groups, fraternities or sororities, or play organized sports the way prior generations got together, belonged and self-identified.

Froshing, hazing and other initiation rituals are less common too. (A positive thing, given all the enduring psychological harm and trickle-down abuses these activities have caused.) Instead, paying a premium for a pair of Nikes, a Dior handbag or the newest Peloton device can be the standing initiation requirement to join a community or social circle.

As Pierre-Yves McSween explains in *Do You Really Need It?* brands are a safeguard against rejection and a kind of social insurance policy. Joining peers by investing in and wearing popular brands also shows a willingness to sacrifice for a kinship based on common trust.[5]

Digital brands like Facebook, Snapchat, X and TikTok directly take advantage of social needs by connecting people in multiple ways and enabling us to instantaneously share all kinds of experiences, from wardrobe selfies and pet antics to life-altering events. It's a novel category that doesn't have any direct precursor in human history, and remarkably has become central to human socialization, how we identify our circles and how we project our identities. Billions of us are fully locked in and need social media brands to sustain valued elements of our lifestyle and even to support the way we've built our relationships.

During the COVID-19 pandemic of the early 2020s we universally had the chance to experience the importance of online social connectedness, through the pain of having our in-person interactions severely curtailed. Many of us learned new ways to reconnect by harnessing available resources. Suddenly, video conferencing was no longer just for soldiers deployed overseas and global executives: it became essential for connecting kids with their primary school classmate, their teachers, and their extended family.

Businesses temporarily transitioned to remote work models — and a surprising number have remained that way. In numerous cases, employees have refused to go back to commuting. Although many miss the easy collaboration and water-cooler socialization, the time and financial costs of these interactions suddenly became tangible. People voted with their feet, showing that while we do value in-person human interaction, it isn't as high a priority as we once believed.

It helped that connecting remotely turned out to be more meaningful than we previously believed. Brain imaging has shown that even through a video screen, we can experience exactly the same range of feelings and release of oxytocin, the "love hormone," as we do in direct person-to-person communication. It will be fascinating to see what we learn in the coming years about our virtual and face-to-face interactions, as social needs evolve through more immersive platforms and AI continues to transform the way we share and who (or what) we're able to consider a "friend."

ESTEEM

NATURE ABHORS A VACUUM. As we find success in fulfilling our social needs, we create new room for concern about our ego or status needs. Marketing visionary Seth Godin tells us status is a principal motivating factor in nearly every nonessential purchase we ever make. It drives nearly every discretionary thing we do.[6]

When we become obsessed with a product or brand, status and esteem are always part of the equation. The products we own and crave become closely tied to our self-relevance.

Self-relevance is a uniquely human trait that plays a central role in our buying behaviors. Your mind at rest automatically finds itself daydreaming, fantasizing, planning and ruminating. All of these involve reflecting on yourself and at the same time reinforcing who you are.[7]

As with your childhood fantasies of playing with that amazing toy you hoped to receive as a gift, or teenaged me fantasizing about the Cateye Solar, any product that successfully navigates its way into the daydreams and plans of its customers, or positions itself as a solution to a nagging problem or fear, establishes a high likelihood of being purchased. Especially when the desire to own that product flips into a status need.

You might notice that status needs overlap social needs. Status is nothing but an aligned set of perceptions, and its existence is entirely dependent on other people. Tom Hanks' character in *Cast Away* agonized over unmet social needs, but had zero status ones.

Our social circles include all the people we associate with and the humans we most care about pleasing, impressing or making envious. Aside from celebrities, human status needs relate primarily to the people with whom we engage in two-way conversations.

Status needs are often prioritized and valued very differently from one peer group to another. While the Amish may not care a whit about brands, some age groups, cultures and cliques are heavily focused on conspicuous consumption and prominently display status brands wherever possible.[8]

Years ago I witnessed a memorable scene in the Tommy Hilfiger section of a department store. A teenage girl was shopping with her mother, while a group of the girl's friends tagged along. The youths were a walking logo farm, in glittering branded hoodies, sweatpants, handbags, shoes and hats. When the mother (who was clearly there to pay) insisted on a particular sweater, the daughter threw a tantrum of sobbing, obnoxious groans and flailing arms. Embarrassed and baffled, the mother pointed out that the sweater was stylish, well-made and the right size. The other teens quietly distanced themselves from what was unfolding.

"But it doesn't say '*TOMMY*'!" the tear-drenched teen finally shrieked out, and stormed off in a fury.

Her mother had entirely missed the point. It wasn't at all about how the clothing looked, what it was made from or how well it fit. Or even what the tag inside the collar said. What was essential in this girl's culture was wearing the brand name conspicuously as a badge.

In individuals with low self-esteem or deep-rooted inferiority complexes, status needs can mean not just acceptance but baseline adequacy to occupy the same space as their peers. In cliques like the one I just described, brands are the dress code, full stop. Everyone who wants access knows it.

Membership-driven product businesses like HelloFresh and Peloton as well as multiplayer games like Minecraft and Fortnite manage to combine status with community, doubling down on emotional needs. Kids know they need Snapchat and WhatsApp to be included in conversations with people in the same classroom. Esteem needs and social needs can intertwine to share tremendous leverage on our choices.

SELF-ACTUALIZATION

WAY UP AT THE PINNACLE of Maslow's hierarchy is a need known as self-actualization. This is all about realizing our greatest potential as human beings. Because self-actualization is a moving target, few of us will feel we've achieved it during our lifetime.

Despite being practically unattainable, self-actualization is a real need for a large number of the first-world consumers you sell to.

Whether it's a midlife crisis motivating a sports car purchase or a desire to reach the top of a leaderboard (if not Mount Everest), self-actualization needs live in us all on some level. They evolve as we grow older, more limited, and more realistic in our expectations.

What's consistent is how self-actualization needs play into our fantasies and become a measure of our overall level of satisfaction with who we have become so far.

Many of us will make huge sacrifices in pursuit of self-actualization, to build a legacy or to see ourselves with greater pride. Successful marketers know this.

In 2019 Procter & Gamble brand Gillette recognized that its then 30-year-old slogan, "The Best a Man Can Get," (originally intended to speak for the quality of shave delivered by its multi-blade razors) could be repurposed to promote self-actualization, just by changing one word.

The result? The very first ad in Gillette's "The Best a Man Can Be" campaign drove up social media conversations about the brand by 11,722 percent, with 1.4 million online mentions in a single week. While the campaign went on to become highly controversial and the slogan returned to its original wording, discussion equals exposure and exposure is relevance.[9] And in marketing, relevance is life — especially for a brand dating back to 1901.

The risk with self-actualization being at the very topmost level of the needs hierarchy is it can seem as disposable as a quintuple-razor blade. Almost any need can trump it, if only temporarily.

And to those with the bandwidth and resources to seek self-actualization (or where it is linked to belonging and esteem), the drive is resilient: it often takes focus and commitment to earn the luxury of prioritizing self-actualization goals.

That said, and while it should face off against status or social needs with caution, self-actualization is definitely not an aspiration reserved for the rich and powerful. It's likely part of your personal motivation for reading this book.

Maslow's Hierarchy of Needs is a motivational theory: it explains how one need takes priority over others and drives us to take a specific action.

While everything within the framework is a motivating need to countless humans, it illustrates much more than how we can trigger select compulsions in a specific order to sell a particular product to the right people. Instead, we can see how these needs are interwoven in everyone's journey, with different combinations coming together as a person's situation and priorities change.

INNOVATION INTERLUDE

GETTING INTO CONSUMERS' HEADSPACE

Headspace, launched in 2010, revolutionized the wellness industry by making meditation accessible through a mobile app.

The product's success stems from its ability to address multiple levels of Maslow's Hierarchy of Needs:

- **Safety needs:** Offering tools to manage stress and anxiety
- **Social needs:** Providing a sense of community through shared experiences and challenges
- **Esteem needs:** Helping users develop self-awareness and confidence
- **Self-actualization:** Guiding users towards personal growth and mindfulness

By gamifying meditation and presenting it in bite-sized, daily sessions, Headspace transformed a traditionally esoteric practice into a mainstream tool for mental well-being. The app's ability to cater to various psychological needs contributed to its rapid growth, amassing over 65 million users across 190 countries.[10]

Headspace's success illustrates how understanding and addressing multiple levels of human needs can create a product that resonates deeply with consumers, driving both adoption and long-term engagement.

And while we usually have no choice but to satisfy the needs at the base of the pyramid before we can spare the resources and attention to climb higher up, each new tier we stand on allows for a wider range of individual choice and concurrent progress. You can renovate your house on the same day as nurturing friendships, choosing a luxury SUV and creating a new charity. As a busy and ambitious person, you could even find yourself pursuing parts of Maslow's entire pyramid in the same hour!

While Maslow's Hierarchy of Needs has been widely influential in the field of motivational psychology, it is definitely not without its limitations and criticisms. Some researchers argue that the real-world hierarchy is nowhere near as rigidly structured as Maslow proposed, and that people often pursue higher-level needs even when lower-level needs are not fully satisfied.[11] Others have pointed out that the hierarchy may not be universally applicable across cultures, as the prioritization of needs can vary based on cultural values and norms. (Think back to my example of the native tribes.)[12]

Recent developments in motivation psychology have led to alternative theories and models that build upon or challenge Maslow's framework. One notable example is Self-Determination Theory (SDT), developed by Edward L. Deci and Richard M. Ryan. SDT focuses on three innate psychological needs: autonomy, competence, and relatedness. According to this theory, the satisfaction of these three needs is essential for psychological growth, integrity, and overall well-being.[13]

Another alternative is the ERG Theory, proposed by Clayton Alderfer. This theory condenses Maslow's five needs into three categories: Existence (what Maslow calls physiological and safety needs), Relatedness (social and external esteem needs), and Growth (internal esteem and self-actualization needs). The ERG Theory supports my notion that people can be motivated by multiple needs simultaneously, and suggests that the frustration of higher-level needs can lead to a regression to lower-level needs.[14]

Despite some limitations, and in the context of the alternative theories, Maslow's Hierarchy of Needs is a valuable framework for understanding human motivation and its implications for product marketing. By recognizing the diverse and dynamic nature of consumer needs, marketers can develop more effective strategies for creating products that resonate with their target audiences.

Also, it is essential to remember that the prioritization of needs is context driven and seldom fixed. If you have to choose between a physiological or safety need and your self-actualization project, the latter will find itself on the back burner in a heartbeat.

But it's what your brain does when it has lots of free rein to make discretionary purchases that gets really fascinating. All of a sudden, dreams, fantasies and Big, Hairy Audacious Goals get air time and budget power.

Just how much depends on the level of freedom and the individual's personality — as well as where they live, who they associate with, what they earn and when they were born. In addition to variations between cultural and socio-economic groups, each generation has its own way of prioritizing needs, based on their values, worldview, prior experiences, finances and capabilities.

While today's Baby Boomers generally have most physiological needs under control, they will start to encounter new safety needs as their strength and mobility decrease. For many, their trajectory on Maslow's pyramid may begin to reverse. Gen X, my generation, will follow suit next.

Millennials, or Gen Ys (born 1991 to 1996) are at the time of this writing in their prime, with many heading into their most productive and highest-earning years. Outnumbering Generation X and living Boomers, Gen Y now has the resources to buy nearly anything it needs — and has the energy and courage to change the world.

Slightly fewer in number are Gen-Z buyers (born between 1997 and 2012), whose earliest memories go back to the 2008 recession and who came of age during the COVID-19 pandemic. These "Zoomers" are showing up to be more pragmatic than the millennial generation who grew up during relatively stable times.

As a result, Gen Zs are much less inclined to own (or even be licensed to drive) a car, more likely to support purpose-driven brands and more likely to prioritize saving for education, instead focusing their spending on the most essential needs — at least for the moment.[15]

AFFLUENCE AND VALUES

THE INCOME LEVEL of your target market can also have a powerful bearing on the way those buyers' psychological needs will be perceived and prioritized. An upmarket product like a luxury car, wearable tech or expensive fashion accessory is unlikely to be associated with a physiological need, because any buyer who doesn't have survival basics under control — even one with the most messed-up priorities on earth — simply can't care about such fancy things.

That considered, think about how many prestige brands are built on values like safety, health, security, property, love and connection. No matter how high a person climbs up Maslow's pyramid, every other level of need is still in the game.

And yet even when a product is able to tick many of these boxes, attempting to do so is seldom the right strategy for positioning. It's much more valuable (and achievable) to decisively own a single point of value than make squishy claims about a plethora of others.

Volvo produces high-quality vehicles that are prestigious, comfortable, high-tech, attractive and reliable, with a reputation for lasting a very long time. The century-old company has the potential to touch on many human needs, yet has built instant brand recognition for focusing on just one of them — safety — more effectively than any competitor. The Swedish automaker is credited for introducing the first three-point safety belt, side-impact airbags, inflatable curtains, blind spot monitors and pedestrian detection systems, setting safety standards for the entire auto industry.

For the 14 years I was a Volvo driver, I can't be sure I was any safer than I'd have been in a BMW or Audi.

Yet one thing is sure: people frequently commended me for prioritizing safety, based on nothing other than the car I drove.

Buyers need focus.

KEY INSIGHTS FROM CHAPTER 5

- Abraham Maslow's Hierarchy of Needs categorizes human needs into five tiers: **physiological**, **safety**, **social belonging**, **esteem** and **self-actualization**.

  - **Physiological needs** relate to survival, including food, water, shelter and air. However, these needs are usually marketed for their additional benefits beyond survival.

  - **Safety needs** encompass protection from harm, security and well-being. Products and services aimed at providing safety often emphasize reliability, comfort and aesthetics.

  - **Social needs** involve belonging, connection and acceptance within communities. Brands can fulfill social needs by offering a sense of identity and community.

  - **Esteem needs** center on recognition, status and self-worth. Consumers may be motivated to purchase products that enhance their self-esteem and societal status. Brand logos can become badges tied to the status their products bring.

  - **Self-actualization** is the realization of one's full potential. Brands can tap into this need by offering products that align with personal growth and fulfillment.

- Products that resonate with consumers' fantasies and self-identity have a higher likelihood of being purchased, as they tap directly into emotional needs.

- Needs are always relative and must outweigh competing needs to motivate action. Buyers prioritize needs based on available resources and personal values.

- Marketers should aim to elevate consumer desire for their products to the level of a need by aligning their offerings with consumers' emotional drivers. Recognize the "flip" that happens when a want is suddenly seen as a need, and how it is triggered.

- Different generations and cultures prioritize needs differently, with external influences such as historical events and economic conditions shaping their perceptions.
- Buyers' income levels and savings influence how they perceive and prioritize psychological needs.
- Brands should focus on owning a single point of value for effective positioning.

—

Remember that understanding and addressing consumers' needs, especially at the emotional level, is crucial for successful marketing and product development.

DO THESE NOW FOR QUICK WINS:

NEED ANALYSIS WORKSHOP

Host a rapid brainstorming session with your team to identify and prioritize the core needs your product fulfills for customers. Use these insights to refine your messaging and positioning.

MESSAGE TESTING SESSION

Develop four or five versions of marketing messages that subtly prompt customers to consider their own needs related to your product. Test these messages with a small audience to gauge engagement and resonance.

COMPETITIVE ANALYSIS BLITZ

Conduct a rapid analysis of your competitors' messaging and positioning strategies, paying close attention to how they leverage the concept of "need." Look for opportunities to differentiate your product based on unmet needs.

CONTENT CREATION SPRINT

Dedicate focused time to workshop compelling content that emphasizes the importance of addressing customers' needs. This is planning, not actual writing. Outline ideas for blog posts, social media graphics, or videos that will highlight real-life scenarios where your product fulfills critical needs.

INTERNAL MESSAGING ALIGNMENT MEETING

Gather your internal teams, including marketing, sales, and product development, to ensure alignment on how the concept of "need" is communicated across all touchpoints. Foster a shared understanding of the importance of customer-centric messaging.

PIN DOWN YOUR PRODUCT'S RELEVANCE

Determine which tier(s) of Maslow's Hierarchy your product addresses. Does it fulfill basic physiological needs, provide safety, enhance social connections, boost esteem, or contribute to self-actualization?

TRIGGER A SAFETY NEED "FLIP"

Safety needs are exceedingly powerful for consumers, so emphasizing these aspects can enhance appeal and pique interest. What less-obvious safety implications can you help buyers bring to the forefront — and "flip" a want to a need?

TAP INTO SOCIAL AND COMMUNITY ASPECTS

Explore ways to position your product as fostering social connections or belonging. Leverage social networks or communities to enhance the product's appeal.

BRAINSTORM STATUS AND ESTEEM

With a group, schedule an hour to brainstorm ways to align your product with status symbols or esteem-building experiences. What connections can you leverage from participants? Make sure everyone understands how your product contributes to consumers' self-image and identity.

FLUSH OUT SELF-ACTUALIZATION NEEDS

Whiteboard or Miro Board how your product can help consumers achieve personal growth or fulfill legacy-building goals. Position it as a tool for reaching their fullest potential.

CHAPTER 6

How Our Brain Recognizes Need

In This Chapter:

- *The role of the limbic system and neocortex in decision-making*
- *Triggering emotional responses to drive product adoption*
- *The importance of visual cues and simplicity in marketing messaging*
- *Real-world examples of products that effectively target the "dog brain"*

OVER A HUNDRED YEARS AGO, Sigmund Freud postulated that our brains are made up of a two-stage processing system: a primary one at the forefront, and another, secondary psychic mode running constantly in the background.

He explained that the primary system is impulse driven and irrational, like a pushy little devil on one shoulder. The secondary system is the angel on the other: more subtle, more cautious and attentive to consequences.

Like a small child, the primary system exists in the present moment and loudly insists on instant gratification.

While the primary system has you grabbing a plate of cheesecake in a cafeteria, it is the secondary system that pushes back, reminding you to think about the calories it contains and whether you really ought to eat that. The same type of dialogue goes on with nearly every buying decision you make.[1]

Modern brain-imaging technologies have not only validated Freud's observations, but have taken them much further, helping us to understand the processes and struggles that take place within the human psyche — and how as product marketers we can finesse our work to trigger purchases.

To understand how customers decide what they need in making buying decisions, we've got to first recognize that our brain does not function as a unified and autocratic command center for all of our functions and actions. It's more like a trio of distinct components, each with entirely different cellular structures and functions — even separate motives, intentions and objectives. Because of this, every decision is a group effort, in which certain participants have more influence and authority than others.

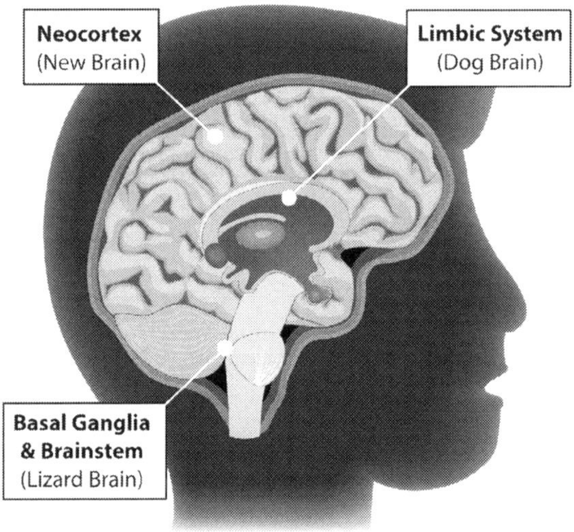

***Figure 6.1. The Triune Brain Model** depicting the human brain's three main components — the rational Neocortex ("New Brain"), instinctual Brainstem ("Lizard Brain"), and emotional Limbic System ("Dog Brain"). This concept helps explain consumer decision-making processes and product appeal.*

The three parts of our brain are put together like a retrofitted Model T, with the oldest parts at the bottom and progressively newer components bolted on top.

Tools like functional magnetic resonance imaging (fMRI) help neuroscientists better understand the operations and triggers of each part and show a surprising amount of ongoing tension between them. There is plenty of interaction, but more passing of the baton and less collaboration than you might expect.

As marketers, it is important to recognize that we are not working to persuade a single decision-making mechanism in each prospective buyer. There are three, each with its own agenda, and two of them tend to dominate.

THE LIZARD BRAIN: OUR SURVIVAL INSTINCT

PERCHED AT THE TOP of the spinal cord is the most primitive part of our brain, the part we share with marine animals and reptiles (which has given it the name "reptilian brain" or "lizard brain"). It includes the basal ganglia and brainstem, among other structures. The lizard brain governs the most basic and essential needs we saw at the bottom of Maslow's pyramid, including those for air, water and nutrition.

The supported functions, although we can choose to forcefully override some of them for a short time, run pretty much on autopilot our whole lives.

Our lizard brain has nearly all the say in life-and-death decisions and is why the bottom tier of Maslow's pyramid can wield such irrepressible power. This most primitive brain is the survival brain, and is likely to dominate only decisions in which serious consequences are imminent.

Most of the time, it's on standby during routine decision-making, keeping our heart beating and various systems operating, while ready to take charge if a situation gets dicey.

THE LIMBIC SYSTEM: OUR EMOTIONAL DOG BRAIN

THE BRAIN'S CENTER is wrapped with the limbic system, including the thalamus, amygdala and hippocampus, all of which we share with dogs and other mammals. It manages nurturing, nursing, bonding and other early mammalian functions. If you think of a dog's intense emotional responses to its impulses, you get a good picture of how our own limbic system responds to things that captivate its attention. By thinking of the dog brain inside us, it becomes easy to visualize how the limbic system can be triggered and excited.

Our limbic responses can trigger us to chase, flee, fight, pounce or cower — literally or metaphorically.

The limbic system operates and triggers our actions at a speed much greater than we are able to recognize.

If I were to flash you an image of a spider, snake or an angry face for just two milliseconds, an fMRI would show your central brain lighting up. At that speed, you wouldn't consciously know you saw anything at all. Your neocortex would be clueless. But your lizard and dog brains would be on high alert.

The limbic system, in particular the amygdala and hippocampus, is the part of our brain that manages emotions, memory retrieval, drives and trust. It is the part of the brain that dishes out dopamine, the "happy hormone" that makes you feel good about eating, getting compliments on social media, playing video games — or taking a drug like nicotine.

Neurotransmitters such as dopamine spark the joy we feel when we come across something exciting. That thrill you feel upon seeing that your new profile photo has 908 likes, with people saying you're gorgeous? That's dopamine making your neurons do the Macarena.

Because of this connection with gratification, our dog brain actually encourages risky or emotion-driven behaviors that are expected to deliver a dopamine hit. The dog brain is here for a good time, and doesn't even have the capacity to care about staying healthy and financially secure.

Brian Knutson, a neuroscientist at Stanford University, used fMRI to study the brains of people as they contemplated a purchase. He found that he could predict whether a prospect would buy or pass just by watching the limbic brain and prefrontal cortex. When brain regions in the neocortex related to feelings of guilt, humiliation and shame were activated, buyers would always take a hard pass. But when the dog brain lit up, out came the credit card.

What Knutson found was that brain scans could accurately translate phylogenetics — chemical changes in the ancient brain's structures — into predictors of buying behaviors. He determined that what people envisioned themselves doing based on need impulses from the limbic brain became the strongest driver of buying behavior — easily overpowering thoughtful rationalization of the consequences. There was no contest.

According to Knutson, if you want to predict what people will do or their willingness to pay, you should look at their *anticipated* experience rather than how they will feel *after* they have done it.[2] What it means is that those fantasies, daydreams and projected outcomes in your mind's eye have a much stronger direct impact on buying behavior than anything else in the real world does.

Take time to digest that, because it explains many things — and ought to drastically impact the way you create your marketing.

The dog brain has an overwhelming amount of influence in purchasing decisions, because it carries a high level of authority in that capacity. It is the oldest part of our brain not only from an evolutionary standpoint, but also from a chronological one in our own bodies.

When our brains begin to take shape *in utero*, our dog and lizard brains are the very first parts to form. The middle brain is usually fully developed between the ages of 10 and 12. By contrast, the frontal lobes, which control rational decision-making, are not fully developed until we reach our mid-twenties.[3]

Knowing this, teenage irrationality makes a lot more sense. It's not simply the current younger generation and too much screen time: most teenagers have always lacked a full neurological capacity to be reasonable.

THE NEOCORTEX: OUR ANALYTICAL TANK BRAIN

THE NEOCORTEX (literally meaning "new bark"), which includes those frontal lobes, aka the prefrontal cortex, is the latest evolutionary addition to our brain. It is 400 million years newer than the limbic system and is mainly what makes us the dominant species on earth. Other mammals also have cortexes, but even those of primates are much smaller than ours. The neocortex, that grayish-pink walnut thing we picture as our brain, surrounds the limbic system and brain center and comprises the rationalizing parts of our mind.

Our neocortex is the reason we're the only species that asks the question, "What if?"

It enables us to thoughtfully contemplate possibilities, using our imagination to fantasize about things that have yet to be seen and gives us the unique ability to strategically plan those visions into reality.

While the neocortex is able to perform complex tasks, it processes visual images about 250 times slower than the dog-brained limbic system. In any race, that's a massive disadvantage.

I think of the neocortex as a slow-moving but powerful battle tank, lumbering alongside the yapping and bounding dog brain, full of analytical and strategic processing power. It burns a lot of fuel — valuable calories — to do cognitively difficult tasks.

But imagining and daydreaming come easily to it. (Remember what happened when you were overwhelmed in a difficult class at school?)

Because of this, the tank brain runs initial protective scans but usually gets fully engaged only after the dog brain has already sniffed things out and locked in its conclusions.[4]

Many neuroscientists have speculated about the "illusion of conscious control," supporting the idea that the slower new brain doesn't play much of a role in decisions at all.[5]

Experts such as Nobel Prize-winning psychologist and economist Daniel Kahneman are certain the neocortex does have the authority to overrule the ancient brain's impulses — it's just that we often don't want it to. We force it to accept and rationalize the exciting, reward-driven decisions made by our dog brain.

Still, it might seem unrealistic to think marketers can simply trigger a need response in the consumer's dog brain and overcome any rational assessment about the risks surrounding a new purchase. Remember, we don't buy the majority of things that intrigue us. We are more in control than that.[6] Right?

Rational assessment and analysis play a role in buying decisions to be sure, but dramatically less of one than was believed even a short time ago. When people buy your product, conventional behavioral economics presumed that most of them would have made a thoughtful, analytic decision to arrive at a choice that's in their own best interests. For that reason, economics, along with psychology, was once a branch of "moral science," concerned with the heart as well as the mind. So it stood to reason that smart buyers would start by comparing features and price options, read reviews and eventually come to the most sensible and value-driven conclusion before hitting "Buy Now."

But new evidence shows that's not exactly how it works.

Our tank brain stands sentry, watching for signals that the offer being presented is not a scam and assurances that buying it isn't going to lead to a major problem in our lives. It does the initial due diligence based on easily obtainable new information and its vast database of prior experiences. Marketing trickery can't deactivate or bypass these safeguards. If the tank brain is initially satisfied, it gives the all-clear.

The dog brain, by contrast, bounds ahead after seeing attractive images. Barring the appearance of something concerning, it has the baton.

It's our impulsive and irrational dog brain that convinces us to rationalize buying on credit, paying interest fees to enjoy that huge TV immediately, rather than wait until we've saved up the money. It's our dog brain that says we need something we merely want.

We may not buy all the products that intrigue us, but when something makes us salivate?

Woof! Cha-ching!

It would definitely be better for us in the long run if we relied entirely on our much smarter, more analytical neocortex to make buying decisions, but that's not the way humans work. We are wired to trust the ancient limbic system, unless we are worried into a slower mode of thinking. And we're hopelessly addicted to dopamine.

So oftentimes we'll abandon a discretionary effort entirely rather than call for the tediously slow, fun-sucking tank brain. That's why most website bounce rates are so high. People click through from an ad, decide they aren't willing to do the brain work in front of them — and hit the back button.

Even if a prospect really needs what you're selling, when you don't immediately entice the dog brain, the excitement and promise of a dopamine hit quickly fizzle, replaced in the buyer's experience by the aching drudgery of rationalization. Disinterest leads to abandonment, with the motivating need quickly dissolving.

It is always important to provide gratification and rewards to the dog brain, rather than turning it off with the technical details. Even for ultra-sophisticated tech products that sell to people wearing pocket protectors and propeller caps, this still holds true. Everyone needs to feel their heart race. Your most important job is to make that happen, quickly and consistently.[7]

MESSAGING FOR TWO BRAINS

IF YOU'RE HOPING to market to the two systems that make up the human brain, it is helpful to have a clear understanding of how each system works and the kind of information it uses. In this table, you can see some of the main differences between them:

Primal (Dog) Brain	Neocortex (Tank Brain)
Autonomous	Can be governed
Fast and energetic Energy efficient	Slow and lazy Energy intensive
Impulsive	Analytical
Intuitive	Self-aware
Sees things literally	Daydreams and imagines
Visual / no language capacity	Understands and uses language
Self-centered	Considers big picture and others
Makes decisions	Rationalizes decisions, including those already made. Can intervene on decision-making
Lives in the moment	Considers past; plans for the future
Pursues gratification; concerned about imminent danger	Desires status, connection, future enjoyment and long-term value
Immediately knows what it likes	Seeks further proof and assurance

Table 6.1. Dog Brain Vs. Tank Brain

When connecting with the dog brain, simple visuals are usually the most effective. An in-store demonstration of Cutco Super Shears snipping through coins sells far more product than the most gripping soapbox oration about how the scissors are forged and heat-treated, or tech specs like the number of serrations per inch.

It's fine to say they never go dull, are guaranteed forever, and pop apart for easy cleaning. But much better is to demonstrate the shears slicing spirals out of pennies and then cleanly cutting through pizza, artichokes and lobster shells.

Demonstrations sell products because visuals speak directly to the non-verbal, highly emotional dog brain. The tank brain does its superficial risk and value assessments, setting a bar the dog brain's enthusiasm is required to clear if it wants the treats.

Intense emotion makes people take action. Boredom, or even contentment does the opposite, keeping people in the warm and muscle-numbing bath of the status quo.

When aroused, we do things, as Johan Berger describes in his wonderful book, *Contagious*. We wring our hands and pace the floor. We pump our fists and run around the living room.

We take action, because arousal compels us to do the most obvious thing. Intense emotion on any level is effective, whether for selling products or enticing people to share a social media post. Berger demonstrated this through an experiment he conducted at the Wharton School at the University of Pennsylvania.

His team tested content-sharing responses to numerous news stories and asked readers to categorize each one as positive, neutral or negative. High arousal emotions like awe, laughter, anger and anxiety dramatically increased sharing activity, while sadness, neutrality or even contentment didn't bring on any response at all.

Despite this evidence, making people angry or anxious isn't intuitive for product makers and marketers. Negative emotions are never our focus when developing and presenting products. We want to make everyone happy — and contentment seems pretty close.

But it isn't. Contentment is that warm, paralyzing bath.

Spark laughter. Make them anxious. Make them angry. But leave your audience feeling content at your product's peril.

HOW GREAT PRODUCTS BREAK THROUGH

GREAT PRODUCTS BEGIN with a problem and the spark of an idea: the need that first inspires an inventor to create. It's the start of a long journey, of countless hours spent focusing on specifications and features. Along the way, through the many convoluted steps to building the product and solving issues, a lot of other stuff piles on. Gradually, that simple idea often becomes devastatingly complicated while the original need gets deeply buried.

In order to make a product fully functional and render it suitable for manufacturing, the inventor, designer and engineers are sucked into cycles of trouble-shooting, adjusting and finessing.

Meanwhile, the product team becomes increasingly aware of competing options to the product and fixates on any minute advantages those alternatives possess. Early testers ask, "What if it also did this?" So, more features are added and refined, hoping to increase value.

But the consumer, who still has that single prevailing need, doesn't see it that way. The prospective buyer looks at pictures and thinks about outcomes in a fairly binary, superficial way. Will it meet my need or not? Will I be delighted — or disappointed … again?

It's essential not to let feature bloat and the elaborate details and thought processes behind your product (as fascinating as they might be) get in the way of your buyers' need for simplicity.

Breaking copy blocks down to bullet points is one of the easiest ways to address this. And any features that require deeper explanation can be linked to from those simple points, if the reader is interested enough or needs more detail. I often suggest to clients, "This is great, but probably belongs in a blog post."

Graphics that show how to use the product and other simple visuals are optimum. Starred reviews are effective because they are universal and speak to our limbic system. They illustrate whether prior buyers were delighted or felt burned, on a visual scale that's instantly parsed. Five yellow stars from prior buyers is a pat of reassurance to a dog brain humping the beautiful product photos, eager to transact before the tank brain mucks things up.

This doesn't mean supporting details can't help sales. They sometimes can. But only if they build confidence or add excitement without extra complexity, which will inevitably pass the baton to the tank brain. An easy-to-scan list of exciting value points can also amp up emotion. Trust-building testimonials and reviews should be readily available and bite-sized. You do need to focus on serving up the dopamine rewards *quickly* and with minimal distraction.

By all means, make it super easy to do a deeper dive on trust points and technical details, but don't force excess thought or analysis into the buying process.

It is worth putting thought into how you will make trust-building content available but not obtrusive, and how you can enable it to continue supporting your buyers' concerns once a sale is completed.

Buyer's remorse is something the neocortex is always processing behind the scenes, and this is where your customer experience becomes critically important. After the sale, more than ever, the neocortex needs to be reassured.

The tank brain often gets rumbling when the buyer tries to sleep, shooting out niggling questions about the day's snap decisions — like buying your product. Web analytics show that often after a purchase is made, nervous customers will return again and again to the online store to read what other customers have said and look for clues that all is well — or is not. Some platforms like Meta's Shops have a "remorse period" after transactions. During that time, sellers are not allowed to ship, in case the buyer has a change of heart.

Order cancellations, returns and churn can be minimized if your order confirmation email hits the buyer's inbox (and not the junk folder) promptly, the product works as promised and the customer's tank brain is freed up to fuss or fantasize about something else.

DIFFUSION OF INNOVATION, IN REAL-TIME

ONE OF THE THINGS I love about running social media advertising campaigns for a good direct-to-consumer (DTC) product is how acceptance and adoption forces can be seen dynamically changing throughout the product launch.

When a product is first introduced — known to no one, devoid of reviews and nonexistent on the internet — who the heck would be crazy enough to take a chance on it?

Fascinatingly, there are people who do. Those buyers are the Innovators, as first described in the Diffusion of Innovation theory developed by Everett Rogers in 1962 and made famous three decades later by Geoffrey Moore's book, *Crossing the Chasm*.[8]

Innovators are the most adventurous of all buyers, often willing to pay for an innovative new product without customer reviews or social proof, and will overlook the inevitable flaws in order to be the first on the block to flash it around.

These buyers have an unusually laid-back tank brain and an alpha dog limbic system. They aren't fools or people with low standards — in fact they are usually knowledgeable mavens who have developed their buying behavior through a history of successful decisions.

They make decisions quickly, requiring little available information. According to Rogers, Innovators represent only about two to three out of every hundred people. You can convert Innovators by effectively targeting the limbic system with enticing, believable and rapidly digestible content.

As those few customers go on to share positive experiences, Early Adopters follow. Early Adopters need a minimal amount of tangible evidence the product is good. They are a little more hesitant than are the Innovators, and may return to look at your product a few times before deciding to commit. Whether or not they love the product, they are highly likely to talk about it and show it around.

Early Adopters and Innovators buy products partly for utility, and partly because they are betting on advancing their trailblazer status.

If the product delights those bold purchasers and is seen to work well for them, more pragmatic Early Majority buyers begin to venture on board. Early Majority and Late Majority buyers make up more than two thirds of most markets, and expect what they buy to be practical, to work well and to last a long time.

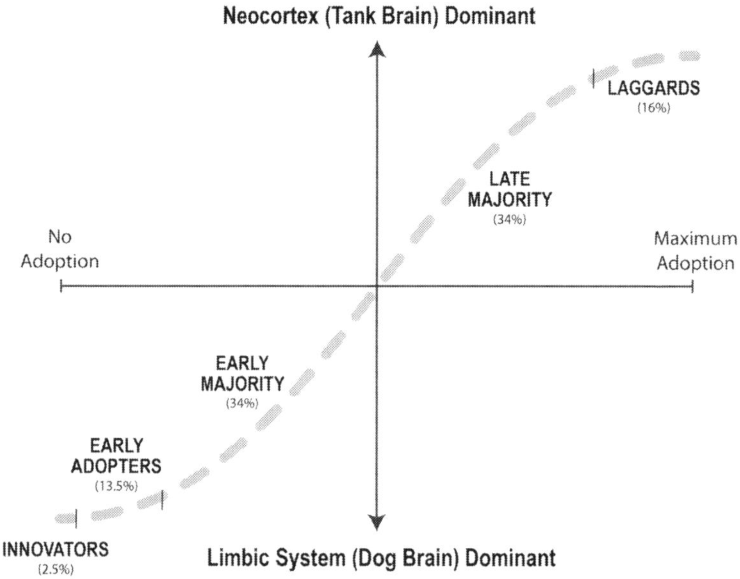

***Figure 6.2. Adopter Type and Brain Dominance:** Each of the adopter types in the Diffusion of Innovation theory reflects a distinct balance of influences from the Dog Brain and Tank Brain. Individuals with a dominant Dog Brain are likely to make a purchase earlier and based on less evidence than Tank Brain dominant counterparts.*

Sometimes the Laggards never show up. These buyers can live with low-tech, old-school solutions, and may even be proud they do. They are so tank-brained that they will devise elaborate work-arounds to keep old systems functioning. They carry paper maps and a magnetic compass in the glove box and do all their banking in person, regardless of how inconvenient it becomes. They will criticize your product and scour the small print looking for reasons not to buy — and will not, unless they have no other choice.

Tony Fadell, who helped develop the iPad, iPhone and Nest, points out that most products go through three distinct generations in becoming ready to satisfy the Innovators and Early Adopters, the Early Majority and eventually the Late Majority and Laggards. Version one (V1) of the product, with its kinks and flaws, is purely for the Innovators and Early Adopters. Others are unlikely to be fully satisfied. Very few products are profitable in V1, and Fadell says profitability should not yet be expected. This is the time to figure out product–market fit and learn what needs to be improved.

With V2, having fixed the things that were wrong with V1, you are ready for the Early Majority. You've identified your problems and fixed them. You're understanding the customer journey and widening your market. This is where profitability can begin to kick in.

And by V3, you are refining your now-great product. You're able to focus less on the product and more on the business, polishing every touchpoint of the customer lifecycle. You may be getting enough sales volume to reduce prices and still make money.[9]

I agree with everything Tony Fadell says, but of course you can't entirely segment your marketing to sell exclusively to select buyer types, locking the others out. While the buyers do tend to self-select, all walks of life might own every version of your product. What differs will be the concentration of each type in your user base, and each one's level of satisfaction.

Over time your marketing content should also evolve to support every viable kind of buyer. That doesn't mean the technical details should be allowed to overwhelm easily digested visuals. We are all led by our speedy dog brain, and have the same basic brain architecture, regardless of what part of it tends to be dominant in our decision-making process. Building out your blog content, linking to new white papers, and adding new publication logos can all be done without dampening the dog brain's excitement.

INNOVATION INTERLUDE:
DUOLINGO'S HOT STREAK

Duolingo, the popular language-learning app, taps into the brain's need recognition mechanisms with its "streak" feature.

The streak counter, which tracks consecutive days of app usage, cleverly engages both the "dog brain" and "tank brain":

Dog Brain (Limbic System): The immediate reward of seeing the streak number increase triggers a dopamine release, creating a sense of accomplishment and encouraging continued use.

Tank Brain (Neocortex): The fear of breaking the streak appeals to our loss aversion tendencies, motivating users to maintain their learning habit.

This feature has been remarkably effective: users with a 7-day streak are 3.6 times more likely to continue using the app long-term compared to those without. Moreover, Duolingo found that users are willing to spend money on "streak freezes" to maintain their counters, directly impacting the app's revenue.[10]

By understanding how different parts of the brain process rewards and risks, Duolingo created a simple yet powerful feature that drives user engagement and supports long-term behavior change.

Gradually, a spectrum of buyers become your entire community, and some go on to become ambassadors of the brand. You know this is happening when skeptics and trolls are quickly called out on social media by proud product owners.

It's fascinating to watch the diffusion of innovation play out in real-time over a product's early weeks, especially considering that the curve originally represented a timeframe of months or even years.

A product's overall sales growth and market share can still continue to follow a similar pattern at scale over a longer term and as it is brought to new beachheads for larger markets. But to do so it has to prove sufficiently needed to excite new audiences of prospective buyers, while continuing to delight existing owners. And as a product matures and new versions are introduced, it can continue to attract the early buyer types — as long as a newer, flashier alternative hasn't emerged.

For you as the product maker, scaling up buyer successes in a big way only happens when you stay true to the motivation that inspired you to create the product in the first place and focus on reverse engineering the gratification you want every customer to feel from using it. It almost never just happens. This means once you target and begin to convert the right people, the product has got to seriously deliver, for every type of buyer.

Instant Pot achieved unprecedented success promising a fast and convenient cooking experience, leveraging Amazon's community of customers who double as product evaluators. Demonstrating the vast range of meals an Instant Pot can quickly cook illustrates the number of ways it will improve the customer's life — while simultaneously triggering a limbic need feeding frenzy. Instant Pot Founder Robert Wang created the new category of multi-cookers out of thin air in 2010 and a mere decade later the product had an estimated household penetration of 26 percent. (For context, auto-drip coffee makers have been around since 1954 and have a household penetration of 58 percent.)[11]

The Instant Pot made impressive promises. And had it failed to deliver, the truth would have been quickly revealed by the switched-on Amazon community, making such runaway success impossible. It not only delivered, but continues to boast new use cases through a large and experimental fan base.

Similarly, Peloton promotes how it delivers motivation, community, pride and adrenaline. It taps into our profound desires to be connected, strong and triumphant. The roster of instructors has become increasingly diverse, to reflect many ethnicities, body types and physical abilities, with adaptive training for members with different abilities. Instructors dish out constant affirmations, cheering community members while cracking jokes and offering tips to break monotony and help users achieve personal goals. Whether you're on a bike, treadmill or rowing machine, a live leaderboard rewards every hard effort with a real-time boost in standings against fellow members doing the same thing at the same time. (You can even voyeuristically peek in on stats like the live wattage output of a competing member.) This is all limbic brain stuff that we can't get enough of — and ongoing positive reinforcement against the tank brain's concerns over the monthly subscription cost.

The success of Peloton's competitive element is not a coincidence either. According to Robert Trivers, one of the world's top evolutionary biologists, competition is among our strongest impulses. Whether we're competing on a leaderboard, trying to outdo the Joneses with our outdoor light display, or earn more money than that annoying brother-in-law, we're suckers for competition. Trivers explains that there isn't a stop mechanism inside of us that says, "Relax, you've got enough," because accumulating excess is a relatively new possibility. We've evolved to be maximizing machines, and we greedily seek to rack up ever more points, more money and more wins, regardless of how much we've already got.[12]

The better you understand how human brains process needs and translate them to action, the more effective you can be at marketing to real-world customers.

Soon, you will begin to recognize how the pieces come together, and you'll start seeing successful marketing campaigns (and creating your own unique ones) in ways you could never have done before.

KEY INSIGHTS FROM CHAPTER 6

- Human actions are driven by a two-stage processing system: the primary (impulsive) system and a secondary (cautious) system.
- The primary system seeks instant gratification while the secondary system rationalizes decisions, often after they have been made.
- The human brain consists of three major parts: the central brain, the limbic system and the neocortex.
- The central brain controls basic needs and is usually in stand-by mode, while the limbic system triggers emotional responses and manages feelings, memory and trust. The limbic system is impulsive and emotional, much like a dog, so we call it the "dog brain."
- The neocortex is the rationalizing part of the brain and processes complex tasks but is vastly slower than the limbic system. It is smart and strategic but slow-moving like a sophisticated battle tank, hence our nickname "tank brain."
- The limbic system encourages emotion-driven behaviors for dopamine rewards, influencing buying decisions.
- Brain scans can predict buying behavior based on limbic brain activity.
- Focus on gratifying the limbic system (dog brain) with excitement and emotions rather than overwhelming technical details which must engage the neocortex (tank brain). Remember the faster limbic system is mainly visual.
- Emotions, even anger or anxiety, trigger action. Contentment equals inaction.
- Post-purchase confirmation and reassurance are essential to counteract buyer's remorse.
- Use visual cues like demonstrations, starred reviews and simple value points to amp up emotion and confidence in a product's value.

DO THESE NOW FOR QUICK WINS:

IDENTIFY CORE EMOTIONAL TRIGGERS

Spend 10 minutes outlining the emotional triggers your product addresses, and connect these with the fundamental needs or desires your product fulfills.

PRIORITIZE EMOTIONAL IMPACT

Ensure your marketing materials evoke the strongest possible emotions in your target audience. Focus on excitement, pride, happiness, or the liberating relief that your product provides. Trigger anxiety or even anger if appropriate, but be mindful not to lull your audience into complacency with messaging that fosters contentment.

PLAN ENGAGING DEMONSTRATIONS

With your team, brainstorm engaging visual demonstrations that showcase the emotional benefits of your product in action. Demonstrate real-world scenarios of your product being used in ways that trigger feelings of excitement and resonate with potential buyers.

FOCUS ON VISUAL CONTENT

Think about how you can craft visually appealing content that speaks to the dog brain. Use lots of images, videos and graphics to convey emotional benefits. The more progress dog brain can make on its own, the better your content is likely to perform.

STUDY SUCCESSFUL CAMPAIGNS

Choose one successful marketing campaign in your industry and analyze how it appeals to different brain components.

Identify one actionable insight you can apply to your own marketing efforts.

MONITOR CONVERSION METRICS

Use a dashboard to keep a close eye on conversion rates and customer engagement metrics. A slip in your online store's conversion rate could be seasonal — or might signal a mistake you've begun to make.

Adjust your emotional messaging based on how well it's currently resonating with potential buyers, testing one small change at a time to understand what is and is not working.

IDENTIFY BRAIN FUNCTIONS IN YOUR OWN DECISIONS

Reflect on two or three recent buying decisions you've made and identify which brain components influenced each decision.

Write down specific examples of how the primal (dog brain) and neocortex (tank brain) played a role. How can a similar approach be applied to your product?

ADDRESS BUYER'S REMORSE

Head off buyer's remorse and draft post-purchase messaging that reaffirms the decision your customers have made.

Plan Getting Started tips, guides, or success stories that encourage buyer success and support the emotional benefits of your product. Create email drip campaigns that help buyers to succeed with your product, guiding them through early adoption into becoming power users.

STREAMLINE POST-PURCHASE EXPERIENCE:

Detail a seamless and reassuring post-purchase experience. Plan to send immediate order confirmations and follow-ups to alleviate any doubts or concerns.

Authenticate emails sent by your online store to come from your company's domain and prevent them being lost in the customer's junk folder.

CHAPTER 7

We Don't Need Another Apple

In This Chapter:

- *The pitfalls of attempting to emulate Apple's success*
- *The importance of uniqueness and staying true to your brand's vision*
- *Strategies for carving out your own place in customers' hearts*
- *Focusing on solving customer needs in a fresh and resonant way*

I'M GOING TO SAY IT. Way too many business books include case studies about Apple.

It's fairly obvious why: Apple is the most successful company in the history of the world, with true cult appeal and beautiful, secure, well-built products anyone can use. Apple almost always comes up in my discussions with a new client around how they want to be perceived. So, I'll apologize now, and explain why this book couldn't help but reference the brand at least a few times — and had to include this one short chapter, dedicated to Apple.

I have loved Apple products for most of my life.

My first connection with the company was in 1978. My father, an elementary school principal, had a friend named John Gray who taught computer programming at a small university. A gentle bachelor with a British accent and a penchant for coral-colored corduroy suits, John drove an enormous wood-paneled station wagon and gave me Christmas gifts wrapped in thick wallpaper that cracked at the folds. He was thrifty and eccentric and generous enough to leave an Apple II computer, often for weeks on end, in the care of nine-year-old me.

I played games from John's stacks of 5-1/4" floppy disks and read books he'd given me about programming in a language called BASIC. I never became a software developer as John might have hoped, but I was hooked on computers years before most of my schoolmates ever saw one.

As a marketing agency owner, I've bought hundreds of Apple products over the decades and have always kept attuned to the company's marketing. When I bought my first computer at 22 to start a magazine publishing business with two journalism school classmates, I needed it to be a Mac.

And now, when my product clients tell me they want to market like Apple, I completely get it. I understand how that brand has resonated with generations of consumers, from the early days to the launch of the first Macintosh, to the iMac, the iPod, iPhone, iPad, Apple Watch, Apple TV, Vision Pro and whatever else. There are so many fascinating twists to the story, from Steve Jobs and Steve Wozniak starting the Apple Computer Company out of a Silicon Valley garage to Jobs' traumatic ousting, prodigal return and untimely death in 2011. It's the subject of numerous books and movies, and I've absorbed many of them.

Here's the thing: your company and product are nothing at all like Apple. At the time of this writing, Apple is the world's most valuable brand, with a market cap of three trillion dollars — more than the Gross Domestic Product of all but the world's top six countries. It's astonishing the company got there and equally surprising it even survived.

Huge companies like Apple enjoy heaps of luxuries that are completely inaccessible to an emerging product maker. Luxuries like massive marketing budgets and instant recognition from decades of reinvesting profits to build a brand that has touched nearly everyone on earth. Each Apple product launch leverages the cumulative benefits of billions of dollars' worth of brand equity, leadership and trust.

Apple events enjoy free worldwide publicity worth tens of millions. Only a handful of brands (like Tesla, Amazon and Google) get anywhere near as much of our attention just for doing their thing. Apple has thousands of marketers, product engineers, designers, developers and expert thinkers. In 2023, its total staff count exceeded 164,000 full-time equivalent employees.[1]

Apple has also made big mistakes and launched several products that utterly flopped. Any one of its nearly forgotten missteps could probably bankrupt your company a thousand times over. (You can, however, learn from those mistakes for free.)

So, you're nothing like Apple — and will never be.

Emulating Apple isn't just unrealistic. Doing so, if you could, would defeat the purpose: copying an innovator makes you a follower, not a leader. It *is* helpful to take inspiration and study the many things Apple has done phenomenally well. It can inspire you to understand what has fueled the passion behind those successes, while you create something completely unique to your own vision.

You should absolutely be obsessed with ease of use and focus on delivering fantasy-inducing messaging for quality products people love to use. Objectives like those are important to any brand's success. But you're not Apple, and that's just fine.

Apple spends most of its time trying to innovate and none trying to be like someone else. That may be the most Apple thing about Apple.

So, what is the most *your brand* thing about your brand?

You have the luxury of carving out your own way to occupy a special place in every customer's heart. That means defining your own distinct values and style. Apple set out to be unique in making tech products that non-techies could use to create things. People needed that in the 1970s and still do.

It's time to think about what your product delivers in standout ways — and what your ideal customers will need from it.

As you continue to develop your product and brand, keep in mind that your success hinges on understanding and addressing the unique needs of your target audience. In the next chapter, we'll dive deeper into strategies for identifying and connecting with your ideal customers.

INNOVATION INTERLUDE:
PATAGONIA'S "DON'T BUY THIS JACKET" CAMPAIGN

In 2011, outdoor clothing company **Patagonia** launched a counter-intuitive Black Friday ad campaign with a full-page ad in *The New York Times*, boldly demanding "Don't Buy This Jacket."

The ad detailed the environmental costs of producing the brand's best-selling R2 fleece jacket, and urged consumers to consider the impact of their purchases. Instead of pushing for more sales, Patagonia encouraged customers to buy only what they needed and to repair, reuse, and recycle their existing gear.

This campaign:

1. Reinforced Patagonia's core value of sustainability
2. Distinguished the brand from competitors focused solely on increasing sales
3. Built trust with consumers by being transparent about their production processes
4. Increased sales and loyalty by aligning with buyer values

The campaign's success demonstrated that staying true to your brand's unique vision and values can be more effective than trying to emulate industry giants. By taking a stand that resonated with their target audience, Patagonia strengthened its brand identity and customer relationships.[2]

KEY INSIGHTS FROM CHAPTER 7

- Your company and product could hardly be more unlike Apple, which enjoys advantages like massive budgets and instant worldwide recognition from decades of brand-building.
- Directly emulating Apple is unrealistic and counterproductive; copying an innovator makes you a follower, not a leader.
- While you are encouraged to draw inspiration from Apple and other leaders, it's crucial to create a brand that's unique to your own vision.
- Apple's emphasis on innovation rather than imitation is a defining characteristic.
- Every brand has the opportunity to carve out its own special place in customers' hearts by focusing on what makes it unique.

DO THESE NOW FOR QUICK WINS:

TALK ABOUT YOUR ORIGINAL VISION

Take some time to articulate your product's purpose and the impact it can make. Write these things down and start working them into conversations. What sets the product and your brand apart from competitors?

Lean hard into your own true values and empower them to shape the brand's identity. Understand how your journey is unique and where your superpowers reside.

Verbalize to others how your product will do that and the impact you hope to make, with the goal of being original. If your brand sounds like a copy of another, it won't feel fresh or true — or be exciting.

When it is uniquely you, it will be a story no one has heard before.

EVOLVE YOUR UNIQUE VALUE PROPOSITION

What makes your product indispensable? Whether it's solving a specific pain point, offering convenience, or delivering a specific experience, pinpoint and refine your unique value proposition.

This is the foundation of your brand's identity, and more discussions will help sharpen it. Try applying your value proposition to a competing option. If it fits that option, it isn't uniquely you.

Keep refining until it is.

DEFINE YOUR BRAND'S VALUES AND AUDIENCE

Just like Apple's original values that guided its innovation and growth, go back to those core values that drive *your* product. Is it about simplicity, empowerment, sustainability, or something else? Is it a unique combination of values and actions, like a new donation model?

Let these values guide your decision-making and not only resonate with, but define your target audience.

FOCUS ON HIGH-IMPACT BENEFITS

Shift your messaging focus from technical features to high-impact benefits other options do not deliver to customers. How does your product enhance their lives?

Use clear, visual and exciting language to convey these benefits, sparking the imagination of your potential customers.

TELL YOUR *OWN* STORY

Every product has an exciting backstory — share yours authentically. Explain why you as the founder embarked on this journey, the challenges you faced and how your product evolved.

Authentic storytelling creates emotional connections that resonate with customers and build empathy. Your founder story should be in the *About Us* page of your website and also on the welcome messages you send to every new subscriber and customer.

SHOWCASE USER SUCCESS

Highlight real-life success stories of your customers. These testimonials provide social proof and demonstrate how your product fulfills its promises. Real-world user stories build trust and establish your product's credibility. They make excellent blog posts, ads and newsletter content.

Prospective buyers often find it easier to relate to others in their situation than most marketing content. True stories add credibility and remove barriers.

—

Creating a product that directly addresses customer needs takes a deep understanding of your uniqueness and the value you can bring. While Apple's success is inspiring and remarkable, your focus should be on solving customer needs in a fresh way that resonates with your values and the product's impact on buyers.

CHAPTER 8

The Elements of Product Need

In This Chapter:

- *The CLIMB™ framework for understanding customer needs*
- *Functional, emotional, transformative, and transcendent benefits*
- *The importance of simple, concise messaging for the "dog brain"*
- *Real-world examples of products that address multiple need levels*

HUMAN BEINGS ARE COMPLEX CREATURES, each of us with a powerful drive to improve our life and feel rewarded.

A desirable product delivers improvements on at least one, and possibly multiple, levels.

It can be a little daunting to identify and understand all the ways even a simple product improves a customer's life, much less how a complex and versatile one can. (A smartphone, for example, can perform an infinite array of functions through installable apps and its cameras, processors, speakers, LED light, connection port, ultra-fast wireless internet, Bluetooth connectivity, touchscreen display and plethora of sensors.)

While desirability is highly subjective, it is valuable to prioritize our messaging and focus down on the most important attributes of an innovative product in order to pull those limbic triggers.

It's something nearly all product marketers struggle with. I am often tasked with helping them identify the needs addressed by a product and rank the importance of the ways it can evoke them. All needs are important, so what do we lead with?

Prioritizing the needs addressed by a product helps the product team avoid distractions. It enables the marketing team to focus on the most important value points from the customer's perspective. Done right, marketing often discovers value that resonates better than what was previously seen to be the main selling point.

To achieve this consistently, I worked out a framework to map, score and prioritize what I call the Customer Life-Improving Mechanisms and Benefits (CLIMB™) — all the attributes that make a product desirable, useful and needed by buyers.

While CLIMB™ can be helpful when applied to simple products like a hand tool or food ingredient, it is particularly enlightening with innovative products that don't fit into an existing product category, or that can deliver a multitude of outcomes.

Regardless of what you're selling, the messaging has got to be simple and concise. The customer's high-speed dog brain lacks the patience or ability to process a lot of complicated content on its own. And in the limited instances when a prospect will opt to dig deeper, they can only do so by using the much slower, more demanding and risk-averse tank brain.

Landing page heatmaps and fMRI scans offer plenty of evidence that if the primal brain is not hooked immediately, the selling opportunity tends to disappear — usually for good. Meaning all the money spent getting the prospective buyer to that point goes to waste.

When you say to someone, "Don't judge me," you're making a request that is beyond unreasonable. It's impossible. Our dog brain sizes people and products up virtually instantaneously, through processes over which we have no control. We may be able to manage our visible responses to some extent, but we can neither turn off judging, nor erase the judgments we've already made.

A consumer's perception and opinion of your product are deeply imprinted at the speed of neural processing.

Multiple benefits, beloved though they are to product makers, end up competing with one another in the audience's mind. They can ultimately drive buyers away by making them frustrated, confused and possibly resentful that you've wasted their time. A customer's focus gets progressively more diffused and diluted, not more aroused, with each additional message or feature you tack onto the list.

An intuitive and impulsive dog brain simply cannot process bunches of desires at the same time. It is out for gratification, not complexity. And while the rational tank brain is capable of processing details, it is generally more interested in uncovering barriers or risks than in encouraging the dog brain's randy and self-centered impulses. It will hold any incoherencies, logic gaps or lack of proof against your product.

So the value your product delivers must be outlandishly clear, as well as more exciting and far simpler than most product marketers (never mind most engineers, God bless them) can succinctly articulate.

As a marketer, you can seldom count on the customer's analytic rational brain to engage and voluntarily dig deeper. Startup company leaders often envision building pages and pages of online store content, including vast libraries of educational material and resources.

But if you've ever studied conversion analytics from a web store, you know what really happens. The vast majority of visitors, especially those coming from paid digital ads, stay on a landing page for only a few seconds.

So the tank brain seldom even shows up at the party.

Even if your ideal customer is highly engaged or ubiquitous, you can't afford to have most audience members instantly peace out. Many otherwise smart startups have learned the hard way that a big funding raise enabling them to throw mega-bucks at marketing almost never generates the expected results. (Cue the next demoralizing wave of layoffs...)

In one visitor after another, the dog brain arrives, sniffs around — and doesn't let the door catch its tail on the way out.

We don't like to believe this will happen for our own product. And it's an easy enough scenario to dismiss based on selective recollection from our personal experiences. Our neocortex loves to trick us into believing it has played a bigger role in decision-making than science shows it really does.

INNOVATION INTERLUDE:
POST-IT NOTES STICK ON NEW NEEDS

3M's **Post-it Notes**, invented in 1968, initially struggled to find market traction. It wasn't until the product was given away as free samples that users discovered its transformative benefits in organization and communication[1].

This shift from focusing on functional attributes (low-tack adhesive) to emotional and transformative benefits (ease of use, improved productivity) propelled Post-it Notes to become a ubiquitous office staple, demonstrating the power of addressing higher-level needs you'll see in the CLIMB™ framework.

In your own experiences as a buyer, you can probably think of times where your rational brain got quite involved in a buying process. A car or home purchase, for example — or a computer system where you had specific compatibility and performance needs to satisfy. Complicated decisions like these (referred to as "considered purchases") can switch on the neocortex to elicit slower, deeper consideration.

Specific performance, functionality or safety requirements, when they are the key motivators or deciding factors, can even overrule desire and impulse. (That minivans exist is proof the rational mind can sometimes prevail.)

The most successful auto sales reps know that if a buyer is interested in the emotional benefits of a car, like speed and aesthetics, they should say, "I *feel* this is the one for you." And if the buyer is evaluating analytically, the winning statement is, "I *think* this is the one for you."

You might also have felt a desire to own a house that's way beyond your budget, or a fast-depreciating sports car that makes no logical sense to buy, maintain and insure. That's your dog brain at work.

Another thing about those bigger or more technical product purchases: the buyer in such cases is usually evaluating offerings from known, admired and trusted brands. That buyer deliberately entered the evaluation process with the expectation of investing more time and effort than usual into making a buying decision. The tank brain was warmed up in advance, leaving the dog brain on a short leash outside the store. Sometimes, though, the dog brain does manage to get involved even in a considered big-ticket purchase — with the expected outcome. The tank brain then gets tasked with rationalizing a splurge after the papers are signed.

For most of us, the car we drive or the house we live in won our hearts very quickly. We were emotionally sold before we went through the motions of creating our pros-and-cons list.

USING CLIMB™ TO UNDERSTAND NEED DRIVERS

IN PERFORMING a CLIMB™ assessment for clients, we work with the client to identify the core motivations that drive purchases based on needs. We then apply a scoring matrix to evaluate the impact of each buying trigger. These "Customer Life-Improving Mechanisms and Benefits" can be visualized as a ladder of four principal sets of motivational drivers that, somewhat analogously to Maslow's pyramid, run from bottom to top: from basic functional needs at the base to transcendent goals that are much bigger than the buyer.

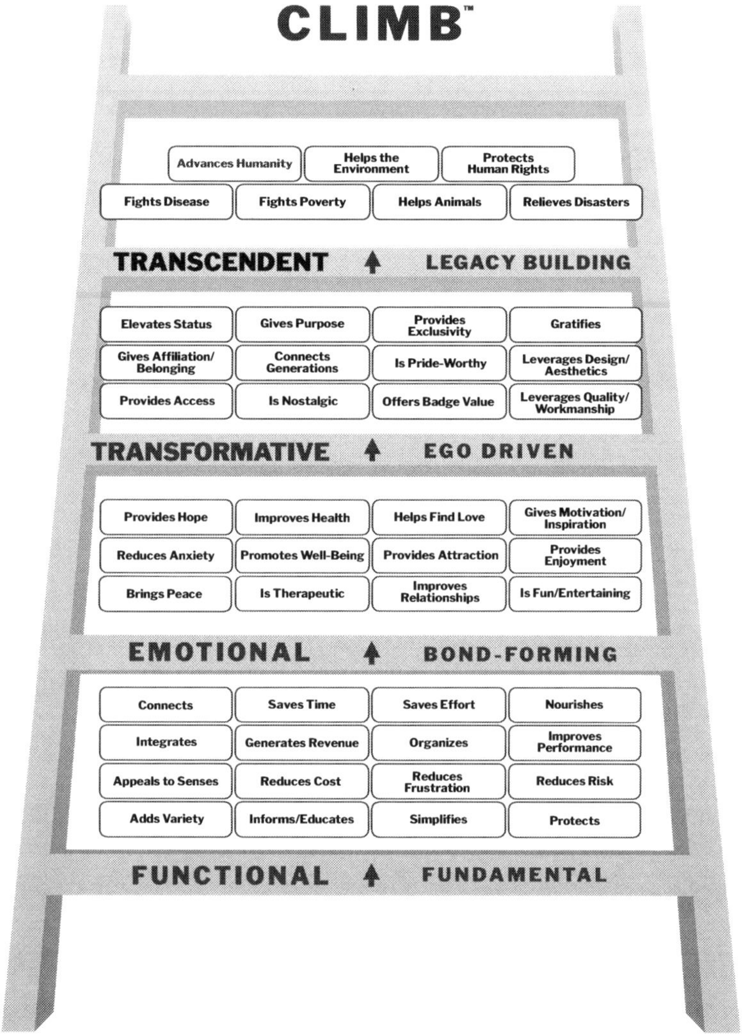

***Figure 8.1. The CLIMB™ Framework.** The ladder rungs represent four ascending levels of product value: functional, emotional, transformative and transcendent benefits.*

FUNCTIONAL BENEFITS

FUNCTIONAL BENEFITS achieve tasks or enable actions with specific fundamental purposes. In order for function-centric products to be successful in the marketplace, the buyer has to recognize such a need exists and be actively looking for a new way to fulfill it. The pain must be great enough that people are willing to risk hard-earned money, abandon their current solution and invest their only non-renewable asset (time) in the adoption curve.

A functional benefit can be one that:

- **Connects:** brings together or unifies two or more products, devices or individuals
- **Integrates:** combines the functionality of two or more existing products or tools
- **Appeals to the senses:** delivers a sensory function enjoyable to the senses of sight, smell, hearing, touch or taste — or a combination of these
- **Adds variety:** brings interest and variation to life or to a routine activity
- **Saves time:** adds speed and efficiency to a repetitive task or process
- **Generates revenue:** monetizes or increases money earned by performing a task or selling a product
- **Reduces costs:** lessens the money spent in achieving an outcome
- **Informs or educates:** provides or facilitates the acquisition of knowledge or skills
- **Saves effort:** reduces the amount of work needed to perform a task
- **Organizes:** creates order, structure, or hierarchy
- **Reduces frustration:** lessens anxiety caused by inefficiency, inadequacy or waste
- **Simplifies:** reduces complexity of a task or lifestyle
- **Nourishes:** provides food, energy, nutrients and sustenance
- **Improves performance:** optimizes efficacy, whether athletic, sexual, functional or intellectual in the consumer, or increases the effectiveness of a tool, vehicle or other product

- **Reduces risk:** lessens the likelihood of harm being done to the owner or loved ones, mitigates possibility of failure
- **Protects:** prevents injury, harm or death; rescues from danger

Products that serve mainly functional needs are among the easiest for consumers to understand, and are sought by buyers who have already identified the need. This means functional product brands can target search engine queries and leverage paid search ads.

Products that address one or two functional needs often sell in extremely competitive categories (think power tools, home appliances and some packaged goods), meaning their positioning has to clearly communicate the value delivered in contrast with other options. Incumbent tools from brands people already know have a huge advantage, even over demonstrably better offerings from a less-known or new brand.

Use visuals and simple language to drive essential messaging to the impulsive dog brain. Clearly connect to the functional need being addressed. Show pictures and punch out — don't explain at length — why your product is the paws-down best solution. Don't invite the tank brain to labor on a dog brain decision.

Most software tools are promoted on the bases of simplifying, saving time and saving effort. Achieving these things exceptionally well are functions of outstanding user experience design. The best functional products seldom win or lose on features and benefits. Their success is nearly always tied to how easy and pleasurable the product is to learn, adopt, use and maintain.

The buyer's tank brain is always ready to ponder whether or not it enjoys the warm bath of the existing solution enough to stay in it — or if the promise of something dramatically better justifies stepping out into the chilly air to brave the shock of transition, along with all the terrifying risks.

EMOTIONAL BENEFITS

EMOTIONAL BENEFITS primarily influence the feelings of the product's owner, with potential ripple effects on others close to them. An emotion-driven product forms a bond with consumers when it:

- **Brings inner peace**
- **Gratifies**
- **Is nostalgic**
- **Leverages design and aesthetics**
- **Offers badge value**
- **Contributes to well-being**
- **Provides exclusivity**
- **Brings enjoyment**
- **Creates attraction**
- **Is pride-worthy**
- **Leverages quality and workmanship**
- **Adds variety**

Products with emotional benefits also natively speak the language of our dog brain, and sparking that connection is crucial to success.

Our desires for enjoyment, inner peace, pride and variety are what drive us to take the biggest risks of our lives. They're why we'll leave the safety, certainty and comforts of our lifelong home to experience a dangerous foreign country. Or wager half of everything we own that a marriage will work out.

Fantasy drives product sales unlike anything else. It is easy to create evocative desires around a product that delivers emotional rewards like attraction and exclusivity — as long as you have enough credibility and trust with the buyer. They have to believe your product can actually make it happen.

This is a big part of why branding is so valuable in the product world.

Take a moment to think of the ONE brand you know, like and trust the most. It might be Apple, Bosch or Lululemon. Your absolute favorite — the one whose logo you'd be most likely to tattoo across your chest (if you haven't already done so).

Next time that brand launches a product you need, what will stop you from buying it? You probably won't shop it against the competition, or sweat the nickels and dimes on price. Or wonder if it will be able to do everything it promises.

And if it is a visible product — one people will see you wearing or using in public — you are even more likely to pay a premium price or wait in line to enjoy a badge-value-induced dopamine high when your peers get a load of you sporting it.

TRANSFORMATIVE BENEFITS

TRANSFORMATIVE BENEFITS bring substantial, undeniable advancements to the owner's life journey and social circumstances. These needs are directly tied to the ego.* They include attributes that affect our status and connectedness to people we care about. A product is transformative when it:

- **Improves health**
- **Reduces anxiety**
- **Provides hope**
- **Gives purpose**
- **Offers motivation or inspiration**
- **Unites generations**
- **Brings affection or belonging**
- **Is therapeutic**
- **Elevates status**
- **Provides access**
- **Helps find love**
- **Improves relationships**

---

* Funnily, clients have asked me to remove "ego" from their Go-to-Market Roadmaps so many times that I seldom use it anymore in that context. Folks don't like the word. But the ego connection is a reality, and between you and me, a very important one.

Transformative products are some of the most fulfilling to create, because they deliver truly meaningful outcomes to the people who use them. And like functional and emotional needs, they can connect directly to the dog brain. Some of our deepest-felt needs are tied to transformative benefits — from status and purpose to our health and our most precious relationships.

Transformative benefits sometimes come from a product's original purpose. Other times, they're discovered along the way.

In 2013, four MIT engineering students entered a design competition with a smart wristband that could warm or cool the sensitive skin on the wearer's inner wrist at the touch of a button. They called it Wristify.

The idea was sparked when the team members were working together in an uncomfortably cold lab space. They wondered if it could be possible to heat and cool a person's body directly by putting a small electronic device in the right place, saving the energy required to climate-control entire large rooms. They began rapid-prototyping and arrived at a working model just a few days before the competition deadline.

They won. The whirlwind of publicity drove the partners to take their idea further. They patented the algorithmic technology that intensified the brain's response to heating and cooling by using waveform pulses.[2] When wearers felt the warming or cooling pulses, they experienced a corresponding sense of temperature change throughout their bodies. While our body core temperature stays remarkably static — within a fraction of a degree — the brain tells us if we're too hot or cold. The device could effectively signal to the wearer's brain that the entire body was warming or cooling using thermal waveforms on a highly sensitive area.

Embr Labs was born, and the product became the Embr Wave. As more and more people began to use it, they discovered that the

Wave was especially helpful for perimenopausal women experiencing hot flashes and night sweats. Independent tests confirmed that most people who suffered from debilitating hot flashes found immediate relief. The tests also validated that the Wave consistently reduced stress and improved sleep quality.[3]

In all, the Wave addresses a boatload of Functional, Transformative and Emotional benefits, by improving comfort, sleep quality and consequently productivity. The companion app adds social connectivity, control and data-driven insights that can be easily shared with healthcare professionals.

In working with Embr Labs, we found the Wave had one of the highest CLIMB™ scores we'd seen among hundreds of evaluated products, despite its apparent simplicity. Together with Embr's teams, we recognized the importance of positioning the product for its ability to quickly stop hot flashes at the touch of a button and even more importantly, to help perimenopausal women regain a lost sense of control over their bodies.

The Wave addresses several very significant needs in a convenient, immediate, drug-free way. And despite the inevitable arrival of competitors, it remains the leader by far.

TRANSCENDENT BENEFITS

TRANSCENDENT BENEFITS create results that help numerous others and may outlive the product's original owner. A product is of potentially transcendent nature when it can:

- **Advance humanity** (regenerative medicine products, Virgin Galactic)
- **Help the environment** (Tentree, Seventh Generation, Lush Soaps)
- **Protect human rights** (Unilever, Marks & Spencer)
- **Fight disease** (Johnson & Johnson, Apellis, Moderna)

- **Combat poverty** (Kimberly-Clark's Toilets Change Lives program, TOMS Shoes, Parallel Sleep, Warby Parker)
- **Help animals** (Jack Black Skincare, Endangered Species Chocolate)
- **Provide disaster relief** (Concrete Canvas Shelters, Rainfresh Water Treatment Systems)
- **Deliver another positive outcome** that's otherwise vastly beyond the reach of an individual consumer

Products with a transcendent component are usually created by purpose-driven enterprises or philanthropic founders who have a goal much more meaningful than profits and market domination. Unsurprisingly, business success often follows for companies that have the winning combination of a transcendent purpose, a great product, strong leadership, and a solid business plan.

Embr Labs' CEO Elizabeth Gazda believes the Wave also has genuine transcendent potential. Sudden hot flashes and menopausal sleep disruptions have curtailed countless women's careers — at what ought to be the peak years of their lives. Using the Embr Wave can help women stay in leadership positions longer. The product can enable its owner to regain lost energy and achieve the confidence to be politically active. The Embr Wave aims to break down barriers that contribute to glass ceilings for women. And with thousands of five-star reviews and many enthusiastic influencers, it seems Embr users are all aboard.

TOMS Shoes achieved a peak value of $625 million in 2014 by donating a pair of shoes to a child in a developing country for every pair of its canvas shoes sold. This gave absolutely no tangible benefit to buyers — in fact they were potentially paying twice as much as necessary to benefit a complete stranger. But buying into TOMS' philosophy added perceived value and made customers feel good about their choice.

The shoes themselves were simple and inexpensive to manufacture. That's generally a good thing, but proved to be TOMS' Achilles heel. The less-than-novel design made it impossible for TOMS to secure intellectual property protection — and very easy for competitors to sell nearly identical shoes for less.

Knockoffs enjoyed much higher margins because they required making and distributing just a single pair per sale. From copycat brands like BOBS (made by sneaker giant Skechers) to counterfeits outright pretending to be TOMS, the market became awash with cheap and confusing alternatives. Sales declined and losses piled up.

While TOMS expanded to coffee and glasses and eventually decoupled from the one-to-one model after being bought out by its creditors, it is considered a groundbreaking purpose-driven brand.[4] Without a doubt, that transcendent purpose fueled its success.

I recently helped launch Parallel, a sleep brand whose flagship product is a pillow — a very nice pillow. It has an ultrasoft outer cover made from sustainable Tencel fibers, an antimicrobial inner cover and a hybrid fill with double the airflow of conventional pillows. The fill is a unique blend: two kinds of precision-cut memory foam plus downy fibers upcycled from plastic water bottles. The Parallel Pillow is sculptable and can be infinitely adjusted by adding or removing fill. (Parallel even ships extra fill for free upon request to avoid the material waste from shipping a bundle with every unit sold the way competing adjustable pillows do.)

So, yes, it's a great product. But there's something else. The Parallel Pillow is branded the "World's Kindest Pillow." Similar to the TOMS' embedded donation model, Parallel gifts a pillow to a person in need with every Parallel Pillow sold. Donor pillow recipients are kids, adults and seniors who have been displaced, without even a pillow to hug at night. Partnerships with national charities give the Denver-based startup credibility and national reach for distributing its donation pillows at scale.

People love the Parallel Pillow, because it is truly an excellent product, designed to suit nearly every type of sleeper. When testing competing products, I slept for months on premium pillows by Purple, Pillow Cube, LAYR, Casper and many others. I was so impressed by the Parallel Pillow that I still sleep on one. It's a remarkable product. The company's transcendent purpose makes consumers feel great about spending a little more to own one — while helping another human. With that, plus a comfortable pillow keeping their neck and spine aligned, they can sleep better at night.

If you're interested in creating a transcendent product, it still has to be new, exciting and hard to copy. Even if people connect deeply with your purpose (and hopefully many will), the reviews they write always reflect their experience with the actual product. Even if they love your transcendent purpose, they won't recommend a so-so product to a friend — or buy it a second time — if something else would do a better job.

The product still has to be fantastic.

Each of the CLIMB™ components your product achieves should help to position your product and brand to speak to ideal customers. But they mustn't compete with each other.

APPLYING CLIMB™ TO YOUR PRODUCT

ONCE YOU HAVE IDENTIFIED which of these elements your product delivers, it becomes easier to rank and prioritize messaging based on the value they bring to the buyer. With my clients, we use a scoring matrix that groups the product's life-improving benefits together by ladder rung, enabling us to compare it to a database of numerous similarly focused products.

For your own product, go back to the CLIMB™ ladder and make a list of the benefits that directly apply to each rung. Be objective and include only those that are a direct result of using the product. For example, a product that "brings inner peace" should do so for the majority of people who use it rather than only in rare and convoluted instances. Although Instagram might be used to share calming images by some users, we know it has exactly the opposite effect on many more.

Step away from the product, or better yet, have an outsider challenge each benefit you identify. Their job is to call you out where you're stretching it, and they may also see legitimate benefits that haven't previously occurred to you.

With that list, you are ready to look at the outcomes a buyer can realistically hope to achieve by using the product.

KEY INSIGHTS FROM CHAPTER 8

- Desirable products deliver improvements to customers' lives on multiple levels, ranging from functional to transformative, emotional and transcendent benefits.

- The CLIMB™ framework (Customer Life-Improving Mechanisms and Benefits) helps prioritize and communicate the ways a product fulfills customer needs.

- Four categories of needs within the CLIMB™ framework:

  - **Functional Benefits:** These benefits are related to how a product performs tasks and functions, such as saving time, reducing costs and improving performance.

  - **Emotional Benefits:** Emotional benefits evoke specific feelings in customers, such as pride, enjoyment and inner peace.

  - **Transformative Benefits:** Transformative benefits lead to significant advancements in a person's life journey and social circumstances, impacting areas like health, motivation and relationships.

  - **Transcendent Benefits:** Transcendent benefits go beyond individual buyers, contributing to larger causes such as advancing humanity, protecting human rights, or helping the environment.

- Simple and concise messaging is crucial, as the primal brain makes snap judgments about needing a product.

- A product's success isn't solely dependent on its features and benefits; the emotional connection and value it provides can be even more important.

- Understanding and applying the CLIMB framework helps marketers position and market products effectively by focusing on the most relevant benefits that resonate with customers' needs.

- By identifying and prioritizing the benefits a product offers, marketers can better communicate its value and create a strong connection with potential customers.
- Transformational and transcendent benefits often require purpose-driven business strategies and can establish a strong brand identity.
- Emotional and transformative benefits tap into the primal brain's desires, while functional benefits appeal to the rational brain's understanding.
- Successful products often fulfill multiple needs simultaneously, addressing different aspects of customers' lives and enhancing their overall well-being.
- Even products with a strong and resonant purpose need to be unique, well-made and hard for competitors to copy.

DO THESE NOW FOR QUICK WINS:

Applying the CLIMB™ Methodology to your product is simple, and can have a huge impact.

Here are four things you can do right now to articulate and convey specific buyer needs for your product:

1. LEVERAGE FUNCTIONAL BENEFITS

Begin by thoroughly understanding the functional benefits your product offers.

Identify the specific tasks or problems it addresses and make sure the tangible outcomes are communicated clearly and concisely in your messaging.

If your product saves time, reduces costs, or simplifies a process, emphasize these aspects to appeal to buyers who are seeking practical solutions to their challenges.

Think deeply about what a person could do with the extra time, productivity or focus gained from using your product and how it could make them happier, healthier and more effective.

2. EVOKE EMOTIONAL CONNECTIONS

Think about how your product can trigger specific emotional responses in its owner.

Write out all the feelings and experiences it can deliver, such as enjoyment, satisfaction, or a sense of well-being, and note realistic examples of how this might happen.

Craft your messaging to resonate with the emotional desires of your target audience via the dog brain.

For example, if your product enhances a sense of pride or exclusivity, convey these emotions through relatable visuals and clear language.

3. ADDRESS TRANSFORMATIONAL NEEDS

There are probably many ways your product can make transformative improvements in the lives of your customers. How can it contribute to personal growth, improved relationships, or increased motivation?

How can you show these outcomes in a highly visual way? Position your product as a catalyst for positive change and personal advancement. If it can help users overcome challenges or find purpose, demonstrate these capabilities.

Brainstorm ways to demonstrate the before-and-after of someone who has experienced such a transformation.

4. COMMUNICATE TRANSCENDENT IMPACT

If your product has the potential to address broader societal, humanitarian or environmental needs, be sure to communicate its transcendent impact in ways the right people will care about.

These things are super important to large numbers of people, and charitable organization membership can be important in targeting ads to reach them.

Highlight how your product contributes to larger goals such as sustainability, human rights, or community well-being. Connect your product's mission to the values of socially conscious consumers who want their purchases to make a positive difference in the world.

Partnering and sharing profits with charitable organizations can be a great way to build meaningful connections with the very people who will value your product the most.

Make a list of groups who will embrace your transcendent goals, and rank each one.

—

By applying these actions, you are on your way to effectively addressing specific buyer needs and can tailor messaging to emotionally resonate with customers seeking functional improvements, emotional connections, transformative experiences and transcendent impacts.

CHAPTER 9

A Buyer in Need Has a Job Indeed

In This Chapter:

- *Customer Jobs Theory and its relevance to product development*
- *Identifying the original driving need behind a product*
- *"The Why Game" for uncovering customers' underlying motivations*
- *Strategies for aligning products with customers' willingness to pay*

SO, WHY DO WE buy a product, anyway?

Sometimes it's obvious.

You need to measure lumber for a deck you're building today, but only have a ruler and a square. Both can be used to measure, but are way too short to be practical.

So, you go to Lowes and compare the available measuring tapes. You might care about the maximum length, how far the tape can stand out without bending, whether or not it gives both inches and centimeters, and the readability of the increments.

You'll compare prices and make a quick value decision so you can get back to your project. In a few minutes, the discovery, evaluation and decision stages of your buyer's journey are complete.

If available products had included a radically new kind of laser measuring device, you would probably not have been interested. That product's ideal buyer is probably prepared to spend more and is up for learning a new way to get a few planks to the right size.

The tape measure example is deliberately simple. For most innovative products, the use cases are a little less commonplace and the buyer's journey more convoluted. The laser tape measure inventor will have to do much more than get hardware chains to stock the new product alongside traditional measuring tapes. He or she must first understand what kind of person will buy it, and what will make that person fully appreciate the extra value it delivers. Otherwise, even if it is the lowest-priced option, the only job it will do is gather dust on a shelf.

(For what it's worth, a variety of high-tech laser measurement tools *do* exist and some even sell for prices competitive with analog measuring tapes. But guess what? The vast majority of tradespeople and DIY aficionados prefer the old-school way. It works reliably, is quick, never needs batteries — and is what they *know*.)

In product marketing there is a thing called Customer Jobs Theory. It was first explained in 1991 by Anthony Ulwick and has been elaborated on extensively by many others.

It goes like this: every worthwhile product has a job to do. When customers buy a product, they are "firing" the old way of doing that Customer Job (whether it's a technology, a tool or a clever hack) and "hiring" the product as a replacement.[1]

This applies to any product worth buying. Without a Job to Be Done (JTBD in marketing shorthand) and a better or cheaper way to do it, we'd all just keep our money or buy candy.

Customer Jobs is that simple, yet so complex that many whole books have been written about it and some marketers have devoted their careers to studying it.

When creating a new product, you're going to be distracted

by shiny things. Everyone in your sphere will suggest features and improvements until you begin to forget the main reason you are making it. When we put the Customer Jobs first in developing a product, however, Ulwick calls the result Outcome-Driven Innovation. Most inventors are driven to solve a problem they have personally experienced and believe must plague a significant number of like-minded people. They are creating a solution that delivers a very specific outcome in addressing a common need.

But down the road, identifying the most valuable driving needs behind a product can take serious consideration.

In the long process of product development, it's easy to get caught up in new features and enhancements. Everywhere you look, you'll find similar and quasi-similar alternatives, and you'll constantly compare your product to them. Your product begins to sprout new buttons and dials, your pitch evolves to include new audience personas and the original Customer Job becomes increasingly murky. The driving need that led to the innovation can even be surpassed along the way by more important needs that may truly be stronger motivators to use the product, as we saw with the Embr Wave. Or forgotten altogether, eclipsed by endless, mostly trivial distractions.

THE ORIGINAL MOTIVATION

WHEN SEEKING to identify the most valuable Customer Job a product does, I first look to the innovators behind it. There is always an initial outcome being sought: the original driving need.

SearBQ inventor Michael Sandeen had ruined a couple of expensive steaks and wanted to create a way of achieving repeatable results while avoiding disastrous flare-ups.

Without a doubt, it was a problem that frustrated millions of other barbecue owners. The SearBQ could also cook all kinds of other foods in half the time of conventional grilling, but Michael's original driving need — to avoid turning pricey meat into useless lumps of coal — was the real Job to Be Done.

We considered targeting restaurant chefs and grilling enthusiasts. But to many of those people, steak is essentially a religion. They have perfected their techniques — and will pontificate with a mounting heart rate about never, ever, under any circumstances putting any weight on a piece of meat.

The notion of a 10-pound press, the key feature of SearBQ, was blasphemy. You'd be sauced and roasted for suggesting it.

So, sauce me up. The results were phenomenal. Searing a cut of meat between two super-hot plates perfectly created what's known as a Maillard reaction, resulting in caramelization and an aromatic, flavorful crust. Steaks cooked on a SearBQ exploded everyone's expectations, and always came out tender and juicy. Smash burgers were amazing. So was seafood. Chicken was even better and best of all were the veggies.

But despite all of this, the SearBQ market wasn't chefs or even grilling aficionados. Not yet, anyway.

Once we recognized that the product was for everyday barbecue owners who just wanted to consistently achieve delicious results, we launched — and sold a million dollars' worth of SearBQs online in the first 140 days.

As expected, many barbecue enthusiasts blasted the product (without ever trying it of course). But it wasn't long before experts like grilling journalist Derrick Riches and publications including *Food & Nutrition* were raving about the SearBQ. And restaurant chefs began buying multiple sets.

But the main audience always was people in the situation where it all started: regular folks who need a little help to cook a phenomenal steak, every time. Ensuring that happens is the number one Customer job of SearBQ.

THE WHY GAME

IN ORDER TO further flush out the driving needs for a product's ideal buyers, it can be helpful to play what I call *The Why Game**. The goal is to repetitively ask "why?," drilling down through the layers of motivating factors, until you uncover the one need that is most important to buyers. It may take five or more "whys" to get there, but what is important is to keep asking until you arrive at the root cause that will lead customers to choose the product over all other alternatives.

Q: Why did you buy this hybrid mattress-in-a-box?

A: It was time for a new bed and a friend had one of these. It was super comfortable.
(Functional Need: Appeals to Senses)

Q: There are several models. Why this one?

A: I'm a hot sleeper and my apartment is south-facing with no air conditioning. This has cooling technology. The better I sleep, the more productive I am the next day.
(Functional Need: Improves Performance)

Q: So does the midrange model. Why the top-of-the-line?

A: I've got a bad back, so I bought the one with the most support. Glad I did.
(Transformative Needs: Leverages Quality and Workmanship and Gratifies)

Q: Still, why not pay less for a premium mattress from a warehouse store?

A: I don't drive. This one was delivered for free to my apartment. And ordering was really easy.
(Functional Need: Simplifies)

---

* Inspired by my two inquisitive young daughters. In their version, "The Why Game" continues until the other participant, always a parent, loses patience and declares it bedtime.

So in this case, the driving need is to provide comfortable, supportive, cooling sleep — sold online with free home delivery. If the mattress falls down on any of these points, it loses this customer.

Any extra features may increase the cost without attracting more ideal buyers. And if this buyer is representative of numerous other consumers, articulating its value with clarity will be vital to making sales.

Here is another example:

Q: Why did you buy this fancy cooler?

A: To keep my food fresh on fishing and camping trips.
(Functional Need: Protects)

Q: But why not get a simple Styrofoam cooler for a fraction of the cost?

A: Had one of those, and it cracked in half the first time out. We were forced to cut our trip short because the food went bad. Now I want durability. Plus, I can stand on top of this one when I'm fishing!
(Transformative Need: Leverages Quality and Workmanship)

Q: You can do that with coolers sold in hardware stores. Why not one of those?

A: This one works better. It keeps things frozen for several days.
(Functional Need: Improves Performance)

Q: Coleman and Igloo make premium coolers that cost less and perform similarly. Why this instead?

A: Those are Walmart brands. This is a cooler I can be proud of.
(Transformative Needs: Elevates Status, Leverages Design and Aesthetics, and Offers Badge Value)

So, this Customer Job is to keep food cold for days on end, in a rugged enclosure — made by a brand that elevates the owner's status.

It's essential to keep asking until the underlying, deal-breaker motivations are uncovered. In both examples, a more limited line of questioning might have missed the primary deciding factor and undervalued the pivotal importance of brand. This customer might not have bought from a startup, no matter how good the product is.

Brand status is misunderstood by many product makers. It is very difficult for a new, unknown company to sell products at a price premium, based on brand equity they haven't yet built.

Many times, I've had a client expect to sell a completely unknown product at an elevated price, on the premise of launching it under a "luxe" brand. But you don't just pop that up overnight. Some of the most valuable fashion names, including Gucci and Prada, have been brand-building for more than a century. Hermès started in 1837 and Louis Vuitton in 1854. Wear those labels and your peers will immediately recognize them. But it took some doing to make that happen.

Yes, branding is important. And it is possible to build a new prestige brand from scratch. But it isn't a prestige brand until the buyer's *peers* think so.

And that comes from delivering many remarkable experiences. It may not always take a century or two, but it does take time, focus and investment.

As Tony Fadell explains in his book, *Build*, the real-world experience a customer has with your product does far more to cement your brand in their minds than advertising or branding activities can. And you have to make great products for years before consumers will buy them just because of your brand.[2] Branding is a long-term endeavor, not a product launch tactic.

Notice how the questions in "The Why Game" examples can help us to understand why the customer seems to have paid a lot more than necessary for functions that are not exclusive to the prestige-branded product. To an objective third party, other options (including products that got fired) might seem comparable. But not to the buyer. And when the Job to Be Done is associated with transformative or transcendent needs, the acceptable price range tends to be higher than when functional and emotional needs alone are fulfilled.

Of course, there are plenty of exceptions. In his JTBD-focused book, *When Coffee and Kale Compete*, Alan Klement tells the story of a low-cost refrigerator marketed in rural India — a hot, densely populated country where few people can afford traditional refrigeration units. The product was expected to be a billion-dollar game changer. (Where have we heard that before?)

It flopped, because most targeted buyers didn't even have electricity in their homes. What did it matter that the refrigerator was available at a much lower cost than conventional fridges? Even rare consumers in India who did have reliable electricity subsisted hand-to-mouth, meaning they would need to forgo eating to save for one! For people with negligible body fat, that isn't even a consideration. Their long-established workarounds continued to do an acceptable job, with far less pain.[3]

For products marketed in affluent regions, the targeted buyer generally does much more discretionary spending. Still, it is important to understand the barriers to paying a premium for a product, even one that does a very useful job. Every consumer has a ceiling to what they will pay.

But here's the thing: when a customer believes achieving the job is a need rather than a want, something changes. Barriers to buying the best solution can be nearly eliminated. For anyone with enough money to spend (which today can be achieved by all kinds of financing options), the difference between what is too big a premium to pay and what is acceptable is merely a construct of the mind — always relative to some fairly arbitrary basis for comparison.

When more money is available through reasonable consumer sacrifices, the price ceiling can be raised, either by increasing desire or by resetting the markers. Sometimes both.

For years, smartphone makers focused on developing a device with a built-in keyboard that could be sold for under $200 — the maximum most consumers said they were prepared to pay. And then the iPhone raised everyone's cost ceiling to three times that amount overnight — without the keyboard — and went on to become the market leader. Today, the most popular smartphones retail for well over $1,000. No market analysts could have predicted the trend would go from racing to the bottom to pushing how high the ceiling can be raised.

Most novel products come from a similar place: the inventor has a problem that's not solved by a product already on the market. A little bit of research confirms the gap, and the wheels begin to turn.

Often, the assumption behind it all is that if one person has had this unmet need, there are likely millions of other people feeling the same itch.

A few years and piles of money later, the product is ready for market. Stress levels peak when real-world results cast light on the possibility that there IS only one person in the world who is sure to love it — and that's not even a paying customer!

Large product brands often face similar challenges when launching new products. Often, it's the brainchild of an executive or product manager that gets developed by the company's engineers, industrial designers and marketers under a shroud of secrecy and with little external validation. They design it, build it and begin to promote it with no sure way of knowing anyone will want the thing.

By that point, the only hope is that the right buyers can be identified, targeted and engaged to buy. It's a hell of a gamble.

Imagine if you went at it from the opposite direction.

Start by finding out what people need to achieve with a product and what they're willing to pay. Then create it.

Great products turn the default product development process on its head, delighting customers by delivering desired outcomes with ease. The people behind them not only work with confidence based on customer insights, but are able to design a user interface that works exactly the way the customer's brain expects it to.

KEY INSIGHTS FROM CHAPTER 9

- Customer Jobs Theory suggests that every product serves a specific job for customers, replacing an old way of accomplishing that job.
- Identifying driving needs and the original motivating factor behind a product is crucial for effective product development and marketing.
- Playing "The Why Game" can help uncover the underlying driving needs and motivations of customers.
- Understanding customers' willingness to pay and barriers to purchasing helps in setting appropriate pricing strategies.
- Novel products often arise from personal unmet needs, with the assumption that if one person has the need, others likely do too. This can be entirely wrong.
- Successful products prioritize delivering desired outcomes with ease and aligning with users' expectations.

DO THESE NOW FOR QUICK WINS:

UNCOVER DRIVING NEEDS

Go back to the driving need that motivated the creation of your product. What were you trying to accomplish, and for what specific situation? Why was your need so significant and so motivating?

Look beyond surface-level features to understand the core problem your product aims to solve. Make note of it.

PLAY "THE WHY GAME"

For each benefit of your product, ask "why" repeatedly to dig deeper into customers' motivations and driving needs.

Why do they want to achieve this outcome?

Why not an alternative solution?

Why does that difference matter enough to change behaviors?

And so on.

Keep asking until you reach the fundamental need that will motivate customers to choose your product over alternatives. Pay attention to supplementary factors that make the product a perfect fit for a common buyer type.

If you arrive at "to stay alive," you've probably gone too far. Unless your central need is a safety one, go back to the prior answer.

When playing "The Why Game," involve multiple stakeholders. Start with the founder and move on to people who represent your key persona — or real customers, if the product is already being sold.

The greater number of customers you play "The Why Game" with, the more you will solidify recurring insights and flush out unicorn cases.

UNDERSTAND YOUR PRICE CEILING

Analyze customers' willingness to pay and seek out potential barriers to purchasing. You can do this by asking people in person or by running consumer surveys.

It can be well worth the cost of having an agency design objective surveys that will have statistically significant results with consumers who closely match your buyer personas.

Determine how your product's benefits align with what customers are willing to invest. Invite someone to play the devil's advocate so you don't allow yourself to be dangerously optimistic.

During soft launch, use a price A/B testing app to scientifically test the impact of varying values and uncover the true maximum before drop-off.

Look at the margin you have across the spectrum: fewer sales at a higher price can be far more profitable than shipping masses of product at a very low margin.

Or the inverse can be true. Do the math to be sure.

CHAPTER 10

A Step Farther: The Coveted Condition™

In This Chapter:

- *The concept of the Coveted Condition™ and its impact on product desire*
- *Moving beyond functional outcomes to long-term transformative benefits*
- *Strategies for incorporating the Coveted Condition into product messaging*
- *Examples of products that effectively tap into customers' aspirations*

I ENJOY THE PROCESS of flushing out a product's Job to Be Done. It feels like turning back the clock with the product's creator, uncovering little treasures that have been buried for a while. And it enables everyone to get profoundly need-centric — thinking about the product through a lens of empathy for the people who will use it.

And in doing so many times, I've discovered something else very valuable. Because the Job to Be Done tends to be directly tied to immediate functional outcomes, it doesn't always reveal how buyers think about their own longer-term goals. This is especially true for business-to-business products, where the person making the buying decision might not even be among those who will use the product.

Our dog brain is impulsive, impatient and self-centered. It needs another hit of that dopamine pretty soon.

Meanwhile, the tank brain is methodically planning needs further into the future and possibly still dealing with the aftermath of prior ingenious choices made by His Doggieness.

It's the usual tension between two misaligned decision-making systems with a 400-million-year generation gap between them. And now here you are with a product to sell to them both — best of luck!

Your product does a job, which is fantastic when a customer needs to accomplish a task and readily connects the dots with your product as the solution. But often it's not so easy.

There's all that friction, remember?

And the risk. *Yarf.*

Plus, the customer often already has a way of solving the problem, which, although imperfect, is the familiar go-to option.

So you need more ammunition, and it exists.

What is far more important than a product that gets a job done?

How about the way the customer's life is better not just immediately, but long after adopting the product? That would be not just satisfaction and achievement, but transformation.

It means building habits and fostering loyalty. To the product and the brand.

I've given a name to that desired long-term future state: the *Coveted Condition.*™

It's an extended projection of the old metaphor of a buyer not really desiring a drill, but in reality, needing a quarter-inch hole.

That's just fine. Except who buys a drill to make just one hole? Borrow or rent a drill for that!

More likely you need a *series* of holes, through which you'll insert bolts that hold together shelf components to organize your books. Or attach pickets to the rails of a fence to make your backyard more private.

An organized library or outdoor privacy would be the Job to Be Done for you as a drill-buyer.

And your Coveted Condition is the new way you'll see yourself as the person who builds and creates useful things. It's the pride and enjoyment you attain through using that power tool. It's a state of being that is better, happier, more capable and prouder than before owning the product.

When an ad shows a Ford F150 bouncing nimbly across massive boulders amidst breathtaking mountain scenery, it's not even attempting to portray something many prospective buyers need to do today, or are likely ever to do. The fantasy is about freedom, capability and the ego boost of commanding a big, shiny, powerful machine. What kind of person could you become? That enviable state is not an F150's Job, but the buyer's Coveted Condition.

If you're a software purchaser for an enterprise business, your Job To Be Done might be achieving higher margins and fewer process gaps, through an integrated project management SaaS tool. But your Coveted Condition as the buyer is being recognized and promoted — and feeling like a corporate rock star — for securing that outcome. The Coveted Condition is deeply personal.

Understanding and conveying a Coveted Condition sounds simple. Yet, like a Job to Be Done, it takes a focused approach to achieve. Product makers get so caught up in refining features and in glamorizing the product itself that real value drivers get snowed under and completely lost.

To help get to a product's Coveted Condition, you also need to think longer-term.

Imagine your customer a year or two down the road, still using and loving the product. Think about how that person's life is significantly better because of it. What has changed? What would be missed the most if you took the product away — including career outcomes, self-image, pride and social status?

Great advertising shows people reveling in their Coveted Condition and connects the dots to the product. In talking to the people who created campaigns that do this successfully, you often learn they arrived there unintentionally. In a Eureka moment, the marketing team stumbled upon the magical, fantasy-inducing rewards the product can bring. They uncovered the Coveted Condition.

CLIMB™ AND THE COVETED CONDITION™

NOW, BACK TO YOUR LIST of CLIMB™ benefits. You *did* make that list, right?

If not, DO IT and look at each of the benefits through the lens of Jobs To Be Done and the Coveted Condition.

What is the most desired long-term outcome of the product doing its Job?

For each Job, ask the questions:

1. **How does this change the customer's life *one year from now*?**
2. **What would happen if this benefit suddenly vanished after a year of regular use?**

See how this alters the way your buyers will see the product? They're no longer thinking about only tangible, obvious outcomes in the moments after laying hands on the product, but about emotional and psychological ones that really last. The kind we're all aching for.

A premium camping cooler is not just about keeping food chilled. There are lots of lower-cost ways to do that. But what if it can mean more time outdoors, because food stays fresh longer (and beer keeps cold), making longer camping trips more successful?

Take that cooler away after a year, and the customer stands to lose out on fresh air, bonding experiences and the rejuvenation that comes only from multiple days off the grid. That has a direct impact on the customer's overall enjoyment of life. Maybe even their longevity.

Instead of immediate comfort from a more supportive mattress, we can think about the things a better-rested person can achieve. Suddenly, it connects to relationships, career success and long-term health outcomes.

INNOVATION INTERLUDE:
A MASTERCLASS ON THE COVETED CONDITION™

Masterclass, the online education platform featuring celebrity instructors, exemplifies the concept of the Coveted Condition™ in its marketing approach and the product itself.

While the immediate Job to Be Done might be "learn a new skill," Masterclass taps into much deeper aspirations:

Functional Benefit: Access to high-quality, expert-led courses

Emotional Benefit: Feeling inspired and connected to elite talent

Transformative Benefit: Building skills in areas of personal passion

Coveted Condition: Becoming a more well-rounded, accomplished individual — with a touch of celebrity-like expertise

The platform's marketing showcases not only the skills users can learn but the type of person they can become - someone who can cook like Gordon Ramsay, write like Margaret Atwood, or think like Neil deGrasse Tyson.

This focus on the Coveted Condition has contributed to Masterclass's rapid growth. Despite premium pricing in a market flooded with free online courses, the company was valued at $2.8 billion in 2024.[1]

By evoking the long-term future self rather than just immediate skill acquisition, Masterclass created a product that resonates deeply with users' long-term personal development goals.

If that beneficial quality vanishes, fatigue and irritability return. Focus is lost. Precious morning connections with one's spouse and kids are spoiled, potentially with far-reaching repercussions. Precious life objectives are once again jeopardized.

We're looking for big needs that keep the customer up at night.

That's why it is valuable to think about one year (or more) from now. While instant gratification is essential to activating "buy" triggers for the dog brain and demonstrating what the product does, those triggers should be tied to bigger, longer-term results that justify investment and patience.

Elevating customers' minds to a bigger picture does a few things. First, it helps the fantasizing mind firmly attach to a coveted future self-image. It shows what is possible and makes high-value goals more likely to be attained. It reduces the frequency of returns by getting buyers to think about the long game.

Returns and churn are often byproducts of buyer's remorse from spontaneous dog brain decisions where the rational mind was ignored or never consulted. When it comes time to justify the purchase (to a partner, to internal late-night misgivings or during a monthly review of the credit card bill), the amount spent needs to feel substantially smaller than the value received.

Understanding the Coveted Condition also raises the bar for the people and teams making the product. The promise grows to be greater than the physical item being built, transforming the business from selling SKUs into supporting dreams and aspirations.

Employees and customers alike begin to see the brand in a more admirable light. The brand begins to build value.

And of course, that value exists nowhere except in people's minds. Aligning with your customers about their long-term Coveted Condition makes value more tangible, so you can build and bolster it.

KEY INSIGHTS FROM CHAPTER 10

- The Job To Be Done might not directly align with how buyers think about their long-term goals, especially in B2B scenarios.
- The Coveted Condition™ is a desired future state that goes beyond functional outcomes and focuses on how a customer's life is changed in a lasting way after using the product.
- Understanding and effectively conveying the Coveted Condition can fuel fantasies that connect the product with a highly desirable future state for the consumer.

DO THESE NOW FOR QUICK WINS:

IDENTIFY COVETED CONDITIONS™:

Go back to your list of CLIMB™ benefits of your product and examine them through the lens of the Coveted Condition™. For each benefit, ask how the customer's life could be better *one year from now* as a result of using your product.

What would be missed if the benefit suddenly vanished after a full year of regular use? The answers should be different from what a new user would miss.

Brainstorm how to demonstrate this in your messaging. How might this way of thinking encourage long-term adoption, build loyalty and minimize returns?

FOCUS ON EMOTIONAL AND PSYCHOLOGICAL OUTCOMES

Shift your perspective from immediate physical outcomes to long-term emotional and psychological changes. How does the customer's mental or physical health improve? How might their relationships get better?

Connect your product's benefits to bigger life objectives that profoundly matter to customers. Is there a potential to step up in social or career status? How does enjoyment or quality of life improve?

What long game is your buyer playing?

ADDRESS BUYER'S REMORSE AND JUSTIFICATION

Help customers justify their purchase by ensuring that the perceived value received vastly exceeds the amount spent. How can you demonstrate value that might otherwise go unnoticed?

While not forgetting short-term benefits that most excite the dog brain, also draw your customer's mind to the long-term, sought-after outcomes your product offers — and the outcomes that stand to be lost without it in their lives.

CRAFT MESSAGING AROUND THE COVETED CONDITION™

Visually integrate the Coveted Condition concept into your product messaging and marketing materials. Don't just recognize or talk about the benefit: demonstrate it to the dog brain through images and motion.

Show not just the functional benefits, but the transformative impact your product can have on customers' lives.

When a customer considers returning a product or canceling a recurring payment, ensure they have considered the Coveted Condition they stand to lose.

Do they really want to leave all that joy behind?

CHAPTER 11

The "Third Self" and Need

In This Chapter:

- *The Three Selves: remembering, experiencing, and the "third self"*
- *The role of the third self in shaping product fantasies and needs*
- *Leveraging peak emotions and endings in crafting memorable experiences*
- *Strategies for engaging the third self in product messaging*

HOW MANY OF YOU are with me now?

No, I'm not prepping for a keynote presentation or talking about dissociative identity disorder (in which a person switches between multiple personalities).

This is about something nearly everyone experiences.

Behavioral psychologist and economist Daniel Kahneman theorizes that humans have two distinct selves: the remembering self and the experiencing self.

The remembering self is the part of us that lives in past experiences, where we revisit and selectively alter memories over time in subtle and unnoticed ways. If you've ever told a story alongside a companion who remembered the same event in an entirely different way, you have seen the remembering self's creative restructuring at work. My wife and I have been together more than 30 years and I am amazed at how much our long-term recollections can differ. I've learned not to place a huge amount of trust in my remembering self about exactly how things happened a long time ago.

Our experiencing self lives in the present moment: savoring and luxuriating, suffering and enduring, laughing and crying. Your experiencing self is always gathering information to hand off to — and be selectively retained by — the remembering self.

It is easy to recognize these two selves, because we move between them constantly. Your experiencing self is reading these words. Some of them may stick with your remembering self.

Everything you know is there in your remembering self — the memories you trigger while reading and relating (yes, even to this text!), the arguments over what *really* happened in a story you told; your entire collection of life memories up until this moment.

And I believe there is also a third self: one that holds our hopes, dreams, fantasizes, worries, dreads and fears. All the promise for our future. The third self needs new achievements and outcomes to materialize in order to become real. It is our motivation and our every remaining hope.

The third self is informed by the other two selves, whose past and present experiences inform, inspire and cultivate realistic new visions of a desired future state.

When you feel the need to own something new, it is because your third self has already envisioned it improving your life, defining future gratification and possibly your Coveted Condition. Fantasies belong to the third self.

To trigger this response in a buyer, draw from their past experiences. Bring awareness to their present pain. The third self is built upon the remembering and experiencing selves. It references troves of experiences and emotions from the past, and crafts vivid reveries that can support and substantiate a newly recognized need.

Not all experiences are treated equally in our minds. In fact, the mind pays no attention to equity or balance. Many studies have corroborated that we tend to remember an experience by how it began and ended, and by the peak emotion experienced during the entire span of time it takes up. Great lawyers and prosecutors focus most intensely on how they begin and conclude trials. They recognize that in a drawn-out process, those are the moments jurors will remember. It works.

Fascinatingly, our remembering self completely disregards the *duration* of pain, boredom or pleasure. Studies show that how long you spent waiting in lines at Disney or undergoing a root canal is hard to recollect at all. You mostly remember peak delight and pain.

And even a near-perfect experience (such as a concert, a meal or even a marriage), no matter how long it lasts, can be completely spoiled for our remembering self if it suffers a bad ending. These phenomena are referred to respectively as *duration neglect* and the *peak-end rule*, and they're universally experienced.[1]

So, to recap, we have three selves:

- **the remembering self**, which holds our past
- **the experiencing self**, which resides in the present
- **the third self**, which lives in our dreams and fears

Understanding our three selves and how they process information is key. It helps you grasp how to evoke and stimulate a customer's need for your product. You can consider the third self in demonstrating a Coveted Condition, recognizing that it must draw from the remembering self and stimulate the experiencing self.

With that in mind, driving customer needs does not have to be limited to obvious sets of experiences and memories that come to mind when you think of your product category. In fact, the obvious scenarios are usually uninteresting or unoriginal enough to make them immediately forgotten.

INNOVATION INTERLUDE:
CALMING THE THIRD SELF

Calm, the sleep and meditation app, exemplifies how a product can engage the "third self" by helping users envision a more relaxed, well-rested version of themselves.

While the immediate Job to Be Done is "fall asleep more easily" Calm appeals to deeper needs:

Functional Benefit: Soothing sleep stories and meditations

Emotional Benefit: Reduced anxiety and improved relaxation

Transformative Benefit: Better sleep habits and mental clarity

Coveted Condition: Becoming a more balanced, energized individual

Calm's interface and content progressively guide users towards their ideal, well-rested self.

The app's sleep tracking and streak features keep users engaged with their aspiration for better sleep and overall well-being.

This focus on the "third self" has contributed to Calm's success, reaching over 100 million downloads by 2022.[2]

By emphasizing the journey to a more rested and focused self rather than just providing bedtime stories, Calm has created a product that resonates with users' long-term wellness goals and their vision of a more balanced life.

Using a SearBQ is not just about cooking delicious steaks in half the time. For many barbecue users, cooking is a pleasurable experience that gets them out in the fresh air, sipping a beer and enjoying the sounds and smells of sizzling food. There's no rush.

But most weekend barbecue chefs have felt the embarrassment of charring a steak or needing to finish pink-inside chicken thighs in the microwave.

SearBQ rose up from the ashes, after its founder incinerated two expensive steaks and spoiled a special evening with his wife.

The product tapped into those universal memories of failure and feelings of inadequacy — and offered the solution of consistency.

When we launched the SearBQ, I recognized that my own remembering self had banked plenty of negative experiences around unsuccessful meals.

Many SearBQ owners are men whose only cooking contribution is made on the barbecue, and the results are closely tied to their ego. Marketing the product was a delicate balance of preserving those consumers' status as King of the Grill, while offering them exciting new claims to fame and improving their future batting average.

For Peloton customers, the need is not as simple as having a quiet, effective workout at home, or gaining the Coveted Condition of sustained fitness. Those things can be achieved using simple equipment, for a much lower price — or no equipment at all.

The fantasy that drives a beguiling need for Peloton is the one in the customer's experiencing self that craves to be motivated on a daily basis, to achieve new heights in the company of a like-minded community, while experiencing the joy of well-being.

Tapping only into obvious prior experiences would have turned Peloton into a commodity. It would have limited Peloton's desirability to a small niche group. For me, the brand channeled my memories of success as a young competitive cyclist, and the challenges I had faced as a business owner and busy father intent on working out consistently. The brand conjured a vision of my future self — built upon the very best constructs of my remembering self and my immediate pain.

But not enough people are like me.

So instead, Peloton got the customer's experiencing self to slide into snazzy shoes and clip into smooth, silent, robustly built bikes. It evoked memories of failed fitness attempts that lacked enjoyment, convenience and validation.

And it put the entire solution in the buyer's own home.

To apply all of this practically to your own product, create a worksheet of all the different drivers of desires and fears.

For each one, think about how it can be linked to the rewards the product delivers.

DESIRE FOR:

Appetite	(hunger, epicureanism, libido)
Ego	(Pride, acceptance, honor, respect, status, self-love, worthiness, confidence)
Ambition	(motivation, achievement, growth, advancement, professional drive, self-improvement)
Hedonism	(enjoyment, pleasure, stimulation, gratification)

FEAR OF:

Shame	(embarrassment, failure, inferiority, inadequacy, rejection, disrespect, diminished status)
Loss	(of identity, meaning, place, purpose, freedom, wealth, capacity, friendships, abandonment)
Waste	(misuse of time, money, natural resources, progress, sunk costs, energy, effort)
Suffering	(future discomfort, pain, aging, injury, disability, decline, death, evil, the unknown)

Make note of all the factors that apply, and be creative in exploring how the less-obvious desires can be achieved through successful use of the product. What universal memories can you tap into?

How would a fantasy look if it arose out of those prior positive experiences — and resulted in savoring the enjoyment of a lasting outcome only your product can deliver?

Now turn that on its head. How can each type of fear relate to a pain point solved by the product? What memories of failure or anguish can you draw from? What bruises can you poke in the present? How exciting does a future look and feel without those dreaded outcomes?

Create a narrative that leads from a common painful experience to the hero discovering and cherishing your product —and gloriously culminates in a Coveted Condition.

Go non-linear and mix up the order, in the way a gripping book or movie might incorporate flashbacks or premonitions.

Bring your product to the here and now with experiential components like in-home trials or point-of-purchase demonstrations.

Go for the most surprising and thrilling combination. It will be the most powerful.

Even if it doesn't become the basis for your next commercial, this exercise flushes out impactful psychological levers to pull, in developing a context of clear and solid differentiation.

KEY INSIGHTS FOR CHAPTER 11

- We have three selves: the remembering self shapes our past, the experiencing self resides in the present and the third self lives in our dreams and fears, crafting visions of a desired future. Recognizing the interplay between these selves sheds light on how fantasies — and needs — arise.
- When you feel compelled to own something, it's because your third self lucidly envisions it improving your life, leading to the long-term Coveted Condition™. Tapping into it drives a lasting need for a product.
- Our memories are influenced specifically by peak emotions and the ending of experiences, disregarding duration. Leveraging this insight, products can trigger needs by referencing past experiences and current pain points. Craft customer experiences to achieve meaningful high points and unique, positive endings.

DO THESE NOW FOR QUICK WINS:

DESIRE AND FEAR MAPPING

Create your own worksheet categorizing desires (appetite, ego, ambition, hedonism) and fears (shame, loss, waste, suffering). Align these with the rewards your product offers.

Consider particularly how less-obvious desires and fears can be fulfilled or mitigated through using your product.

CRAFTING NARRATIVES

Build narratives that connect fears to pain points addressed by your product, culminating in the buyer's Coveted Condition.

Find powerful combinations that surprise and resonate emotionally, offering differentiation and psychological leverage.

ENGAGING THE THIRD SELF

Set a timer for ten minutes to brainstorm all the ways your product's outcomes fulfill the buyer's long-game aspirations.

Develop scenarios that journey from feared experiences to the hero's discovery of your product, triumphantly resulting in a lasting and cherished Coveted Condition.

—

Understanding the constant interplay between our three selves — the past, present and future-driven self — will empower you to present your product in ways that strike deeply emotive chords.

By leveraging memories, feelings, desires and fears, you trigger needs to fulfill people's most meaningful dreams and their long-term aspirations.

CHAPTER 12

The Intersection of Goals and Beliefs

In This Chapter:

- *The role of customer goals and beliefs in driving purchasing decisions*
- *Strategies for aligning products with customers' pre-existing beliefs*
- *The importance of identifying and addressing "no-go" beliefs*
- *Crafting targeted messaging to resonate with customers' motivating belief*

MODERN HUMANS HAVE a crazy number of needs. We're confronted by thousands of products vying for our attention wherever we go.

Most of them, we quite effectively block out. So at what point does our brain decide a particular product–need combination is worth the risk, cost and trouble of buying?

It happens at a specific point.

The need that drives you to purchase a product lives at the intersection of your Coveted Condition (your ultimate goal) and your deeply held beliefs.

Let's dissect that. If you are truly committed to becoming fit, you'll look at the various ways to get there: personal trainers, wearable fitness trackers, group exercise classes and in-home virtual training.

In making your choice, you will use the process of elimination. You'll cross out most of the options, referencing your existing beliefs about what will actually work for you.

If you believe personal trainers are too expensive, you'll rule them out immediately. If you believe wearable devices are gimmicky and ineffective in the long run, those are off the list. And if experience has taught you that the only way to stay committed is by signing up for a scheduled group exercise class with friendly workout companions and a fired-up instructor to hold you accountable, that is where you'll end up.

And your choice will be directly at the intersection of the goal and your strongest beliefs.

This is the heart of product positioning. It's the practice of identifying people who will most appreciate a product's value and succinctly communicating that value to them. When you make that connection through your marketing, it is what we mean by achieving product–market fit. Suddenly, you're selling to exactly the right people, with minimal wasted spend or effort.

It's essentially the holy grail of selling the maximum amount of product and continuously delighting your customers.

TWO PATHS TO ALIGNMENT

THERE ARE TWO WAYS to achieve this alignment. The easiest by far is to go after the people who will intuitively see that your product can deliver their Coveted Condition and are able to support that notion with their pre-existing beliefs.

If those people are readily available and identifiable, you're off to the races. It can be as simple as popping the puzzle pieces together through your marketing. Your target audience members know their long-term goals and can easily be reminded of the flaws in existing options. Your product gets them there, faster and more easily — with no bitter aftertaste or ring-around-the-collar.

INNOVATION INTERLUDE: IMPOSSIBLE FOODS ALIGNS GOALS & BELIEFS

Impossible Foods, the plant-based meat company, illustrates how a product can succeed by aligning with customers' deeply held beliefs and goals.

While the immediate Job to Be Done is "eat a tasty burger," Impossible Foods appeals to deeper motivations:

Functional Benefit: Plant-based meat alternative that tastes like beef

Emotional Benefit: Enjoying familiar foods without guilt

Transformative Benefit: Reducing one's environmental impact

Coveted Condition: Being seen as an environmentally conscious, forward-thinking individual

Impossible Foods' mission to reduce meat consumption for environmental reasons aligns perfectly with many consumers' growing concerns about climate change and sustainability.

This alignment of product with customer beliefs has been crucial to Impossible Foods' rapid growth. By 2024, their products were available in over 11,000 retail locations worldwide.[1]

Impossible Foods is seen as vastly more than veggie burgers; it delivers a way to enjoy familiar foods while expressing sustainability values.

By operating at the intersection of customers' goals (eating delicious food) and beliefs (reducing environmental impact), Impossible Foods has created a product that resonates on a deeper level than traditional meat alternatives.

Except most of the time it's not quite so simple. Maybe the majority of people don't see your product and immediately "get it."

So the second way is to target the best-fit prospects and fill in the gaps. Educate your market, helping prospective buyers to clearly visualize the link between their prized end result, their deeply held beliefs — and your product.

Usually, you can draw out existing beliefs. Lead your audience to look at their goals through the lens of their established perspectives. Help them see your product come into focus.

What never succeeds is when deeply held beliefs or values go directly against any part of what your product promises to do, or clash with any significant thing it has to execute to achieve the customer's goal.

GOALS, BELIEFS AND YOUR NO-GO LIST

I SUGGEST A SIMPLE EXERCISE where you go back to the list of Coveted Condition(s) your product achieves. These are the most meaningful outcomes it provides for the buyer. If you have more than one distinct buyer type or use case, or if the product can lead to multiple life-changing outcomes, there may be different Coveted Conditions.

Create a second list for each of these Coveted Conditions. These will be the current beliefs a buyer might have that make it easy to embrace your product as the ideal solution.

Some of these beliefs could center around commitments to environmental or social objectives, like reusability or ethical sourcing.

Or they could be built on performance expectations, whether those relate to personal relationships, athletic achievements, improved mental focus or the completion of a household project. Prior experiences supporting performance expectations are usually at the heart of these beliefs.

The deeper the burn, the deeper we learn. How have your prospective customers been burned before? What deeply held beliefs are embedded in that scar tissue?

What's most important is that a large number of prospective buyers can be expected to hold the beliefs you identify. If you are unsure, do the research to ensure a belief is held by a minimum viable audience.

Third, create the No-Go List. These are all the showstopper beliefs that will make a prospect refuse to (or be unqualified to) buy your product. A No-Go List can be nearly as important as identifying your ideal buyer.

For example, if you use a marketing platform that enables you to target or exclude specific interests, your No-Go List can save a lot of money by avoiding showing ads to people who will definitely not buy what you're selling — or worse, will buy it, return it and post scathing reviews.

If your product is an auto accessory, you want to market only to people who are vehicle owners, or who show an interest in buying a gift for someone who is.

If you're selling ham sausages, even the most delicious ones on earth, you don't want to pay for advertising directed at vegans, people who shun nitrates, or anyone who avoids pork. These are deeply held beliefs that define your no-gos.

With a clear, documented understanding, you can begin to assemble the messaging that will reinforce the connection between the strongest motivating beliefs held by your prospects, their goals — and the truly relevant value your product delivers.

KEY INSIGHTS FROM CHAPTER 12

- The decision to purchase a product is determined by the intersection of one's ultimate goal (Coveted Condition) and deeply held beliefs.
- There are two main strategies for aligning a product with buyer goals and beliefs: targeting individuals who already intuitively see the product's value and educating the market to bridge any gaps between their beliefs and the product's ability to deliver.
- It is valuable to understand the beliefs that make it easy for buyers to embrace your product as the ideal solution. Consider barriers to buying competing products, commitments to environmental or social objectives and performance goals based on past experiences.
- The No-Go List includes showstopper beliefs that would make a prospect refuse to buy your product. This list can help save money by avoiding targeting individuals unlikely to purchase or who may have negative reactions to the product.
- Use your knowledge of buyer beliefs to craft messaging that reinforces the connection between their motivating beliefs and the product's unique value proposition. This ensures effective communication that is fresh and different enough to strike a chord with the target audience.

DO THESE NOW FOR QUICK WINS:

UNDERSTAND ESTABLISHED BUYER BELIEFS

Conduct real-world research to understand the beliefs and values of your target audience.

Running objective consumer interviews with strangers is a sure way of uncovering what real prospective buyers deeply believe. Identify unshakable beliefs that align with your product's value proposition and flush out any that would be no-gos to a purchase.

Don't try to guess what these are: find out definitively.

CREATE ALIGNMENT STRATEGIES

Develop strategies to align your product with buyer goals and beliefs. Think first about targeting individuals who will intuitively see the product's value and then plan to educate the market to bridge any gaps. (The first is much easier.)

COMPILE AND EXPLAIN YOUR NO-GO LIST

From your research, make a list of beliefs that would prevent or disqualify a certain type of prospect from purchasing your product.

Use this list to avoid wasting resources on individuals unlikely to buy or who may have negative reactions. Write out an explanation that you can share with marketing partners to be sure everyone is keenly aware of the No-Go List and why it applies.

CRAFT TARGETED MESSAGING

Use this knowledge of buyer beliefs to craft fresh messaging that leverages the connection between motivating beliefs and your product's value proposition.

These are hypotheses still, so test variations to be sure your messaging resonates with the right audience and addresses their needs and beliefs effectively.

Low-budget digital ad campaigns are a fast and effective way to run real-world tests.

CHAPTER 13

Why Do I Need *This* Thing?

In This Chapter:

- *Addressing customers' subconscious question: "Why do I need* this *thing?"*
- *Crafting compelling positioning statements that articulate unique value*
- *Targeting the most appreciative audience for your product*
- *Leveraging social proof and influencer marketing to influence behaviors*

AS WE LEARNED IN CHAPTER EIGHT about Customer Jobs, even the most innovative products have to displace something else in order to be bought. Your customers might have to stop buying another product in order to budget for yours, or step away from a work-around they've habitually used, possibly for years.

Buying your product means so much more than a cash outlay. It requires smashing existing habits, rebuilding workflows or abandoning behavior patterns. It can mean literally carrying a prior investment to the trash can. And then finding the time and energy to learn something new.

So the question your customers will subconsciously ask (that is, if you can get them interested enough to care) is, "Why do I need *this* thing?"

Your answer has to be arresting, compelling — and brief. It should be built directly into your product positioning, so customers don't need to go searching or figure it out for themselves by piecing together various pages of content. (Two things the majority are sure not to do.) That answer may even be your core positioning statement.

And in the last chapter, we looked at how positioning exists at the intersection of goals and beliefs.

There is, of course, another element in that mix: the audience itself. The prospective buyer who must appreciate and be willing to pay for the value your product delivers.

Your positioning statement is the clearest articulation of that value to the most appreciative audience. It isn't all the findings you have been noting, the aha moments and your product's Coveted Condition. It is the words you use to articulate the essence of all that glitter and jet fuel.

Crafting a positioning statement is always harder than it seems.

Because. Every. Word. Counts.

You can't include every wonderful thing, because nobody will absorb it all. Your positioning statement should probably not be anywhere near as long as you'd like it to be.

In *Why Should I Choose You?* co-authors Ian Chamandy and Ken Aber set a seven-word limit for differentiating a product or service, based on the seven-item capacity our brains have for quick retention — the same reason telephone numbers and many countries' license plates are capped at 7 characters.

As Ian Chamandy told me in an interview, it's all about communicating what it is that most remarkably makes your product a clear choice, in a way people can retain:

"Every product has an essence to it," Ian says. "A thing that makes it uniquely remarkable, and then it has features and benefits that come out of that. And part of the problem is companies only think in terms of features and benefits, figuring out what those are and making sure that list is as long as possible to appeal to as many people as possible. Or if they do think about what the essence is, the process they have for doing it is so superficial that it renders the answer meaningless. And then without the essence, all of the rest of it falls apart."[1]

Distilling the essence of why someone should buy your product down to a brief sentence is hard to do. But it's a valuable undertaking, and not only so that audiences will read and remember it.

Creating a short positioning statement forces you to avoid shotgun pitching and look for the most meaningful differentiation, that is most likely to jolt an ideal buyer out of complacency.

Done right, it becomes the tagline that you use in marketing, at the top of your online store and anywhere you want prospective buyers to see it.

And you've already done most of the work in creating a great positioning statement.

Now you just need to carefully craft it, and distill it to be super short.

Go back to the lists you compiled in understanding the connection between motivating beliefs and your product's value proposition. Which of those speaks to the largest pool of prospective right-fit buyers? Can some of the most powerful elements be combined?

A great positioning statement often follows the format "It does X for Y."

X represents the unique value delivered, and Y represents the ideal buyer. Sometimes the value delivered intrinsically identifies the ideal buyer, because it's fairly obvious who that would be. A top chef may not be looking for the speed and ease of use an Instant Pot delivers. (And the results, however *magnifique*, may not be in alignment with what the restaurant's patrons expect.) But for regular folks seeking to cook a multitude of meals, easily and super-fast, Instant Pot is the bomb.

The acid test is that your positioning must trigger an "aha" with the people who matter most. It should feel like it speaks directly to them, providing a thought-provoking and compelling answer to the question, "Why do I need *this* thing?"

As for those people who matter most, it's vital you understand not only how they behave, but where to find them.

WHERE THE FISH ARE

"FISH WHERE THE FISH ARE." It's a great metaphor in marketing, because it's so relatable — and so important. Pricing coach and author Jonathan Stark says something like this about it:

There are an estimated three trillion fish in the ocean. Now imagine if you filled a backyard swimming pool with fresh water and stocked it with a thousand rainbow trout.

Would you be more likely to catch supper in the backyard pool, or the ocean with literally three billion times more fish?

It's so obvious.

And yet marketers rush straight for the ocean, mesmerized by the allure of a greater perceived opportunity.

Kamooki Lures has focused for more than a decade on going where the fish are and it's worked out well.

I remember my amazement when Kam Sheikh first showed me pencil sketches of his fishing lure idea, for the fledgling company he gave his own boyhood nickname: Kamooki. Kam's drawings were beautiful and precise. At the time, the product was a hand-carved wooden prototype and Kam was working on patenting his technology while searching for a manufacturer.

I had a great feeling about it and could see Kam was ready to do what was necessary to make the lures succeed.

When he was a college student, Kam had spent his summers

working as a fishing guide in some of the greatest trophy lakes on earth. He went back to his network and recruited fishing aficionados to help him test and perfect the prototype. The lure was a miniature engineering marvel, able to balance underwater on the tip of a nail or hop rock-to-rock across a lake bottom without snagging weeds, while making a rattling sound.

Predatory fish went nuts for it. While Kam had proven the lure worked, he also recognized that his peers' enthusiasm was not a valid measure of what the real market would think.

So, with his first batch of lure models and a large aquarium, he set off for ICAST, the fishing world's biggest trade fair.

He was fully prepared for rejection, so he was stunned by the excitement the lure, now dubbed SmartFish, stirred up. His live demonstration captivated the dog brain of fishing aficionados in attendance and he became the center of the show's attention. Pro anglers were itching to use it, trade media journalists queued for interviews, and retail buyers started calling to place orders.

Except Kam wasn't ready yet. He took plenty of notes and went back to improving his designs, making SmartFish even better and more lifelike. Then he went to lakes, rivers and oceans, capturing underwater video of fish after fish attacking the lures —irrefutable proof that his product worked.

A year later, he took the finessed versions and went back to where the fishermen were. By this time, we had his positioning down: The World's Smartest Lures.

The lures were smart because they used physics and fluid dynamics to achieve unique balance and movement characteristics. And smart fishermen saw the value.

Before long, Kam's growing range of colorful SmartFish lures appeared in tackle shops and fishing stores across the United States and Canada, and were selling briskly in Kamooki Lures' own direct-to-consumer online store.

It didn't end There. Kam attended fishing competitions with a pickup truck, boat, and team, thoroughly decked out in attractive branding.

He built a network of brand ambassadors dubbed the Kamooki Pro and Kamooki Field Staff, populated by enthusiasts and personalities known and trusted in the fishing community. Long-established fishing show hosts, pro fisher-folk and a new generation of younger, often prettier fishing influencers shared their love of Kamooki Lures across social channels, proudly sporting Kam's logo

The hard proof was in their photos and videos: trophy-sized catches with a SmartFish lure still dangling from the fish's mouth. It's the kind of visual the dog brain gobbles up and the tank brain can't refute.

Once consumers feel the need to own a product, they look for signals that support their inclination to buy it. And many times, that search doesn't stop with the initial purchase.

The work you do to build community and show up in the right places will continue to pay off, often in ways that will surprise you.

What watering holes attract your best-fit customers in the greatest concentrations? And what community members have the most influential voices in those places?

PEER PRESSURE: HOW NEEDS ARE INFLUENCED

NOBODY THINKS OF THEMSELVES as a buyer persona.

When it comes to our personal style and tastes, each of us wants to be uniquely "me." Completely independent and free in every choice we make. No one can tell us what we like. We explore, discover and pave our own way, constantly blazing trails, exercising our free will.

But as consumers, do we really?

In his book *Nudge*, economist Richard Thaler describes how an artificial music store tested the extent to which a song's popularity could influence customers to download it compared to less popular songs. It was a controlled experiment, with participants split into two groups. Half could see the popularity of available tracks and the other half could not. All could hear samples of the songs before making their choices.

The popularity rating was completely fabricated and randomized. It was no indication at all of how good any song actually was. And as you're probably guessing, the songs that appeared to be popular were downloaded by the test subjects at a dramatically higher rate over the same tracks in the control group where popularity was not a factor.

The experiment showed that the perceived popularity of a product can strongly influence desirability to buyers, even with a product as subjective as music. This is why early wins and proof of popularity can be tremendously important to a product's overall success.[2]

Platforms like Amazon have created "early reviewer" programs that help products to establish social proof soon after launch, recognizing how important social influence can be.

I've seen product sales plummet after a surge in negative reviews. And when one reviewer complains about a previously unmentioned issue, that issue suddenly begins to surface in subsequent reviews — even if nothing has changed with the product.

Often the problem is not even the product itself, but another satisfaction factor like delays in fulfillment or gaps in customer service. These are relatively easy things to resolve, and are vital to building social proof.

Why is social proof so powerful?

As Arizona State University behavioral science professor Robert Cialdini puts it, 95 percent of consumers are imitators and only five percent are originators.

The vast majority of us are persuaded more by the actions of others than by any other proof a product brand can offer. Even as reviewers, we imitate other reviewers.[3]

So, when your dog brain is captivated by the demonstration of an enticing new product in your social media feed, you go to the comments.

You want to see what other people are saying.

Then, when you click through to the product's online store, you look at the testimonials, the "As Seen In" logos and the product reviews. What other people say carries more weight than anything the product maker can say, even in a highly curated context.

"Influencer" has become a legitimate career title on platforms like TikTok and Instagram, and celebrities are now the world's most valuable brand spokespeople.

For buyers, a celebrity endorsement signifies that the product is trustworthy, reliable, and fashionable. From George Clooney's $40 million Nespresso deal to the hugely successful product lines of YouTuber Jimmy Donaldson (better known as Mr. Beast), the power of leveraging a trusted person's credibility is proven to have tremendous potential value.

In recent years, a new category of micro-influencers has emerged, where the content creator has fewer than 100,000 followers and usually has an organically grown following. While micro-influencers provide a more affordable route to creating user-generated content (UGC), the challenge has become in managing multiple ambassadors with a lower general level of professionalism to achieve return on investment (ROI).

Likes and shares appeal to the dog brain, but they don't directly translate to conversions. Product makers often learn this lesson the hard way.

Even with lower-cost content creators, it's very important to engage individuals who align closely with your buyer personas and are genuinely excited about using the product. It may be worth the investment to hire an agency that specializes in influencer marketing.

Any way you go about it, the influencers you cultivate must be able to articulate (and fluidly explain) your positioning statement, and should frequent the same watering holes as your customers do. When we talk about "authenticity" we refer to the natural and seamless alignment between all these elements.

For your buyers, it's all about getting a meaningful answer to the question, "Why do I need *this* thing?"

KEY INSIGHTS FROM CHAPTER 13

- Before they will buy, customers must be convinced to abandon existing habits or workflows. The question they subconsciously ask is, "Why do I need *this* thing?"
- Positioning statements should succinctly articulate the unique value of the product to the most appreciative audience. Every word counts in crafting a compelling positioning statement.
- Distilling the essence of why someone should buy your product into a brief sentence is challenging, but it's a valuable undertaking. The resulting statement is easy to remember and becomes the tagline used in marketing efforts.
- Identify the audience most likely to appreciate the product's value. Then go fishing where the fish are by targeting the optimum audience concentrations.
- Social proof, such as perceived popularity and influencer endorsements can significantly influence buyer behavior. Leveraging social proof through reviews, testimonials, and endorsements is a proven way of boosting product success.

DO THESE NOW FOR QUICK WINS:

ANALYZE CUSTOMER MOTIVATIONS

Spend 20 minutes reviewing customer feedback, reviews and testimonials to identify common motivations for purchasing your product.

Look for recurring themes or needs that your product fulfills, and consider how these can be incorporated into your positioning statement. Condense this information into a concise positioning statement that answers the question: "Why do I need this thing?" Aim for a maximum of seven words to differentiate your product effectively and in a way that's easy to recall.

ENGAGE WITH MICRO-INFLUENCERS

Research micro-influencers within your niche who will have a genuine interest in your product and have an engaged following. Many online tools are available to facilitate this kind of research and validate engagement.

Reach out to best-fit prospects with a personalized message highlighting the value proposition of your product and proposing a win-win collaboration. Think about what's in it for the influencer beyond monetary compensation.

Based on what you know of their goals and beliefs (which they probably share) why would they love to see your product succeed?

NURTURE INFLUENCER RELATIONSHIPS

Spend 15 minutes crafting a communication plan to engage and nurture relationships with selected micro-influencers.

Provide influencers with clear guidance on how to articulate your product's positioning in their content and encourage authentic endorsements.

Have them use the product and present it to you before creating content. They won't want to do a number of retakes and edits, and few will get all the key points right the first time.

MONITOR INFLUENCER IMPACT

Set up tracking mechanisms to monitor the impact of influencer collaborations on key metrics such as website traffic, engagement, and conversions.

Analyze the effectiveness of each influencer partnership and adjust your approach based on the results.

OPTIMIZE CUSTOMER TOUCHPOINTS

Make a complete list of your product's customer touchpoints, including website messaging, packaging, and post-purchase communications.

Ensure that your positioning statement is consistently communicated across all touchpoints to reinforce its impact on potential buyers. Repetition is how people remember.

GATHER, ITERATE AND REFINE

Build a repository to continuously gather feedback from customers, influencers, and customers to refine your positioning statement and messaging.

Use a Google Doc or Sheet you can access from your phone whenever a new bit of input comes across your radar. The more often you add to your repository, the more valuable and top-of-mind your data will be.

Create the file right now, and make the first entry. You're on your way!

Every time a review or comment comes in, look for the insight behind it. Why does this person need (or not need) the product? Add the insight to your repository. Capture good testimonials before they get buried.

Iterate on your approach based on these insights and how they reflect evolving market dynamics to stay relevant and effective.

CHAPTER 14

Suddenly, You Need Bacon

In This Chapter:

- *The surprising story of repositioning bacon as a breakfast staple*
- *The role of Strategic messaging and influencers in shaping consumer habits*
- *Examples of revolutionary products transforming consumer perceptions*
- *Strategies to leverage credible endorsements and media*

IN THE EARLY 1900s, most Americans tended to eat breakfasts similar to what Europeans consume today. A roll with jam or a bowl of cooked cereal were the norm. Folks didn't feel they needed anything more.

Then, in the 1920s, the Beech-Nut packing company found itself diversifying and wanting to sell more high-fat pork sides, with their shelf life extended through smoking and adding plenty of salt.

Better known as bacon.

Trouble was, few people were very interested in bacon at the time. It couldn't compete with other cuts as a dinner meat, and lunch breaks were too restrictive for workers to fry some, eat it and clean up. (And if the smell of popcorn is too pervasive for the office, imagine bacon!)

INNOVATION INTERLUDE: *OATLY FROTHS UP A FRESH NEW NEED*

Oatly, the Swedish oat milk company, exemplifies how a product can create a need by reshaping perceptions and habits.

Oatly's clever marketing focused on the barista community, positioning oat milk as the superior non-dairy option for coffee drinks. This strategy created a need among coffee enthusiasts who previously hadn't considered plant-based alternatives.

The company's quirky branding and transparent messaging about sustainability appealed to consumers' desire to make environmentally friendly choices, further driving adoption.

Oatly's success in creating a need is evident in its rapid growth. After its U.S. launch in 2016, Oatly's revenue skyrocketed from $15.5 million to $783 million by 2023.[1]

By focusing on a specific use case (coffee) and aligning with emerging consumer values (sustainability), Oatly created a new category of consumer need, transforming oat milk from a niche product to a mainstream staple.

Bacon had no clear place, and people didn't feel a need for it in their lives

So Beech-Nut hired Edward Bernays, a New York press agent who had recently opened a public relations business — one of the first of its kind.

Bernays, who had worked as a medical editor early in his career, wondered if bacon could be repositioned as a breakfast food. He asked his doctor about the possibility of serving bacon as a breakfast companion. The doctor concurred that a substantial meal would be helpful to hard-working people starting their day, most of whom would not have eaten anything since early in the evening before.

Bernays persuaded the doctor to write a few letters.

It turned out to be more than a few. In all, he mailed 5,000 of his colleagues nationwide, asking for support of the idea. And 4,500

American MDs wrote back (a 90% response rate!) stating that a hearty breakfast — specifically bacon and eggs — was a smart and healthy way to start the day.

Next, Bernays used his media connections to push these results into the newspapers.

The story made front pages nationwide. Many articles even included a photo of bacon and eggs, promoting breakfast to Americans for the first time as the "most important meal of the day."

It was high-powered influencer marketing, long before anyone knew what that was.

Bacon sales took off and breakfast was transformed forever.

In pre-television America it would have been a costly uphill battle to convince the public to change its daily breakfast routine to something more time-consuming and expensive (to say nothing of being packed with sodium and cholesterol).

But by combining the day's powerful credibility of newspapers with the American public's trust in medical doctors, millions soon believed they absolutely needed bacon and eggs to achieve the Coveted Condition of being their healthiest and most productive selves.

By changing the belief to align with the goal, millions of people changed their habitual behavior.

Today, revolutionary products use similar techniques to transform buyers' habits. Peloton got people to abandon the belief that they could work out more effectively at the gym than at home. Apple made us believe an expensive smartwatch could make us safer, healthier and better accepted by our peers. Tesla showed auto buyers that electric motors are sexier and more powerful than internal combustion engines. Nike uses the allure of great athletes to reset regular people's beliefs about their inner potential.

And suddenly your brain says you need a smartwatch, a fitness subscription, an EV, those expensive shoes — and bacon.

Woof! Cha-ching!

KEY INSIGHTS FROM CHAPTER 14

- Bacon, once a marginalized dinner meat, was successfully repositioned as a staple breakfast food in American culture.
- Beech-Nut packing company sought to boost sales of bacon by diversifying its offerings.
- Edward Bernays, a New York press agent, led a strategic campaign to reposition bacon as a breakfast staple.
- Bernays collaborated with a doctor to portray bacon and eggs as a hearty and nutritious breakfast option.
- Through targeted PR efforts and media influence, Bernays propelled the idea of bacon as a central part of the "most important meal of the day" onto front pages nationwide.
- The bacon repositioning story demonstrates how strategic messaging and influencer marketing can drive cultural shifts and shape consumer habits.
- Revolutionary products like Peloton, Apple, Tesla, and Nike have similarly transformed consumer perceptions and behaviors through strategic messaging aligned with pre-existing beliefs and goals.

DO THESE NOW FOR QUICK WINS:

GET CREDIBLE ENDORSEMENTS

Research and identify authoritative figures, professionals, or experts related to your product's domain who can provide credible endorsements.

What role, experience or position makes someone especially qualified to say your product addresses significant needs?

Establish connections with right-fit influencers and experts to gain their support and validate your product's benefits.

Lead the discussion with how your collaboration can help your influencer — and how your buyer will benefit.

LEVERAGE MEDIA

Use media platforms and influencers to amplify your product's story and benefits to a wider audience.

What platforms do your ideal customers gravitate to and who do they trust?

Think about hiring a PR agency with experience in your space.

A good one can craft a perspective-flipping narrative and will already be connected to excellent publications, bloggers and influencers.

ANALYZE MARKET DYNAMICS

Spend 20 minutes analyzing the market dynamics and historical examples of successful product transformations, similar to the repositioning of bacon as a breakfast food, or eggs for dinner.

Identify key strategies and tactics used to change consumer beliefs and behaviors and consider how they can be applied to your product.

ENGAGE WITH TRUSTED PROFESSIONALS

Dedicate 20 minutes to engage with trusted professionals or recognized experts who can validate the benefits of your product from a health, wellness or scientific perspective.

Seek endorsements or recommendations from credible sources to strengthen the perceived value and credibility of your product among consumers.

DEVELOP STRATEGIC PARTNERSHIPS

Explore potential partnerships or collaborations with complementary products or services that can dovetail with your product.

Identify opportunities to bundle or integrate your product with existing solutions to create a more compelling offering for consumers.

What are the eggs to your bacon?

CHAPTER 15

The Need for a Better Product

In This Chapter:

- *The concept of "escape velocity" for products*
- *The importance of creating an excellent product*
- *Key attributes of successful products*
- *Strategies to improve your own products*

"The best way to increase sales of a product is to improve the product."

— David Ogilvy

"Tell ten people. If they don't tell the others, make a better product."

—Seth Godin

IN CELESTIAL MECHANICS, there is a thing called "escape velocity."

Escape velocity is the speed a rocket has to achieve to break free from a planet's gravitational pull and exit its atmosphere, after which it will need no further propulsion. Once an object reaches escape velocity, it won't fall back, and will continue to travel on its own indefinitely.

A similar dynamic exists for products.

At launch, every new sale you make requires massive energy and effort. A small number of innovators and some early adopters may bite, and your biggest supporters may be willing to buy nearly anything you are selling.

But the rest of your buyers need to be identified, attracted, engaged and convinced through marketing.

The product has only just begun to exist, and a web search for it comes up dead empty. There is no social proof, and little to provide buyers with confidence the product is legit, much less amazing.

With the exception of unicorn brands like Tesla (which for years has leveraged founder Elon Musk's celebrity appeal to access massive free publicity) and Instant Pot (which exploded through perfect timing after being featured on Amazon's Prime Day), marketing is consistently the most reliable way for a product to become known and be recognized as needed by the masses.

There was a time when a million-dollar marketing budget and a crafty advertising team could give pretty much any product a chance at selling enough units to reach escape velocity and become a household word. (Or when you could write letters to thousands of physician friends and literally have them save your bacon through the print media.)

Those were the bad old days, unless you were one of the shysters. Plenty of mediocre and sometimes even horrendous products flourished, just by becoming well-known and easily recognized brands. The mechanisms didn't exist for buyers to reveal their disappointment to others, aside from one to one.

When you saw an infomercial or received a flier in the mail, you had to judge the product based on nothing but the ad copy. There were no customer reviews, no social media comments, no online forums. The consumer was alone in the wild, and unethical product makers had a heyday.

Fortunately, that world is nothing but a fading, if fascinating memory. The only way to succeed and thrive today is to begin with an excellent product. One that a large number or people need enough to actively look for and buy, even when you aren't paying to reach them.

That's not to say you're likely ever to stop marketing. But at some point, you've got to largely decouple cost and effort from individual sales, so that every single unit is no longer costing you directly. And the sooner, the better.

If you decide to buy a new phone tomorrow, it probably isn't the direct result of an ad or because your old one lost its ability to make calls, but because you have come to feel you need the latest model — for a better camera, faster processor or longer-lasting battery.

The same goes for when you buy the newest all-electric Volvo, or upgrade your Instant Pot to one of the company's air fryers. You already have functioning ways to get around and cook, but will begin your research based on what you know and what you believe, supported by things you've seen smart and fashionable people using recently. While ads may push products onto your radar, successful companies aren't counting on an immediate conversion.

The best advertising for a sleek new vehicle is having people admire it on the roads. I mentioned earlier that I was a Volvo driver for years. My parents, uncle and grandparents had Volvo cars, and while I wasn't a fan of the vehicles' signature boxy look at the time, I did know they were built for safety.

So, when kids were in my future and I spotted the curvaceous, newly released Volvo S60 on European roads, I vowed to get one as soon as it was available at home. I'm quite sure I never saw an S60 ad before signing the papers.

Similarly, the most powerful advertising for a new smartphone or cooking device is your maven friends raving about how those products have improved their own lives.

Achieving escape velocity, so that the product can sell itself, depends on having a product that is needed, enticing, and understood — and performs really, really well.

With the ubiquity of product reviews for nearly anything that can be sold, mediocre products can never sell themselves, even if you spend millions to have them universally recognized. And lousy ones are lucky to get used as boat anchors or doorstops.

We've all got better things to do than build and flog a product that isn't superb in every possible way. Why would anyone even want to? And yet we see it happening every day.

Most failed products have at least one Achilles' heel that should never have been overlooked. Competitive disadvantages, points of failure, quality gaps, or flawed economics of production or distribution.

Successful products have plenty in common too. Virtually all hugely successful products achieve the following very well:

OUTCOMES

WHILE IT'S SUPER OBVIOUS that a successful product must deliver the desired results and fulfill buyer needs, product makers often give themselves too much slack when it comes to outcomes.

To succeed at scale, your product has to work flawlessly every time, for a long time.

That means it is not acceptable to sometimes have parts missing, the odd quality issue or a moderate failure rate.

Dealing with these problems post-sale eats up profits, and the effects always show up disproportionately in reviews. Even if exactly half of your customers are satisfied, the disappointed buyers are two to three times more likely to write a review than the happy ones.

When sales begin to scale, so do problems.

That can turn your dream of success into a complete nightmare. It's not unreasonable to focus on consistently achieving perfect outcomes.

ADVANTAGES

THE IMPORTANCE OF BEING much better than competitors on every level can hardly be overstated. Brands like Apple and Tesla haven't succeeded just by topping competitors' offerings in one or two minor ways.

They have blown up the industries in which they play by offering completely fresh approaches and huge, easily seen advantages over the status quo.

You want to eliminate every significant basis for comparison, and be far superior in any remaining way your product can be compared.

EASE

THE EASE OF ADOPTING a product is far underrated in the perception of too many of the people involved in designing and building one.

If most product makers could 10X the effort they invest in achieving simplicity, minimizing learning curves and reducing part count, marketplace failure rates would be quite different.

It's no coincidence that the most successful products are also the easiest for consumers to learn to use and adopt painlessly into their day-to-day lives.

EXPERIENCES

SUCCESSFUL PRODUCTS are often the result of exceptional customer experiences. "Delight" should be not an aspirational goal, but the baseline.

Your online store has to be inviting and engaging, and it must immediately build confidence in the product and brand.

Customers' dog brains should be squirrel-called by beautiful, elegant industrial design.

Buyers should delight in the feel of buttons and the product's ergonomics. At every touch point, the experience should ratchet to a higher level, including — no, especially — when something goes wrong.

Never overlook customer experience, sales and support when building a product brand. Customers need these things from your product, or they don't need the product.

ECONOMICS

I'VE SEEN MANY good products fail because their business models were not economically viable. Imagine writing a business plan in which you predict to sell a $50 automotive part direct-to-consumer, but it will cost $5 to manufacture, $8 to pack and ship — oh, and each online conversion will average $40 in ad media spend.

Simple math ought to herald the end of that whole notion, yet countless products start out on similarly ill-fated journeys.

Some product makers bank on an initial marketing blast to reach escape velocity early on (which is extremely hard to do).

Others set out to price the product higher than existing options, attempting to position it as a luxury or prestige alternative, but without convincing consumers how it will improve their status.

In some edge cases it works, but not often enough. Intense launch campaigns are quickly forgotten. Jacking up the price can cripple conversion rates, trigger price-gouging complaints and increase media costs.

Other approaches to "fix" bad economics can be equally risky. Quickly adding more products to increase average transaction value can lead to the business losing focus and working harder — usually still at a loss.

Entering the very expensive, high-risk world of retail distribution is a huge undertaking and commitment that requires financing production costs, offering wholesale discounts, and agonizing waits for payment — provided the product even does sell well in stores.

The only real answer is to deliver a product that is at least ten times better than any other option, making it enticing enough (in the buyer's mind) to justify the price tag.

A product people really need, love to use — and will happily go out of their way to acquire.

INNOVATION INTERLUDE: DYSON AND THE NEED FOR A BETTER VACUUM

Dyson exemplifies how creating a significantly better product can revolutionize an existing market to fulfill unmet consumer needs.

When James Dyson introduced his cyclonic vacuum cleaner, he addressed several pain points in existing products:

Functional Benefit: Consistent suction without performance loss

Emotional Benefit: Pride in owning a cutting-edge appliance

Transformative Benefit: Less time and effort spent on cleaning

Coveted Condition: The enjoyment of a clean, efficient home

Dyson's approach to improving the vacuum cleaner went beyond incremental changes. By completely reimagining the technology, he created a product that was demonstrably superior to existing options.

The company's focus on transparent design, allowing users to see the cyclone technology in action, reinforced the product's innovative nature and appealed to consumers' desire for understanding and control.

From its launch in 1993, Dyson grew to become a market leader, with global revenue reaching £7.1 billion in 2023.[1]

By addressing fundamental issues with existing vacuum cleaners and creating a visibly superior alternative, Dyson redefined consumer expectations for the entire category, and proved that focusing on creating a genuinely better product can drive market success and fulfill previously unrecognized consumer needs

KEY INSIGHTS FROM CHAPTER 15

- To increase product sales, improving the product itself is crucial.
- Successful products achieve "escape velocity," where they sell themselves (and customers sell them) without continuous marketing effort.
- A strong marketing budget and effective teams can't compensate for a mediocre product, much less a lousy one.
- Universal recognition doesn't guarantee success; excellence is essential.
- Mediocre products no longer sell themselves, because product reviews and customer feedback are easily shared and accessed by prospective buyers.
- Successful products share common attributes: delivering outstanding outcomes, providing clear advantages, offering intuitive ease of use, creating exceptional experiences and having sound economics.

DO THESE NOW FOR QUICK WINS:

EVALUATE PRODUCT QUALITY

Block out 30 minutes to conduct a comprehensive review of your product's quality and performance.

Identify any potential areas for improvement, including experiences with missing parts, quality issues, or failure rates, and prioritize addressing them to ensure flawless outcomes. If your product is not yet being sold, establish a time-based plan with the manufacturer for rapidly addressing and eliminating issues when they arise.

FOCUS ON USER EXPERIENCE

Dedicate 20 minutes to enhancing the ease of use and overall user experience of your product.

Prioritize simplicity, minimal learning curves, and intuitive design to ensure seamless adoption into customers' daily lives. Where do people trip up? How can user error be eliminated?

ANALYZE ECONOMIC VIABILITY

Set aside 30 minutes a day for one week to understand the economic feasibility of your product, including industrial design and manufacturing costs, overseas freight expenses, tariffs, shipping fees to your customer and marketing spend.

Learn the extent of brand assets like photos and videos you will need, as well as monthly retainer fees you will pay to a marketing agency.

Confirm your Return on Ad Spend (ROAS) expectations by talking to a product marketing expert. Seek to know what similar products are paying per conversion, and how that cost is affected by scaling. While these data points are highly variable over time, it is important to understand how they work — and whether they work for your product. Build a spreadsheet to track all of this and do the calculations for you.

Confirm that your pricing strategy makes sense and will generate profit, while leaving room for operations, contingencies and R&D.

SEEK VALID REASONS FOR PREMIUM PRICING

Allocate 20 minutes to brainstorm valid reasons for consumers to perceive your product as luxurious or high-value. Understand what new luxury products do to convey their value, without being able to leverage brand recognition.

Focus on showing how your product is significantly superior to existing options and justifies its price tag through unmatched performance and reliability.

AVOID RISKY BUSINESS MODELS

Spend 30 minutes devising fallback approaches to economic challenges, such as launching intense marketing campaigns or entering retail distribution. These should be significantly different from your Plan A. They might even be better, because they are not what everyone else is doing.

Don't be a flash in the pan. Aim for a sustainable business model that delivers long-term value to both your company and your customers.

REVERSE-ENGINEER ESCAPE VELOCITY

Set ambitious goals for achieving escape velocity, where your product can sell itself without the need for high-cost marketing efforts. Identify what escape velocity looks like for your product, and work backwards to where you will start out at launch.

When you reach that magic threshold, what forces will be propelling you ahead the most efficiently, and what steps can you take to ensure they are in place?

Focus on continuously enhancing your product's quality, performance, and overall value proposition to drive organic growth and widespread adoption in the market.

Map pathways and build mechanisms for customers to recommend the product to multiple friends. Plan to invest in search engine optimization rather than paying high costs per click for search advertising. Remember — these things take time and don't happen on their own.

CHAPTER 16

What's So Bad About the Status Quo

In This Chapter:

- *Addressing pain points to amplify product desire*
- *Poking bruises while respecting emotional attachments*
- *Learning from successful campaigns that tackled the status quo*
- *Tapping into pain points to create resonant content*

REMEMBER HOW DESIRE really gets amped up when a buyer begins to fantasize about your product? Sometimes it happens simply because the product delivers a commonly sought Coveted Condition and aligns with the same people's pre-existing beliefs.

But very often it takes more. Remember, friction and internal resistance are powerful forces that act aggressively against people's buying impulses. The status quo is our biggest enemy.

As a product maker, you've got to fine-tune your combat chops, and take on the status quo directly.

When Steve Jobs introduced the iPhone, he started with what people already knew was wrong with their smartphones. Bad web browsing, cumbersome physical keyboards, and "touch screens" that responded only to light gouging by a clumsy, easily lost stylus.

Any other presenter would have jumped straight into the technical details.

But Jobs' approach was much better. The status quo had left costumers with a lot of bruises, but bruises don't hurt enough of the time. (As Seth Godin says, the status quo is very good at one thing: sticking around.[1])

Recognizing this, Jobs gave each of those bruises a good, hard poke, offered a truly fantasy-worthy solution — and *Woof! Cha-ching!* Hordes of buyers needed an iPhone and literally queued up to fork over their money.

Same with my Cateye Solar. I was a cash-strapped teen, but seeing what had just become available, I could hardly bear to look at my crappy mechanical speedometer. Suddenly, the bruises were unbearable and my constant daydreams of the alternative made buying it non-negotiable.

Marketers often forget about the importance of showing what's wrong with the solution people are already using, and that can be a huge mistake. For people to feel they need a product, they must strongly desire to have it in their lives — and something else. They must be not only ready, but extremely eager to ditch the status quo, along with all the habits, sunk investment and emotional attachment that go with it into the trash bin.

If you can bring them to resent, despise and feel pained by what they are using, you eliminate a tremendous amount of resistance.

But a caveat: poking a bruise is something that should be done with precision and thoughtful consideration for your audience.

Why? Remember that people have strong feelings for what they spend a lot of time using. Those can include brand loyalty or a burden of pride, possibly from years of telling others about it. At one point, it was what aligned with their deeply held beliefs. Maybe in some ways it still does. You don't want to insult a brand they love, and by extension, offend your prospective buyers.

But Steve Jobs did, right?

Sure. Except that unlike the Apple fandom watching Jobs' keynote, your future buyers probably don't even *know* you yet.

You're pledging to help them, saying you've got something ten times better. And they do know the shortcomings of what they've been using, even if they've been ignoring those issues. So, you've just got to carefully poke each bruise, evoking vivid memories of the pain and frustration and then demonstrating how your product is so much better at achieving those jobs — and fulfilling their Coveted Condition.

You may already know the pain points from personal experience. They are what led you to create the product. Even when this is the case, it is valuable to include pain point questions in your validation and Voice of Customer (VOC) research. Often, you'll gain insights about what issues are the most frustrating, and be able to define the true value of providing a solution.

TURNING PAIN INTO GAIN

UNDERSTANDING HOW CUSTOMERS perceive the challenges they face with existing products can also be a fantastic starting point for your content marketing. If plenty of people are searching for a workaround to a problem your product solves, not only does that demonstrate you're on the right track with the product, it also identifies an opportunity for you to create blog posts, podcast episodes and other sought-after content targeting those search queries by people actively looking for a better solution than their status quo one.

As you gain insights into each pain point, it becomes easier to bring them all to people's attention in ways that feel like a bruise being poked.

Think of the Snickers campaign slogan, "You're not you when you're hungry." Prior to it, most candy bar buyers had probably never considered how being "hangry" affected their personality.

Snickers was working to position its compact, high-calorie candy bar as a way to power up, rather than being seen as just another junk food option like other candy bars that were full of wafers, crisps and things that didn't fill you up. Plenty of fans had already found that a Snickers was a quick, satisfying way to bridge meals. There was clear potential to acquire market share from within and outside the candy bar market. But plenty of incumbent products had a place in consumer's snacking habits.

With that in mind, Snickers developed clever ways of reinforcing that reality through exaggerated plays on the energy kick you can get from eating a Snickers bar. In the ads, NFLers tackle Betty White, and ninjas botch a stealth attack because of a bumbling Mr. Bean. Then, in each case, a bite from a Snickers bar transforms the misplaced celebrity into the character's true, elite self. It's hilarious and gets the message across in an unforgettable way.

It's about repositioning the product as a far better replacement for the status quo, while aligning with what buyers already know. We all believe hunger makes us irritable and hampers our performance. When hungry, we're not the best version of ourselves.

Snickers' was able to double down on that need-driven belief. It poked the bruise and made consumers reach for its product instead of an energy bar or a handful of nuts the way prior beliefs would have led them to do.

SHOW THEM YOU CARE

VRBO'S ADS DIRECTLY target the frustrations travelers have experienced with Airbnb, the vacation rental industry leader. People renting with the incumbent often found themselves experiencing awkward dinners with a stranger at the table, or weird encounters with hosts who rented out rooms in their own home.

But Vrbo offers only private vacation homes, where these scenarios couldn't happen.

The company knew many travelers hated the compromise of

sharing a space during their precious vacation time. So it spoofed these painful scenarios in funny, memorable ways.

In one ad, an overly enthusiastic host asks "Do you believe in ghosts?" When the uneasy guests reply that they do not, the host says dryly, "Good. Mother is buried in the yard."

Vrbo posed the question: "Why would you ever share your vacation home with someone you wouldn't share your vacation with?" It was a less-than-subtle poke at a commonly felt sore spot for people using Airbnb. Importantly, the tone and messaging were respectful to the audience, who possibly felt some loyalty to Airbnb. It urged them to relax, and get the private vacation *they* deserve.

Think about what your buyers despise most about the status quo, contrasted with the change your product brings — while recognizing the attachment they may have to the solution they are using.

How can you most effectively poke those bruises, in a way that feels thoughtful and empathetic?

You want your audience to say, "Hey, yeah! I really DO hate that!" And to see your product as the pleasurable, exciting alternative that is a non-negotiable need.

KEY INSIGHTS FROM CHAPTER 16

- Effectively addressing customers' pain points and shortcomings of existing solutions can amplify their desire for your product.
- Gently remind customers of the frustrations and limitations they experience with current solutions to evoke a strong desire for change and "poke the bruise."
- Connect your product's benefits with pre-existing beliefs and goals, reinforcing that your solution can achieve their Coveted Condition.
- Approach pain point discussions with empathy, careful not to insult customers' current choices or brands they are loyal to.
- Pain points identified during research can be used as blog post, video and podcast topics, creating valuable content that resonates with your target audience and can be found in web searches.

DO THESE NOW FOR QUICK WINS:

IDENTIFY PAIN POINTS

Dedicate 30 minutes to conduct thorough research and identify the pain points specific to the existing solutions your target audience is using — not the need itself.

What do people hate most about the status quo? What would they like to smash?

Explore forums, social media discussions, customer reviews, and conduct Voice of Customer (VOC) research to gain insights into the frustrations and challenges your audience faces.

RECOGNIZE EMOTIONAL ATTACHMENTS

Spend another 20 minutes analyzing the emotional attachments your audience may have to their current solutions, including brand loyalty and pride.

Consider how to approach poking these bruises with precision and thoughtful consideration to avoid insulting their existing choices.

LEARN FROM SUCCESSFUL CAMPAIGNS

Set aside 30 minutes to study successful marketing campaigns that effectively poked at the bruises of the status quo and positioned their products as far superior alternatives.

Analyze how these campaigns aligned with existing beliefs and emotions while communicating how the product is a breath of fresh air.

CREATE ENGAGING VISUALS

Plan to develop visual assets that vividly illustrate the frustrations of the status quo, contrasted with the transformative power of your product.

Consider using storytelling techniques and humor to engage your audience and make your messaging memorable.

STAY AUTHENTIC AND RESPECTFUL

Throughout your marketing efforts, maintain authenticity and respect for your audience's experiences and choices.

Laugh together at the flaws of the competition, but remember that the customer may hold years of brand loyalty.

You aren't the new best friend, yet.

Avoid alienating potential customers by acknowledging the value of the incumbent's place in the customer's world while positioning your product as a compelling alternative.

Make notes of how this looks to your customer.

CHAPTER 17

What the World *Doesn't* Need Now

In This Chapter:

- *Staying true to the product's original mission*
- *Avoiding Need Neutralizers that undermine effectiveness*
- *Addressing bad customer experiences and product shortcomings*
- *Recognizing when to pivot or discontinue a product*

ANYONE WHO TAKES a product to market becomes acutely aware of what can go wrong.

Their biggest fear is always that people won't buy. Even the most confident product makers know it can happen. And even the most successful ones have experienced it.

But failing to sell enough of a product for profitable commercialization is just one way you can fall down.

You stand to disappoint the very people you set out to help in the first place. You may take their money, but what if they never get the satisfaction they'd hoped for — and was central to your vision?

Whether the product fails to meet expectations, is hard to understand, is confusing to use, doesn't work well, breaks easily or wears out prematurely, you're disappointing supporters and generating bad deals.

That always makes me feel unhappy when I'm the customer, and I do my best to avoid being involved in marketing any product that fails to deliver as promised.

A product becomes unneeded in a few predictable ways. And only by recognizing them and deliberately taking steps to steer clear of each one can you be sure to avoid finding too late that your product has strayed into dangerous territory.

BAD EXPERIENCES

WORD OF MOUTH has always been important in marketing. Not so long ago, referrals could entirely build a business and while negative customer experiences could leave customers fuming, they didn't necessarily lead to failure.

Even outright scams could live on for ages — think of ads in comic books selling useless "X-Ray Specs" or brine shrimp marketed as "Sea Monkeys." Disappointed kids had nowhere to post their complaints, so generation after generation of new victims continued to mail in their allowance money.

In the digital era though, bad customer experiences surface instantly and can haunt brands forever. If the product is generally good and the brand is committed to satisfying customers, each complaint can become an opportunity to learn, resolve the problem and improve the product.

But when the product consistently falls short on the very needs it promised to satisfy, there is no possibility of a happy ending.

NEED NEUTRALIZERS

IN THE SUPERMAN TV shows, movies and comics, there's a green, crystalline substance called kryptonite. It comes from the Man of Steel's home planet, Krypton, and if any gets near him, he becomes weak as a kitten. It can even kill him.

And while solving a true and widespread need can be a product's superpower, there are forces that are like kryptonite even to powerful, commonly felt needs.

I immediately think of an air purifier that I once helped market. The product maker had achieved huge success in a niche electronics space, and secured a partnership to manufacture and sell a promising new consumer device. In all the excitement, the train got rolling quickly, and production began before any doubts could emerge.

This air purifier had some remarkable superpowers. It used a new technology that made it more effective than conventional HEPA air purifiers — by a margin of three thousand times. Plus, it came with two hot-swappable batteries that gave it a 24-hour battery life. Those two features alone gave it true portability and a unique selling proposition that was vastly superior to anything else on the market.

Slam dunk, right?

But there was kryptonite — lots of it.

Because of the innovative new technology, virtually every component was unique. This meant that to be profitable, it had to be priced significantly higher than other small-space air purifiers.

Except it cleaned air at a much lower rate than any incumbent. Even small rooms often exceeded the specified maximum cubic feet it could effectively handle.

And it had a high cost of ownership, forcing the owner to replace four expensive air filters, on two different schedules. Those consumable sales were seen as awesome recurring revenue by the manufacturer, who was proud that the machine would shut down when any filter needed to be replaced. Even if a third party offered replacement parts, the technology ensured nothing but original filters would work. Unsurprisingly, consumers despised this "feature." Many were enraged when they discovered how much it cost just to keep their pricey gadget working.

Worst of all, the thing was LOUD. When I tried one, I couldn't believe nothing was wrong with it. Half the settings were not even recommended for use while people were present in the room. (Who the heck purifies the air when they're away?)

Of all these Need Neutralizers, the loudness was the most potent. Not only did the device hit surprising decibels, but the fans' high-pitched whine could quickly become unbearable.

Consumer reviews panned all these things. And the need, along with the product itself, was effectively neutralized.

It's important to recognize what Need Neutralizers exist for your product — and do whatever it takes to eliminate them. As hard as that can be while you're still in product development, overcoming the kryptonite later on may be impossible. You can't market it away.

There are three types of Need Neutralizers that can kill a product:

1. PURCHASE FRICTION

These are the barriers that get in the way of acquiring the product in the first place, or becoming a repeat customer. A glitchy online store, inconvenient payment methods, or complications further down the line like shipping delays or customs fees are a turnoff to the customer.

Mail-in rebates are a type of post-sale friction sellers willfully build in, knowing most buyers won't go to all the trouble it takes to receive the discount. When buyers do, it's referred to in the industry as "breakage." But what really gets broken is love for the brand. The air purifier I told you about tried to use mail-in rebates to artificially reduce sticker shock, with breakage expectations central to the strategy. It didn't increase sales, but made new work for the support team — and you can probably guess how pleased consumers were. The anticipation of mail-in rebate frustration is like hitting the dog brain with a water hose. It can make people less inclined to buy than offering no discount at all.

No form of purchase friction is acceptable to the customer, and every kind leads to a direct reduction in sales. It's worth testing and retesting your buyer's experience to remove friction at every step.

2. INCONVENIENCES

Issues like a loud or irritating noise can make your product unbearable to use, especially if the inconvenience presents frequently or for long durations, and if it impacts people beyond the principal user. Running an air purifier that is a little loud may be acceptable for the person who bought it, but if other members of the household are constantly complaining about the noise, it will soon hit the refuse heap — or the seller's Returns desk.

Design flaws and counterintuitive user interfaces are Need Neutralizers customers notice every time they try to accomplish something they bought the product to do. These problems make up a majority of negative online reviews, even when a technically functional product falls just marginally short of expectations. If a product requires constant fiddling and adjusting simply to do its job, it becomes an inconvenience, not a solution. Busy people need consistently stellar outcomes, and won't tolerate products that under-deliver or are less than delightful to use.

3. OWNERSHIP COSTS

These include expensive consumables requiring ongoing servicing, battery replacement, frequent repairs — or products that have to be replaced outright. Even if a product solves a bothersome need, many owners will be put off by a high ongoing cost of ownership.

Desktop printers and multi-blade razors are two categories that have succeeded as glaring exceptions to this rule. Gorgeous, ridiculously cheap handles lock buyers into using Gillette's expensive razor heads. Many color printers by Epson and HP sell for little more than a single set of replacement ink cartridges. High-margin ink sales subsidize the low printer costs, and people are baited to buy an amazing printer for a great price. Often only after the sale do many discover that it came with low-capacity "starter" cartridges — enough to print just a small number of pages. Amazingly, most of the time, these consumers opt to accept the high ownership costs.

In the printer market, it's a game of economics. The same manufacturers make units that use high-volume ink tanks with more affordable ink. Not by coincidence, these unsubsidized printers cost more and come with fewer features, slower output speeds and downgraded print quality. It's engineered to be a better long-term deal, but one that's hard to swallow at the time of purchase.

Naturally, the vast majority of buyers opt for the lower initial buy-in but much higher ownership costs. Or the sexy free razor handle and expensive blades. The rational, long-term focused tank brain loses again.

It's important to remember that desktop printer and razor manufacturers are fairly unique in their success at harnessing high ownership costs. They succeed by delivering a precise balance of value and performance that is very hard for competitors to beat. Customers hate these games, but discover there is no ideal alternative.

As a product maker, you want people to love your creation, and for it to be the best alternative possible. And even if disappointing a large percentage of customers is something you can live with, that usually has disastrous consequences for the product brand.

RETURNS

IF YOURS IS A physical product, one of the worst things that can happen is to be left with a massive monument to your failure in the form of thousands of neatly stacked boxes of unsold units. Even if you are able to unload them on a liquidation reseller, it's a disastrous and embarrassing way to end.

The next worst thing is when a product continues to boomerang back to stores and online sales channels in the form of customer returns. Even if the product doesn't end up in a liquidation heap, getting it into stores may have been costly and difficult. Every return statement jeopardizes future procurement deals.

Product returns reduce your net sales, meaning each one erases its value (and then some) from your net profit. Enough of them can be the end of your business.

CHURN

FOR SOFTWARE PRODUCTS, "churn" is the equivalent of returns. Most successful cloud-based products are sold as subscriptions, because the model is so much more lucrative and consistent than endlessly flogging individual license sales. But the downside is that customers experience subscription fatigue and are increasingly on the lookout for subscribed products that no longer fulfill their needs. They scour their bank statements in search of recurring costs that can be cut. Enterprise customers do the same, and specialized apps now exist to assist in subscription assessment and cost-cutting.

In the B2B world, the end users are often not even involved in making such decisions. If someone isn't highlighting the product name on that list and saying, "No! I NEED this one," it risks becoming a churn statistic.

THROWING IN THE TOWEL

WHEN A PRODUCT IS NOT catching on in the market, at what point is it time to declare it a failure?

It's a tough question. Failing fast is a popular strategy: it means testing fresh approaches and entering new markets, while limiting losses by getting out quickly when there's no clear sign of traction. It's knowing "when to fold em," as Kenny Rogers famously sang.

It makes sense and we've all heard stories about massive hits that came only after countless painful misses. Thomas Edison said, "I have not failed 10,000 times. I've successfully found 10,000 ways that will not work."

The trick is in failing forward, quickly extracting what *does* work from what does not and in avoiding repeatedly making the same mistakes. Then using those lessons to build a new, winning formula.

The key is to combine successful elements to create a truly needed product. And crafting the exact version of it people are excited to use — not tricking them into buying a flawed or undesirable version 1.0.

Sometimes, no new and improved iteration of the product will work, and it's smart to throw in the towel.

How do you figure all this out, without burning through mountains of money?

It's called validation. And the earlier on you begin, the better.

INNOVATION INTERLUDE:
JUICERO AND THE UNNEEDED JUICER

Juicero serves as a cautionary tale of a product that failed to address a genuine need and ignored critical Need Neutralizers. Launched in 2017, Juicero aimed to revolutionize home juicing with fresh, cold-pressed juices anyone could make.

However, Juicero overlooked multiple Need Neutralizers:

Price Point: At $699 (later reduced to $399), it was significantly more expensive than conventional juicers.

Complexity: The machine required proprietary juice packs and an internet connection just to function.

Unnecessary Technology: The juice packs could be squeezed by hand, rendering the expensive machine unnecessary.

These powerful Need Neutralizers zapped the product's value proposition. Despite raising an eye-popping $120 million in funding, Juicero shut down just 16 months after launch.[1]

The Juicero case highlights the importance of addressing real consumer needs and avoiding over-engineering.

It demonstrates that even with substantial funding and sleek design, a product that doesn't solve a genuine problem or that introduces unnecessary complexity is likely to fail in the market.

KEY INSIGHTS FROM CHAPTER 17

- Ensure your product stays true to its original mission of addressing pre-existing needs. Beware of losing focus amidst spontaneous feature requests and suggestions.
- Failing to meet customer expectations can lead to disappointment, bad deals, and damaged brand reputation. Strive to deliver on promised benefits and functionality.
- In the digital era, bad customer experiences can surface instantly and haunt brands forever. Rapidly addressing product shortcomings is crucial for brand credibility.
- Identify and eliminate factors that neutralize the effectiveness of your product, such as purchase friction, inconveniences and high ownership costs.
- Product returns and churn can erode profitability and damage brand reputation. Minimize returns and churn by pouncing on customer concerns.
- Recognize when it's time to course-correct or discontinue a product that fails to gain traction in the market. Embrace failure as a learning opportunity and prioritize quick adaptation and iteration.
- Avoid wasting resources on developing products that don't meet customer needs or expectations.

DO THESE NOW FOR QUICK WINS:

KNOW THE MISSION

Clarify and document your product's purpose to maintain focus throughout development. Sanity-check frequently with others who understand your fundamental goals.

IDENTIFY NEED NEUTRALIZERS

Make a list of factors that neutralize your product's effectiveness, such as purchase friction, inconveniences, and high ownership costs.

Streamline the user experience to optimize product adoption and minimize the impact of Need Neutralizers. How can you eliminate or compensate for each one you identify?

ADDRESS PRODUCT SHORTCOMINGS

Hunt down and proactively address any product shortcomings. Keep track of negative experiences reported by customers and investigate them.

A lone complaint could be a wrong-fit customer or fluke user screwup. Three or more is definitely an issue.

Swiftly resolve issues to maintain brand credibility and customer loyalty, while improving the product in meaningful ways as you go.

MONITOR RETURNS AND CHURN

Devise a simple system to track product returns and churn rates so you can use these to gauge customer satisfaction levels.

Minimize returns and churn by addressing root causes to permanently solve every problem. (This can be done in a method similar to "The Why Game," systematically drilling down to uncover the one problem that must be resolved to eliminate the issue forever.)

How can the next version of the product be returned much less frequently?

PIVOT OR DISCONTINUE

Prepare in advance to pivot or discontinue a product that fails to gain traction in the market, rather than pressing onward in a robotic death march.

How will you know when it's time? Put it in writing now.

Embrace failure as a learning opportunity and use that market intelligence towards meeting customer needs more effectively.

STAY INFORMED AND ADAPTIVE

Dedicate 15 minutes each day to staying updated on industry news, market trends, and competitor activities.

Set up Google news alerts to let you know when important keywords pop up in news stories.

Follow relevant blogs, news websites, or social media channels to gather insights and adapt your strategy accordingly.

CHAPTER 18

Validating for Needs

In This Chapter:

- *The importance of adopting a validation mindset*
- *Common validation methods and their applications*
- *Avoiding common validation mistakes and biases*
- *Testing prototypes with real users for valuable feedback*
- *Assessing the value case and justifying the product's price*

TO ANYONE WITH the gumption to create a new product, it always seems profoundly (and somehow increasingly) clear that people will be blown away by its value and feel compelled to own it.

And that's a big problem.

As the product maker, you have zero objectivity.

Truth is, no human being on earth is *less* objective about your product than you are. You are much too close to the concept to perceive it the way strangers will.

You have completely understood why it exists, since ... before it even *did*.

Prospective buyers will see the product from all kinds of different angles, with mindsets that don't align with your own. Remember, we do not buy most things we see — even many products we want.

So, how do you find out if they'll feel enough of a need to pony up the money for your product?

Many product makers will do what Ken, the phone accessory entrepreneur, did.

They will go out and pitch the product to friends, colleagues and relatives. Which is a terrible idea.

You like these people and trust their opinions. And they like you.

So they will almost always lie to you in such a situation. They'll say they LOVE the idea, and that buying it would be a no-brainer. (But as Ken discovered, they would probably not buy it if they randomly happened upon one and didn't know the person who created it. And even though they do know you, they may not be willing to pay for it with their own real money.)

They are simply saying what you clearly want to hear. It costs them nothing and makes you both feel good — at least in that moment.)

And so off you go, feeling wonderful. And you invest your life's savings (or your investors') on a product no one, or not nearly enough people, will need to buy.

You do all the work to build it, and excitedly go to market.

Probably to what Peloton's John Foley referred to as "crickets."

Then, what happens next is incredibly frustrating. You dig in to fix the problem. You run endless different ads, trying a multitude of headlines, images and text variations.

More crickets.

You might hire Conversion Rate Optimization experts, and redesign your online store ten times over. It will cost a fortune, and probably none of it will work. The crickets become maddening.

I've heard innovators say, "just send us enough traffic and if one percent buy, we'll be a huge success." But often closing that one percent turns out to be infinitely harder — and costlier — than they ever thought.

It really is possible to send millions of people to a beautiful, technically excellent online store, and get close to no conversions. If you are not able to trigger an irresistible need to own what you are selling, people just won't buy it.

Yet even experienced innovators can't help projecting that some specific, tiny percentage of the (always overblown) Total Addressable Market will be absolutely certain to convert.

It's never the case. Pre-launch expectations are almost always wrong — no matter who did the math.

When Segway founder Dean Kamen introduced his self-balancing upright personal transporter in 2002 with support from Jeff Bezos, investor and venture capitalist John Doerr predicted the company would be the fastest in history to reach $1 billion in sales. Steve Jobs said the Segway would have an impact as great as the personal computer. The concept was protected by a solid patent portfolio and initial production was geared to manufacture a half million units a year, after the company spent more than $100 million on research and development.[1]

It was as much a sure thing as the world had ever seen. Right?

Indeed. And in the first seven years, all of 23,500 units were sold.

What went so wrong?

Segway was a fascinating, truly novel invention. But the company was unable to do what Clayton Christensen, who coined the term "disruptive innovation," says is the very most important thing in launching a product. That is, to fulfill an unmet need and then position the product as the one that does it better than anything else.[2]

The thing is, the need Segway fulfilled wasn't unmet.

People in cities were already getting around quite well with cars, bicycles, skateboards, scooters, inline skates and motorcycles. Very few saw justification to drop $5,000 for a new way of doing something that was already working — and have to lug 100 pounds of Segway up and down stairs. (In truth, most consumers never even got far enough in their buyer's journey to lift one, or to learn the batteries would cost more than $1,000 to replace.) The Segway required big changes in how its owners did things, with questionable gains and a crap ton of friction.

Few people felt a compelling enough need, and Segway never managed to spark tempting fantasies in the minds of many buyers. It was hard to even conceive of one. Riding a Segway wasn't sexy; it looked plain nerdy.

Non-owners observing Segway owners didn't glaze over with envy and desire. So, seeing one was not the best ad to buy a Segway of your own. Early adopters complained about being called lazy, and were often ordered by police to get off the road — then off the sidewalk.

With a device that appeared to defy the law of gravity in how it balanced, perceived danger was a built-in barrier. And the danger was not just in people's minds.

President George W. Bush was photographed (and widely mocked for) falling off a Segway while on vacation, and journalist Piers Morgan broke three ribs in a similar way.[3]

In 2010, British entrepreneur James Heselden bought the company — and died nine months later by riding his own Segway straight off a cliff.[4]

Then in 2015, China-based Ninebot acquired Segway, only to cease production in 2020 due to — you guessed it — lack of sales.

Luckily, Segway has more lives than Super Mario. Recently, the company has been resurrected as a maker of e-bikes and of hoverboards — basically smaller, cheaper and lighter versions of the original, failed Segway. Probably what it ought to have been in the first place, had Dean Kamen only gone directly to the market to find out what buyers really needed.

It's a wild cautionary tale that shows how a product with perceived promise can do an awkward lip stand, regardless of investment, backers, hype and marketing effort. None of that matters if you can't trigger a sense of unmet need (and practicality) in consumers that is so strong, it compels them to ditch their old ways.

You've got be dead sure your product *will* — and that you'll be able to position it solidly around a Coveted Condition. Confirming there is an unmet need and triggering recurring fantasies are not optional. They are critical to overcoming buyer resistance.

But why are customers so violently resistant to adopting something new?

There are numerous reasons, beyond the obvious dislike for parting with their money:

- **Psychological costs of change:** People tend to overvalue products and systems they already have, ignoring depreciation and inflation while clinging onto prior investments like life preservers on the *RMS Titanic.*
- **Obsolescence costs:** No one wants to abandon accessories and workflows that go with current products, to waste investments like a library of compatible media — or be disconnected from friends and colleagues who are still using the old systems.
- **Loss aversion:** Studies prove that we fear loss two to three times more than we value potential gain. One study found that college students experienced much stronger emotions about risking a decline in their relationships than about potential improvements in the same ones. And in a UK experiment, homeowners were 45 percent more inclined to switch energy providers in order to avoid a loss than if doing so could achieve equivalent savings.[5]
- **Expectation of sacrifice:** In adopting a new product, buyers expect they will have to give up some benefits of their current solution, such as compatibility or workflow efficiencies.
- **Risk avoidance:** Humans steer clear of a learning curve. We're creatures of habit because experience says there is risk, sacrifice, and often loss in deviating from what we know to work.

Just like Ken, innovative product makers tend to believe all of this resistance will crumble when consumers see how amazing their solution is.

Often, they feel consumers have no real alternatives, because no other solution can do what their product does. That's why they made it.

I've heard plenty of smart entrepreneurs say, "We have no competition."

And they were wrong. There is always competition to address any problem faced by a significant number of people. Whatever it is people are already doing or using to get around the same problem your product solves – that is your competition. It might be what they have cobbled together using resources they already own, or could acquire at little or no cost. (Think free apps or tools, or parts on hand.) The cost of that alternative may have been zero.

Competitive products be damned. The prospective customer not shelling out for your product, or for anything else, may be your biggest competition.

If no similar product has yet gained popularity, it could be an indicator that not enough people have felt they needed a solution badly enough to pay for one. Meaning your product won't likely be viable in the marketplace.

And as with Segway, it doesn't necessarily help if your product is super-innovative. Product makers completely misunderstand how buyers' brains work when they expect a radically unique solution to have mass appeal because it's so unusual. In fact, the opposite usually holds true. While the dog brain may start slobbering, the tank brain roars, "Too new!"

The more innovative a product, the greater the change in behavior that's required for a mass market to adopt it. The most successful products provide sizable benefits, but only require minor changes in behavior.

The DVORAK keyboard layout offered measurable performance

gains over QWERTY, moving the most common keystrokes from the left hand to the right. About 85 percent of people are right-handed, and could benefit from that change. But becoming proficient at typing with an entirely new keyboard layout required a big learning curve. The people who would most appreciate the improvement were the same ones for whom QWERTY was already second nature. (Never heard of DVORAK? There you go.)

CONFIRMING THE NEED

VALIDATION CAN BE TERRIFYING.

It's not fun, and you desperately want to avoid doing it.

Because you're enamored with the dream of success. Your own gigantic Coveted Condition™. A positive outcome already exists for your third self, built on all your fantasies.

And, like an expectant parent, you have embedded that success into your whole vision of the future.

Validation might reveal what you least want to hear, and ruin everything. You're not willing to allow that. The third self is the happiest you've ever seen it.

No one likes being advised post-conception to question their suitability for parenthood, and that's essentially what I'm saying you've got to do.

And that reluctance is totally normal. Scientific, even. An innovator's optimism-driven resistance to seeking the truth about a product's chances of success is something psychologist and economist Daniel Kahneman refers to as "the planning fallacy."

In *Thinking, Fast and Slow*, Kahneman explains that in the grip of the planning fallacy, we tend to make choices driven by unrealistic optimism instead of thinking objectively about potential outcomes. Kahneman affirms that as we learned in Chapter 3, we tend to overstate potential gains and underestimate associated costs.

We happily envision successful scenarios while ignoring the likelihood of errors or misjudgments.[6] This in part explains why product makers ignore daunting statistics in relation to their own chances of success. They believe their product is a clear outlier — which it may be, but probably is not.

They aren't Steve Jobs, and their company isn't Apple. That's the world's biggest unicorn example, not a stinking template.

So, the responsibility *should* be to prove to themselves, to their investors and to their collaborators that the product will be the next big thing — not bow to their risk-loving primal brain, like thousands of innovators before them who have fallen prey to the planning fallacy.

Where your own product is concerned, it's much wiser to learn and confront the truth early on, so you can fix each problem, try a different target audience — or refocus your energy on creating something that really is needed by a critical mass of buyers.

Almost as importantly, asking the right questions can help improve the product and your messaging so the greatest possible number of people DO feel they need it.

ADOPTING A VALIDATION MINDSET

VALIDATING PRODUCTS IS STRATEGIC work that can paralyze even experienced product teams and inventors.

You don't want anyone to talk you into killing a game-changing product just because they lack the vision to fully understand it, especially before you've refined it and perfected your positioning. There's a reason why successful artists and architects don't let critics see the preliminary sketches.

Likewise, validation efforts might miss the point, and will kill the product development momentum. The cake will flop if you open the oven too soon.

Perhaps these are some of the excuses you'll give yourself. So, instead of validating the product scientifically, you will passionately present your vision to friends.

Do a good enough job, and they will tell you it's a fantastic idea. Of course, that's the polar opposite of proper validation. We're not doing that, right?

To create products people need, you've got to escape that validation-fearing and self-deluding mentality and embrace the power of learning from genuine future customers. Listen to lots of them, pay close attention to what is missing in their world, and design the solution to those unmet needs with an elegant, intuitive human interface.

Then build THAT, and you've got something people will buy.

Do whatever mental acrobatics it takes to get excited about the validation process. *It is the most important work you will do to create a product that will be needed.*

Read that last sentence again and again, as many times as it takes for you to fully believe and embrace it.

Seriously, you must adopt this perspective, or you're going to mentally negate any validation you do, and dive in with the kind of false expectations that nearly always lead to failure.

CONCEPT VALIDATION

BECAUSE YOUR PRODUCT doesn't yet exist in people's actual context, the natural tendency you'll have is to paint a picture that explains how much they need it. And in doing so, you'll go straight into pitch mode. Pitch mode is the opposite of validation, because it shuts out the truth instead of seeking it. People hearing your pitch will intuitively say what you're so desperate to hear.

You don't want to tell the people you interview *anything* about your product until you've first heard as much as possible from them. While this is strongly counterintuitive, it will be very hard for you to describe the product without jumping into pitch mode. As soon as you do, it re-frames the conversation around what you are working on rather than what they need. It puts you in the position of seeking approval — and blows up the validation process.

Instead, the first thing to ask your subjects is whether they have experienced the exact problem your product solves — without mentioning a single thing about the product. If not, they aren't a good validation subject.

Next, find out what steps they have taken to solve the root problem. How hard have they tried? Have they searched online for solutions?

The amount of effort they have expended in real life is an important indicator. If people have never done a quick web search, put in significant effort, or spent any money looking for a solution, the problem is probably too minor to justify paying for a product that solves it. The resistance already appears to outweigh the benefit.

If hordes of people are actively searching for a similar solution, it makes things much easier. The current is flowing your way, and your main task is to set up downstream and become a top search result. (While that's not nearly all it will take, being sought is a very strong start.)

But if few are searching, you'll be paying to reach every prospective customer — with the task of captivating, engaging, educating, and winning over each one. So, you'll start off swimming upstream, and the current will be stiff.

There are several ways to conduct validation research. The most common are surveys, focus groups and one-on-one interviews.

All of these are helpful only if you are able to target people who closely resemble your future customers, in terms of comparable regions, age groups, income levels and social situations.

SURVEYS

IF YOU HAVE AN UNDERSTANDING of survey design and are prepared to learn how to conduct them scientifically, running your own survey can be highly informative.

A downside of surveys is that they're by nature simple and uniform, especially when designed to reach a statistically significant number of participants. The responses won't give a lot of nuance, suggest alternate approaches, or reveal answers you haven't already considered. You ask the best questions you can come up with, simplifying them for candidates to understand easily, and are constrained to limited forms of quick responses. Still, the results can be insightful and can be a credible reflection of how your future audience thinks. Whenever I run surveys for a client, there are always at least a few surprises that shape how we take the product to market.

FOCUS GROUPS

BACK IN THE 1940s, radio soap opera sponsors (literally detergent companies) began testing their advertising concepts on real people. These "focused interviews" run by sociologists brought meaningful insights and tended to improve sales. Similar techniques were adopted by the military for testing propaganda during the Second World War.

I've orchestrated many focus groups over the years and have absolutely seen the good and bad of them. Visionaries tend to strongly dislike this approach, because it deliberately seeks input from people external to the brand culture, who lack the context to think about innovation and future value. Often, participants in traditional focus groups were people who would not buy the product under any circumstances and didn't represent ideal buyers, so their feedback could easily become counterproductive.

If you've ever been part of a focus group, you probably remember being one in a group of strangers sitting around a table, aware that you were being recorded and watched through a two-way mirror while responding to a long series of questions. You could hardly devise something further from how people make a buying decision in real life. Luckily such sessions are run by professionals who know what to ask, how to draw useful insights — and usually what to ignore.

And while that format is still employed, most focus groups have moved to virtual, and in doing so have become much more effective at recruiting participants who represent a product's true audience. Participants work efficiently from home in their free time, and can be carefully vetted. Because it's become such a simple, easy paying gig, there are always many eager candidates to choose from.

For product and marketing validation, there are plenty of good reasons to use online focus groups. To do it effectively, you will usually run three or four groups, each with between eight and twelve members. Research shows that less than eight members can turn out unreliable results, while more than a dozen can become unwieldy and expensive. One online focus group agency owner I know likes to say an online focus group can be run for the cost of buying lunch. (How accurate this is will depend on where you buy that lunch, how many people you invite, and what they are eating. But it makes the point that we're talking hundreds of dollars and not tens of thousands.)

ONE-ON-ONE INTERVIEWS

WITH NARROWLY TARGETED or B2B products, it is often easiest and most informative to reach out directly to people who fit the profile and interview them. As always, remember to focus clearly on the problem — and how badly your potential buyers need to solve it. Keep your solution out of the discussion.

The easiest, lowest-cost approach to one-on-one interviews is to talk to people in your own circle who are likely to be ideal buyers for your product. Especially at an early stage, before you have invested in design and development, this is a good way to validate the need and concept.

As you progress and begin moving forward (preparing to bring in investors, use your own savings, or take steps to expand a product line), it's time to consider professional one-on-one interviews. We do these all the time at Graphos Product and the process includes carefully recruiting participants who match the client's buyer personas. The interviewer does not know the participants, which brings objectivity the client can't possibly achieve by talking to their own contacts. And the sessions are structured to find gaps, reveal opportunities and uncover insights.

Even if you intend to use surveys, focus groups and one-on-one interviews conducted by a professional, it can be a good idea to begin with informal interviews of your own.

Early validation like this gives you a direct view of how buyers perceive their needs in relation to the product you're working on. It gives you a low-stakes opportunity to rethink and pivot. Or to go back to the drawing board, which is never fun but seldom a mistake.

IDENTIFY YOUR CUSTOMER (AND HOW TO FIND THEM)

THIS IS GOING TO BE super important when your product is ready to buy. Almost no product is right for everyone. More likely, there is a specific, relatively tiny subset of people who are almost certain to love your product, will be willing to pay top dollar for it, will learn quickly how to succeed with it and will automatically talk about it to like-minded consumers.

Identifying who those people are and how to reach them is called *segmentation*. You're identifying a niche out of the general population, into a segment you can target directly, to make efficient use of your marketing budget and maximize the number of early successes. Segmentation work never ends, but it always begins in earnest at the validation stage.

There are a number of ways to use audience segmentation to target right-fit buyers. Social media platforms can let you target ads by factors like interests, affiliations, age, marital status, income and gender. For a business-to-business product, you can buy lists of prospects sorted by industry vertical (specific sector or niche within a broader industry), or advertise in media or on websites whose audience includes those individuals. You can connect with influencers who are part of your segment's community and attend trade shows where your tribe can be found.

The same styles of segmentation are used in selecting candidates for surveys, one-on-one interviews or focus groups.

When you're conducting validation research, here are my best tips:

1. **Talk to the right people.** If you've developed an innovative long-distance running shoe, don't query people who only ever run in video games. A much better choice would be marathoners looking to shave seconds off their best 26.2-mile time. Seek out and speak to people who fully represent your ideal buyer. If finding them is hard now, it won't get much easier when you're marketing the product.
2. **Don't talk about the product,** especially when validating the underlying need. Focus on the problem, and on identifying whether there is a desire and preparedness to pay for a better solution to it.
3. **Avoid the obvious questions.** It would be silly to ask a competitive marathon runner if she would be interested in a lighter, faster shoe. But that is essentially what a lot of product makers do in their validation attempts. Of course, she would! But that doesn't mean she would abandon what has been working well, risk injury and gamble her money and years of training on something radical and unproven. When the desire for the job the product does is obvious, probe for the barriers to understand what it will take to overcome them.
4. **Ask ideal buyers if they have ever searched** for a solution to the problem your product solves. If they have googled it, you are probably on the right track. That shows motivation and willingness to take action. If not, your product may be entirely unsought, or the problem it solves might not even be sufficiently troublesome that people would justify paying for a better way.

5. **Have the prospect walk you through** what they do to solve the existing problem. This will give you an idea of how much better your product is (if it is) and what people are currently investing in time and money for a solution. It will also elucidate the full value your product can deliver. These walk-throughs can also help you uncover additional value your product provides, or that it can be tweaked to deliver.
6. **Probe to find out what people like** about the existing way of solving the problem and understand the friction for your buyer in making the change to something new. Hiring your product always means firing another method. How loyal are they to the existing solution or the brand behind it? A lifetime devotee to Adidas may refuse to run in something new and unknown, even if it is verifiably superior to their Adios Pros. I might be highly motivated to replace Zoom, but am I prepared to convince all my colleagues and clients to download and learn a new video conferencing app? That's way too much friction, without enough for me to gain. I like that people I need to talk to already use it. An element that is not even a product feature, like the "network effect," can be a tremendous barrier to change.
7. **Understand their Coveted Condition.** Once you understand the job people are trying to do, ask how achieving it quicker, better or more easily would change their lives a year from now. How do they envision that improved experience? How would the outcome be central to a happy daydream? And what would be the very worst thing about going back to the old way if the amazing new solution disappeared?
8. **Ask what they would pay.** Asking straight out how much an ideal buyer would pay to solve the problem is much better than suggesting a price and asking if they would pay that amount for it. Not wanting to hurt your ego and with nothing to lose either way, they're likely to affirm whatever price you suggest. Having them

put a value on the solution engages a different kind of thinking. Although no one can tell you how to price your product, they should be able to tell you what they would be prepared to spend right now (or commit ongoingly) to solve the problem effectively.

At what bottom price would they become concerned about the product's quality and what is the dollar ceiling where the cost would not be justifiable, regardless of how well it works? If you can get these answers, you will have an approximate low-to-high range.

Continue asking the same questions of people with similar needs and pay attention to their level of interest and how much they are willing to pay. You will need this information to determine if the economic fundamentals are plausible.

While there are sophisticated tools and techniques for conducting pricing research, you can learn a great deal in your own interviews by carefully asking the right questions. (Note: I have consistently found both ends of the price sensitivity scale to be much lower coming from professionally sourced interview candidates than the results clients obtained from polling friends and family members. That should tell you something.)

9. **Take pre-orders.** Once you have confirmed the need, a price range and preparedness to overcome other friction, ask your ideal buyers to pre-order at a slight discount from their own suggested price point. Even if the product is nowhere near ready, asking for real money flushes out someone who is unintentionally falsifying a willingness to buy. Lean into the awkwardness, because this is a valuable moment of truth in your conversation. Don't avoid it. Point out that taking pre-orders is critically important at this stage, and offer a written guarantee to refund payment if the product is not delivered when expected. Having pre-orders truly is valuable. It gives you a strong positive

talking point for backers and prospective partners. Always take the payment, even if you plan to refund it later. Until the moment people put skin in the game, *nothing* is real. And while you are securing these first customers, you are building a valuable team of testers, champions and reviewers. Thank them and encourage their ongoing active support — it can make a huge difference through critical early times.

VALIDATION MISTAKES TO AVOID

OPINIONS

AS ROB FITZPATRICK SAYS in *The Mom Test* (my favorite book on validating product ideas early on and without a big research budget), you never want to ask for opinions about your product — least of all to your mother, who is sure to say it is perfect, just like you.

Except I believe friends can be even worse. You naturally choose as your friends the people who make you feel good. If they didn't, you wouldn't still be friends. So, while your true friends may tactfully alert you if there's spinach in your teeth, they are never going to say you've got a messy house, an ugly baby or a ridiculous product idea. Nor are they able to experience your validation work with real objectivity, even if they are the poster child of your ideal buyer persona. Friends are predisposed to encourage your dream and they would be thrilled to watch you create something cool. Like your mom, they have an innate, subconscious duty to protect your ego — except friends usually don't expect the relationship to be unconditional. If they offend you badly, they anticipate repercussions.

By all means, tell friends and family members about your product. It'll feel good for everyone and they will be pleased to be in the know and to support your brilliant idea. Some may be your first customers and will become vocal supporters. They will share your social media posts and comment enthusiastically.

Friends and family will also support you through the toughest days.

Just don't make their responses central to your validation results.

PITCHING

As I mentioned earlier, pitching becomes second nature when developing a product. You will become adept at pitching the product, and it will find ways to sneak into your validation interviews.

"If you're talking most of the time, it probably means you're pitching," Rob Fitzpatrick told me in an interview. "You've made the conversation about your product instead of about your customer. Don't take hypotheticals or guesses at what people may do in the future. Don't ask, 'Might you ever do this?' Of course, they might, someday, maybe. Instead ask them the specifics: 'How did you do it today? How did you do it last time?' No opinions, no hypotheticals and as much as possible, shut up and let them talk." [7]

It's great advice. Because you've set up the discussion, you'll be inclined to lead, and they will happily let you. Plan your open-ended questions, and let silence happen, avoiding the urge to fill in the gaps yourself.

COMPLIMENTS

Keep in mind that you don't want to tell an interview candidate about the product until later in the validation process, once you have confirmed the need and learned as much as possible about how the problem is currently being solved. When you do describe the product or show a prototype, it's a time for extreme caution.

There are various kinds of bad data traps you want to avoid, the worst of them being compliments, and now is when they're likely to come.

Compliments are what Fitzpatrick calls the "fool's gold" of customer learning. If you or someone else close to the product is conducting the validation research, your subconscious but unavoidable goal is to prove that people really do want it. That's a dangerous mistake, and one your ego will push you to make.

In need validation, you are never looking for someone to say your idea is brilliant and a game changer. The true goal is to identify a fit with real-world buyers that will convert to market demand for your product.

Train yourself to recognize compliments as a sign that you've been pitching the product, or signaling a desire for praise rather than validation of the need. If compliments become a trend, engage an objective third party to conduct (or help assess) the validation process to watch for blind spots and avoid faulty data. Stick to your list of validation questions — and start taking paid pre-orders if candidates consistently get completely psyched about the product. If that succeeds, you probably are onto something good.

Genuine excitement at the right time is more than just a positive signal. It's essential that your concept excites the right people even more than it excites you.

Excitement can mean your product solves a need that is causing big pain right now. People currently have to work around the problem in an expensive, time-consuming, perhaps agonizing way. Your product must deliver an expectation of reward that will arouse enough excitement in the buyer's dog brain to overcome the pain responses that come with instigating change and parting with money.

If you are successful in validating the need and a willingness to pay for your product, you are ready to design and build a prototype.

For a physical or hardware product, the earliest prototype can be almost ridiculously simple. In fact, it should be.

While you can fairly easily have a prototype 3D-printed in high fidelity to look and feel like something straight off a store shelf, one made of paper tubes, duct tape and wood blocks can be even more helpful early on. That's because users can easily see it for what it is: a rough physical draft of your concept, with plenty of room for improvement.

Software products and mobile apps should also be prototyped to test the user experience (UX) and interface design on real people before development begins. User experience is not only a huge factor in adoption, but it is the battleground where mature software products will compete to gain and retain customers. Doing UX well from the early days gives you a competitive edge out of the gates and establishes your users' experience as a cornerstone business priority.

PROTOTYPE VALIDATION

THERE ARE TWO LEVELS of prototyping:

1. **Functional prototyping** (establishing user experience; activating need through performance)
2. **Aesthetic prototyping** (establishing design; activating need through visual appeal)

When you've developed your first working prototype, take it to your original validation subjects. You can now tell them what it seeks to achieve, but nothing about how to use it. You might even hand it to them backwards or upside down, to see if, and how easily, they correct the product's orientation. In the real world, buyers have to figure these things out on their own.

Carefully observe, or ideally, record a video of their interaction with the product. Do they try to slide a push-button, or twist a component that isn't meant to turn? Struggles are more important to note than successes. If testers put torque on a weak spot by holding it wrong, you will know to fortify the structure, or find a way to emphasize the proper place to grip, for example, by adding design features like knurled finger indents.

Ask the test user to speak constantly and narrate their thought process. Getting a valuable window into the minds of customers at prototype stage will give you valuable, truly exciting insights. Capturing them and responding in the next iteration is how you create a product to be loved, not one that you simply hope and pray will be appreciated.

Then go back a third time to the same people with the next version of your prototype and repeat the process with even less instruction from your end — and further narration from the tester. Things may go better, or not. Be ready for regression and see it as an opportunity to improve the product. Take each revised prototype to a good number of entirely new test subjects as well, because they will better represent early consumers. By the second go-round, any prior experience will make it look like the product has become more intuitive, regardless of whether it has or not.

THE VALUE CASE

ANOTHER REASON IT IS surprisingly hard to sell something new is that consumers are inexplicably cheap. If they don't feel they need your product badly — and that it's a once-in-a-lifetime, now-or-never deal — most will take a pass. Validating a need and desire without balancing the price and value component in the customer's eyes can be a critical error.

The value case becomes an even bigger challenge with oversized or heavy direct-to-consumer products, or products with low margins. Consumers have been conditioned by services like Amazon Prime to believe shipping ought to be free, even if delivery costs the seller more than making the product. Online shoppers now feel so entitled to free shipping that many will post angrily, write negative reviews and forever boycott if asked to pay shipping costs. Consumers don't care what it costs the seller — to the extent that it is fully your problem to solve. Trying to explain it just feeds an endless cycle of frustrating discussions.

Likewise with return shipping. Many DTC businesses opt to abandon their returned products rather than pay return shipping costs. While it's a part of the value case that often makes no sense at all, today's consumers demand free shipping, both ways. Failing to solve the economics of this can be the death of your product.

Remember SearBQ? The product was made from solid cast iron and weighed nearly 30 pounds in the packaging.

After our successful launch, I handed off the marketing to another agency. It wasn't long before a number of economic complications started kicking in. Spiking commodity prices made all that iron increasingly expensive, and in an environment of rising delivery costs, the weight was more and more of a problem. When free shipping was no longer feasible, the company founder would plead with irate customers that "We're shipping bowling balls here."

And the message back was consistent: that wasn't the customer's problem. Shipping ought to be free.

Getting the product from the factory to the customer soon cost more than manufacturing it, and inevitable return costs further deepened the impact crater. Between the pressure for free shipping, rising production costs and ever-increasing digital marketing expenses from auction-based ad platforms, it became too much. The cost of doing business began to exceed what most customers would pay. Despite having a remarkable product, SearBQ stopped selling online in 2024.

Pay close attention to all the cost factors as you plan, and recognize that they are seldom consistent or predictable. Sudden increases in one or more can take down an excellent product, or eat up all of your profits. And unless you have an amazing new delivery system of your own or will sell only in retail stores, budget to offer free shipping and returns. Customers will demand it.

Mobile apps are another logic-defying example of customer cheapness. Everyone knows that a useful application takes a tremendous amount of time, skill and investment to create. Yet a high percentage of users choose to endure endless productivity-killing ads and work around stripped-down functionality in a free version, rather than pay a few dollars to upgrade. It's a confounding phenomenon that can be fatal to businesses. Rather than opt for your in-app upgrade, most will simply delete the app.

The same hardwired inclination applies to most consumer decision-making, until some even stronger perception of need forces it to give way. Presenting any new approach to solving a pre-existing problem puts the onus on you to overcome a neurologically painful human resistance to spending good money.

When you're selling to highly motivated buyers who know, love and trust your brand — or who emotionally need the status boost of being seen using your product — the barrier to your value proposition gets lowered.

But a new product by an unknown brand faces a steep and slippery incline. This is why I recommended asking prospective ideal buyers during your validation testing to put up real money. If these people hesitate, your existing value case is definitely too weak. Know how you will help real-world consumers understand the true cost of their current approach, and how much happier and better off they will be with your amazing product.

CROWDFUNDING PLATFORMS AS VALIDATION MECHANISMS

Clients often ask me if crowdfunding sites like Kickstarter and Indiegogo are a useful form of product validation. After all, they can put the product in front of a lot of real people, with the opportunity to explain and show why it's great. And the ultimate validation test: people are asked to put up real money to back it.

In fact, there are many potential benefits to using these platforms, as well as repercussions, resulting in famous success stories and (many more) fizzles. I've worked with plenty of clients who experienced each end of the spectrum and can share a few significant caveats:

- In order to be ready for a crowdfunding platform, your product has to be quite far along in the development process. Many products on crowdfunding platforms are already in factory production — far past the stage when validation can save you the most money and enable major course corrections.

  By the time supporters have backed your product, you are committed to a fairly rigid design and spec set. You're heavily invested not just in going forward, but in a specific way forward. Optimal validation is not a binary job of confirming viability or predicting failure. It should be used to better understand your ideal customer's needs and Coveted Condition so you can tune the product to delight the right people.

- While sound validation needs to target those ideal customers, crowdfunding platforms are often populated by and supported by early adopter personalities. These people may not represent the people you can easily find in the regular marketplace. Often 90 percent or more of a campaign's backers are existing members of the crowdfunding platform. If your product is for a general "everyone" audience, this is possibly less of a problem. But for products with a specific ideal buyer who has rarer needs or interests, it will be up to you to find these people and bring them to your campaign. That's a sticking point if your target market includes seniors or people less likely to be active in crowdfunding.

  All of this can be good practice and help refine your positioning for the actual launch. But you chance putting off otherwise enthusiastic supporters who are simply uncomfortable with the strange process, to say nothing of the waiting game it often involves. The result can be that someone who would happily buy the real thing from your online store shows up in your crowdfunding data as a "nope."

- Because targeting on crowdfunding platforms can be less than ideal, you'll need to filter the feedback you receive. With every negative comment or feature request, carefully evaluate whether a true ideal buyer would feel the same way. Don't be distracted or disheartened by the peanut gallery when you might be inadvertently pitching to folks with peanut allergies!

- Finally, consider the risks associated with putting your product out there and making your idea public too early. If you are thinking of patenting the product, running a crowdfunding campaign is a very prominent public disclosure and will disqualify your intellectual property from being patented in most of the world's jurisdictions.

Product counterfeiters and potential competitors watch these platforms closely. Your success could be kick-starting a product knockoff — or informing a one-upmanship plan. Copycats can see your design, just as you're eagerly proving there's a market for it. Their goal is to get there first. Even if they do not beat you to market (and many succeed), low-quality imitations can harm your product's reputation.

Worse yet, an even better version by an established brand (think Amazon Essentials) with superior logistical and buying power can make it impossible for you to compete at your own game.

All of this is not to say you should avoid crowdfunding. Far from it. Many successful brands have used this approach effectively, and the platforms continue to evolve.

Just remember that real validation begins very early.

And that while crowdfunding can be a fierce sword for an innovative product maker to wield, it definitely has more than a single edge.

KEY INSIGHTS FROM CHAPTER 18

- Product makers often struggle to objectively assess their product's market appeal due to their inherent optimism.
- Feedback from friends and family tends to be misleading.
- Even extensive marketing efforts may fail if the product doesn't fulfill a genuine need, or isn't seen as uniquely valuable.
- Effective validation involves confronting uncomfortable truths early on and listening to potential customers.
- Adapt the product for unmet needs identified during validation.
- Avoid "Pitch Mode": instead of explaining why people need your product, focus on understanding their Coveted Condition™ and the barriers they face in achieving it.
- Assess the efforts people have already invested in solving the problem to gauge its importance. Lack of effort may indicate the problem isn't significant enough to justify a solution.
- Determine if there's existing demand for a solution by analyzing search volume and consumer behavior.
- Surveys, focus groups, and one-on-one interviews are common validation tools, but be sure participants closely resemble your target customers.
- Identify and target specific customer segments to efficiently allocate marketing resources and maximize success.
- Opinions from friends and family may be biased and not reflective of genuine market demand.
- Compliments can inflate your perception of market interest; focus on objective validation methods instead.
- Test prototypes with real users to assess usability and gather feedback for improvements.
- Highlight the value your product offers compared to existing solutions to justify its price.
- Crowdfunding platforms can validate demand, but be cautious of early public exposure and risks to intellectual property.

DO THESE NOW FOR QUICK WINS:

CONDUCT TARGETED SURVEYS

Design surveys to gather insights from potential customers who closely resemble your target audience. You can use platforms like SurveyMonkey or Google Forms to reach a broader audience beyond friends and family. *(Hitting a wall? See next Action Item)*

SEEK PROFESSIONAL VALIDATION HELP

Consider hiring validation experts or agencies specialized in market research and product validation. Their expertise and impartiality can provide valuable insights and ensure thorough validation processes.

ORGANIZE FOCUS GROUPS WITH DIVERSE PARTICIPANTS

Host focus groups with individuals who represent different demographics and backgrounds relevant to your product.

Consider seeking out professional facilitators to ensure unbiased feedback and valuable insights.

USE ONLINE COMMUNITIES AND FORUMS

Engage with online communities related to your product's niche or the problem area.

Participate in discussions, ask questions, and observe conversations to understand real consumer needs and pain points.

PERFORM A COMPETITIVE REVIEW

Look at competitors' products and marketing strategies to identify gaps and unclaimed opportunities in the market.

What are areas where your product can offer unique value and address unmet needs? Where do your product's superpowers give it a unique advantage? Focus on them instead of playing me-too, or worse yet, trying to compete on alternatives' strong points.

INTERVIEW INDUSTRY EXPERTS

Seek out industry experts, influencers, and thought leaders for one-on-one interviews. Their expertise can provide valuable perspectives and help validate the market potential of your product.

PROTOTYPE TEST WITH BETA USERS

Develop prototypes and offer them to beta users for testing and feedback. Use platforms like TestFlight for mobile apps or create a beta testing program for physical products. Gather user feedback to iterate and improve the product.

CREATE LANDING PAGES FOR PRE-ORDERS

Build landing pages to take pre-orders and gauge interest. Offer incentives such as early-bird discounts to incentivize pre-orders and validate demand before full-scale production.

ANALYZE SEARCH TRENDS

Use tools like Google Trends and keyword research tools to identify search volume and trends related to your product or the need it solves. High search volume indicates existing demand and market interest, but pay attention to the level of competition for high-volume keywords and run the searches yourself to study the pages that already rank well. Grab every advantage: top-ranking competitors have been investing in their organic search strategy for years, and you'll be starting from scratch.

ADOPT USER-CENTRIC ITERATION

Continuously gather feedback from the prototyping phase on. Observe how people interact with the product. Probe for pain points or struggles, and iterate the design to enhance familiarity and usability.

Every advancement in intuitive design means smoother adoption, better reviews, fewer returns — and a more successful product.

CHAPTER 19

Need vs. Resistance

In This Chapter:

- *The concept of MAYA (Most Advanced Yet Acceptable)*
- *Balancing innovation with familiarity for mass adoption*
- *The conflicted tendency to be drawn to novelty, yet resistant to change*
- *Integrating familiarity in product design and user experience*
- *Applying natural mapping for intuitive usability*

THE FAILURES OF SEGWAY, the Apple Newton and Google Glass were not because those products lacked innovation or utility. They represented a dramatic re-thinking of how people traveled, planned and used personal devices. The market just wasn't ready for them. They pushed beyond acceptable thresholds — and buyers pushed right back.

A French-born American named Raymond Loewy (1893–1986), considered the father of industrial design, came up with a theory that ought to have been helpful to the people behind these and many other failed innovations. They didn't take it seriously enough. (But you can.)

Loewy called his theory MAYA. It had nothing to do with the ancient people of Mexico and Central America and everything to do with product adoption. It stood for *Most Advanced Yet Acceptable.*

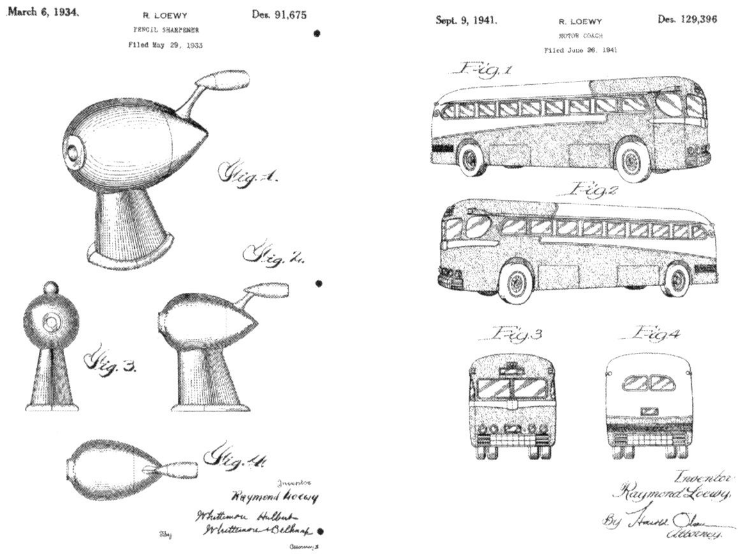

***Figure 19-1. Designs by Raymond Loewy:** A futuristic pencil sharpener (1934) and motor coach design (1941) reflect Loewy's visionary streamlined design style that maximally advanced innovation while maintaining familiar elements.* *(U.S. Design Patent 91,675, U.S. Design Patent 129,396; USPTO.)*

The idea is that a mass market will not embrace something that is too radically different, even if it is a phenomenal product that delivers on a clear and painful need. As we've seen, there is that powerful status quo bias, and consumers are spooked off by big changes.

Yes, customers are intrigued by novelty. It's a trait that has driven us to become the dominant species on our planet, enshrouded in human-made comforts and assisted by amazing tech in everything we do. But until recent decades, humans have always progressed by baby steps, knowing that uncharted territory brings unknown but certain dangers. In our dog and lizard brains, a powerful fight or flight reflex is triggered by things that look too unusual.

This fear of new things is hardwired into our nervous systems. Yet at the same time, as explorers, trailblazers and inventors, we hunger for progress. We are at once *neophilic*, and *neophobic*, craving novelty while recognizing the next big thing could well be the death of us.

Being human is a mass of contradictions and inner conflicts.

Loewy, who designed the Coke bottle, the Greyhound bus, the Shell logo and many other icons of twentieth-century living, would agree. He famously said that in order to sell something surprising, you need to make it familiar; and to sell something familiar, you need to make it surprising. "One should design for the advantage of the largest mass of people," he said, explaining that familiarity is not only helpful, but essential to large-scale adoption.

Loewy probably understood adoption better than anyone ever has. By the 1950s, he could take credit for the look of the world's most iconic car (the Studebaker Starliner), the most popular beverage bottle (and its fountain too), the best-known American airplane (Air Force 1) and the country's most used locomotive (the Pennsylvania Railroad S1).

Loewy's theory can be used to explain ear-worms in music, blockbuster movies and even successful Internet memes. When something new, challenging or surprising evokes a feeling of comfort, meaning or familiarity, it is called an aesthetic *aha.*[1]

Similarly, the "Mere-Exposure Effect" is a concept that's been proven not only through the success of Loewy's designs, but through numerous studies. Social psychologist Robert Zajonc (1923–2008) used laboratory experiments to demonstrate that exposing people to a familiar stimulus makes them view a subsequent experience far more positively than similar stimuli to which they have not yet been exposed.

In an experiment in 2000, Zajonc showed random polygons and Chinese ideographs to different groups of Western subjects for a short interval. He later showed group after group various combinations of shapes and asked whether each one created positive or negative feelings. In all cases, and regardless of the combination or sequence, people preferred the images they had very briefly seen before.

Through hundreds of studies and meta-studies using songs, audio tones, shapes and physical objects, the results are the same:

people have an affinity for things with which they are familiar — and are uncomfortable with what is not familiar.

Zajonc also demonstrated that even words in every semantic category, and even individual letters and numbers, show a strong correlation between ratings for preference and frequency of usage.[2]

So, it's quite possible that the more frequently we hear, read and say the word "need" (remember the graph in Chapter 4?) the more intent we become on servicing our perceived needs.

The connection happens subconsciously in our dog brain. In an online advertising study, participants were flashed banner ads for a camera between zero and twenty times as they read an article. Despite being focused on reading and unable to notice the ad, the more often subjects had seen the camera, the more inclined they became toward later desiring it.[3]

Does this mean that large-scale adoption isn't possible for innovative products?

It depends. What is clear is that human consumers move slowly — if they do at all — into unknown waters.

Despite having deep pockets, strong vision and phenomenal publicity, it took Elon Musk's Tesla 17 years to sell enough electric cars to achieve profitability — even though, on the surface, Teslas looked remarkably similar to conventional vehicles.

EMBEDDING FAMILIARITY

FOR MOST INNOVATIVE PRODUCTS, the solution is a design and user experience that intentionally embeds familiarity at every level.

There are two steps to this.

First, you should integrate familiar patterns and functionality into the product's design to make it inviting and intuitive to anyone who sees it. Tesla cars introduced an innovative, powerful electric motor and tablet-based interface, controlled by logical, intuitive actions very similar to those used on Apple touch screens.

There is a very short learning curve and a recurring sense of familiarity, even on a car that continuously pushed the acceptable limits of technological advancement as far as they could safely go. The Segway, on the other hand, used unfamiliar steering and balance mechanisms that made people feel physically uncomfortable and oddly conspicuous.

And second, try to match innovative functions to systems in the real world. "Natural mapping" is a principle of design in which a system's controls logically correspond to the desired outcome. It's often a relation between sets, where one set is the controller and the second set is what is being controlled.

Natural mappings work through similarity and familiarity:

Spatial similarity, in which the controls mirror the layout. A good example of this is when the controls of a gas stovetop mimic the layout of the cooking elements. (It's shocking how most stove controls are aligned horizontally rather than in intuitive positions!) Likewise, if you have used multiple screens on a desktop computer, you have probably appreciated how the display arrangement control allows you to align your screen layout in a way that offers spatial continuity by replicating the real-world layout in your settings.

Conceptual similarity, in which scrolling up means more — whether volume, brightness, speed — or green means "go" and red means "stop." Conceptual similarity can be affected by differences in how the related functions are represented in various geographic locations and cultures: in parts of Japan, there are still blue traffic lights that mean "go." Be aware of these differences when planning user experiences for varying markets.

Behavioral similarity, where raising or turning your smartwatch wakes the screen, or how the movement of your fingers on a trackpad zooms or rotates an image in a corresponding way. In other words, a natural-feeling action is used to trigger a corresponding outcome. With behavioral similarity in an interface, adoption happens naturally and nearly immediately.[4]

On-screen interfaces and physical products benefit equally from familiarity and the intuitive usability that comes from it.

In fact, any time a product is accurately referred to as "intuitive" or "user-friendly" you can be sure it draws from similarities to what people already know how to do. The product simply does what the brain first expects, without any work to figure it out.

Put another way, a lengthy instruction manual indicates a less intuitive product. And most of us don't like manuals.

That's why in testing prototypes, it is so important to observe what people attempt to do when using a product for the very first time. If they tap an on-screen graphic expecting it to function as a button, or reach to the upper right corner of a device for the power control, that is a strong signal as to how those elements could be made more intuitive.

Instead of a longer instruction booklet or more tutorial videos, how can your product be made more familiar, more similar to what people already know, and as easy as possible for buyers to adopt unassisted?

KEY INSIGHTS FROM CHAPTER 19

- Innovative products like Segway, Apple Newton and Google Glass failed not due to lack of innovation or utility but because they pushed beyond what the market was ready for.
- Raymond Loewy's "Most Advanced Yet Acceptable" (MAYA) theory explains that mass markets don't embrace radical changes easily; familiarity is essential for adoption.
- Humans are both drawn to novelty and resistant to change due to deep-rooted fear of new things. Innovative products must balance both.
- The "Mere-Exposure Effect" shows that exposure to familiar stimuli makes people view them more positively.
- Integrating familiarity in design and user experience helps address the need for innovative products.
- Natural mapping, using spatial, conceptual and behavioral similarity, enhances intuitive usability.
- Products referred to as "intuitive" or "user-friendly" draw from familiar concepts for ease of use.
- Prototyping should involve observing how users interact with products in order to align design with their expectations.

DO THESE NOW FOR QUICK WINS:

SEEK MAYA IN PRODUCT DESIGN

Avoid the trap of assuming your idea is a sure success without evidence that it is neither too radical nor too similar to existing products. Find the line where Most Advanced Yet Acceptable lies for your product. How hard is it for a fresh audience to understand what it does, how to use it — and why?

Start paying careful attention to this, and make changes to bridge any gaps. Don't be Segway.

DEMONSTRATE FAMILIARITY

Understand that while innovation is at the heart of what you are doing, ensuring familiarity in design and user experience are crucial to driving mass adoption. If your product is highly innovative (and if you've ever used the word "disruptive" it probably is), write a list of attributes that align with what users already know because they are analogous to things those people habitually do.

Point out in your product videos and marketing content how easy the transition is to make, because it involves actions and thought processes they already use.

Train your micro-influencers and content creators to do the same. The more easily customers make those connections, the less they will fear adoption.

APPLY NATURAL MAPPING

Integrate controls and functions that mirror real-world interactions, ensuring spatial, conceptual and behavioral similarities for intuitive usability. Point these analogies out for prospective buyers, to melt away any fear of failure.

Think about new ways your product can incorporate mirroring and natural mapping to make it second nature to use. Experiment with your prototypes, varying placement of inputs, and observe which ones first-time users catch onto most easily.

CHAPTER 20

Scaling for Needs

In This Chapter:

- *The amplifying effect of scaling on both strengths and weaknesses*
- *The importance of optimizing processes before scaling*
- *The value of incremental testing and gathering real consumer feedback*
- *The need for flexibility and adaptability during the scaling phase*

WHEN YOU SCALE ANYTHING, from a marketing campaign budget to a returns process, you scale everything associated with it — including the flaws and all their consequences.

That means you can't expect to 10X your sales and revenue without doing the same to every functionality glitch, cost factor and customer support challenge associated with selling an individual unit.

If just one in every twenty deliveries arrives broken or infuriates the customer through a recurrent manufacturing flaw, you honestly don't want to scale sales to a million units.

Doing so will create 50,000 angry customers (equal in military terms to a full army corps of enemies) and unleash a deluge of returns.

INNOVATION INTERLUDE:
NETFLIX AND THE ART OF SCALING FOR NEEDS

Netflix exemplifies how a company can successfully scale by continuously adapting to changing consumer needs and technological advancements.

Initially a DVD-by-mail rental service, Netflix transformed into:

Functional Benefit: Convenient access to a vast library of content

Emotional Benefit: Freedom of choice and control over entertainment

Transformative Benefit: Personalized viewing experiences

Coveted Condition: Being a trendsetter in entertainment consumption

Netflix's scaling strategy involved several key elements:

Anticipating technological shifts: Moving from DVDs to streaming before broadband was ubiquitous.

Content creation: Investing in original programming to reduce reliance on licensed content.

Data-driven decisions: Using viewer data to inform content creation and recommendations.

Global expansion: Adapting content and interfaces for each market.

Through the power of strategic scaling, Netflix grew from 7 million subscribers in 2007 to over 230 million by 2022.[1]

Netflix's success in scaling highlights the importance of anticipating future needs, continuously innovating, and adapting to changing market conditions.[2] By staying ahead of technological trends and consumer preferences, Netflix transformed from a niche service to a global entertainment powerhouse.

It will bog down human resources, cost a fortune, and quite possibly destroy your brand.

In ongoing cost components like product usability, engineering, manufacturing, marketing and fulfillment, it is vitally important to optimize as comprehensively as possible before you scale.

A mistake you make early on in product development or your core processes will stick with you through every order, every customer, every sale — until the root cause is found and fixed.

On the bright side, processes for making good decisions also scale with growth. Each optimization pays greater dividends the more you sell.

PRESSURE TO SCALE

When you're launching a product, you will feel tremendous pressure to go huge, right out of the gates. Whether it is to appease nervous stakeholders, to bolster egos, to recoup startup investment or to achieve better buying power, most product creators and their teams want to see amazing results, and aim to ramp up production as immediately as possible.

Often expectations and priorities are out of whack from the start. I've seen experienced product makers build 100,000 units of an untested product on a cannot-fail belief, only to be stuck with 90,000 of them sitting in a warehouse a year later. Or receive a convoy of shipping containers, just as a major defect in the injection molds is discovered.

EXPECT THE UNEXPECTED

The biggest unknowns, including unforeseen needs and barriers, only begin to reveal themselves on Day One of actual sales. Even with a great go-to-market plan, you can't predict with certainty how real consumers will behave or what combination of stimuli will motivate most of them to buy. Not until the rubber meets the road and you start real-world testing of messaging, images and platforms — with the product ready to ship.

With a need-centric product, your job is to always be watching and listening. As your sales numbers grow, so should your awareness of how people are using your product to succeed.

There are always lessons and surprises. That should be part of why you are choosing to take on this adventure. Solving one need often reveals others.

Scaling is not just bigger numbers. It is a process that tests your skills, your culture and your commitment. Every day you will find yourself in a place you've never been before. And every morning, when you check the product's sales statistics and traffic analytics, you will wonder if this is when the breakthrough will materialize.

And when it does, hopefully you will have optimized everything you could have. Then and only then, you can strap in, enjoy the ride — and prepare for the next exciting stage of creating helpful, intuitive products people really need.

KEY INSIGHTS FROM CHAPTER 20

- Scaling a product amplifies every aspect of your product and operations, both positive and negative. In the same way a magnifying mirror enlarges blemishes, scaling sales magnifies strengths and shortcomings alike.
- Before multiplying investment in ads and growth marketing, fix any existing flaws or problems at the source. Their impacts will inevitably be scaled up along with — and at the expense of — your successes.
- It's crucial to optimize your processes before embarking on a large-scale production. Thoroughly test your product, refine your operations and ensure that your foundation is solid before ramping up production.
- Take the same approach to running ads. Test images, video and content at a macro level, then scale only what works. (And continue to A/B test some more, for as long as you run ads.)
- While planning and strategy are vital, true insights into consumer behavior and preferences emerge only when your product is made available for purchase. Don't rush into large-scale production without testing the waters first.
- Engage potential buyers with your product, messaging and platforms to gather valuable feedback that can guide your scaling efforts effectively. Expect customers to uncover surprising flaws or quality issues — and be prepared to make improvements.

DO THESE NOW FOR QUICK WINS:

EMBRACE PRE-SCALING OPTIMIZATION

Before even considering scaling your product (or equally, your ad spend), meticulously review every aspect of your operations.

Search for any potential flaws, inefficiencies, or weaknesses in your product, manufacturing, support, marketing and fulfillment processes. Address these issues to ensure you have a strong foundation that can withstand the rigors of scaling.

INCREMENTALLY TEST EVERYTHING

Rather than diving headfirst into large-scale production, plan to adopt an incremental approach. Begin by soft-launching on a smaller scale and gather feedback from real consumers who know they are in an "early adopters" group.

Test various combinations of messaging, images and platforms to understand what resonates best with your target audience.

Use this data to fine-tune your strategy before scaling up. Such a patient approach is counterintuitive and pushes against the pressures you are likely to feel, but can make a massive difference in reducing costs and building a strong product brand.

BECOME FLEXIBLE AND ADAPTABLE

Understand that scaling is a dynamic process that thrives on flexibility. Never expect to sit back and cheer when the sales graphs spontaneously shoot upwards in a hockey-stick curve.

Be prepared to rejig your strategies based on consumer response to your product, which will change over time and vary with each initiative, season and audience group.

If you encounter unexpected challenges or opportunities during the scaling phase, be ready to adapt your approach accordingly.

Focus on continuous improvement and learn from the scaling experience. It can be the most exciting part of your product journey!

CHAPTER 21

Compel Responsibly

In This Chapter:

- *Ethical responsibility in need-centric product development*
- *Navigating ethical gray areas and avoiding exploitative practices*
- *Prioritizing transparency, honesty, and user well-being*
- *Ethical decision-making frameworks and collaborative reviews*
- *Contributing positively to society through responsible product development*

WHEN I WAS A KID, Saturday morning was cartoon time on television. Every few minutes that I sat glued to the TV, I'd get bombarded with commercials for toys, sugar-coated cereals and junk food like Pop Tarts and Twinkies.

McDonald's even created a fictitious world called "McDonaldland," populated by a bizarre cast of characters designed to capture kids' hearts and imaginations, ultimately leading to relentless pleas to visit the restaurant and collect the latest Treat of the Week.

It was an exploitative free-for-all that started in the 1950s and went on for generations.

But in 1990, the US-based Federal Communications Commission created the Children's Television Act, which mandated commercially supported TV networks to program at least three hours per week of educational content, most of which landed on Saturday mornings. It also limited Saturday morning TV ad space to ten and a half minutes per hour. Cartoon time would never be the same.[1]

While advertising to children is still technically legal in the United States and Canada, both countries have adopted fairly restrictive regulations, and most North American advertisers have scaled the practice back substantially. In Sweden and Norway, any kind of advertising to children is prohibited, and in the Netherlands, ads for candies or sweets are required to display a toothbrush to remind kids to brush their teeth after enjoying the product.[2]

Kids are among the most vulnerable and susceptible humans. The dog brain is essentially all a child has, as their frontal cortex won't be fully developed for another two decades. In my mind, children should never be the target of advertising. Likewise with any other sensitive or easily manipulated audience. We can do better.

While creating products that fulfill genuine needs is a noble pursuit, in doing so it is crucial to tread carefully and ethically. As a product maker, you have the unique power to shape consumer behavior — and you know what comes with great power. (Can't say I learned nothing from watching Spider-Man all those Saturday mornings.) It's important to think about the ethical considerations of need-centric product development and how to balance innovation and enticement with responsibility toward the people we touch.

I expect you have no intention of tricking people into buying a product they don't understand or won't need. Even if you might get a bang out of slipping town-to-town like the classic snake oil salesman, it wouldn't be a feasible option today. (And back when it was, you were still likely to wind up scrubbing off tar and feathers from time to time.) I'm betting that isn't who you are.

But where is the hard line? To me, it's about true value for the buyer. If nearly all of your customers feel the product is worth what they've paid and more, you're in a great place. On the other hand, if you detect consistent signals of poor value delivery, underperformance or lingering dissatisfaction, take a critical look at how you've been presenting the product.

It's normal — and expected — to get the occasional one-star review. The best, most successful products in the world can't please everyone. Some people won't read or take time to understand the description. Others might shop when they aren't in a condition to make sound decisions. A few are bound to have unrealistic expectations, no matter how honestly and clearly you present the product's capabilities. And the occasional buyer is just plain unreasonable by nature.

As you begin to scale, listen to the voice of your customer and invite feedback. Unless you're completely tone-deaf, you will soon know if you're attracting and delighting ideal buyers and will be able to make adjustments, even hard turns, to get things right.

When starting out, it is easy: as discussed in the last chapter, you should be testing on small audiences and scaling what works, which generally keeps costs and risks minimal.

But even minimum viable audiences are made up of real people, so pay close attention to the feedback. Social media ads can be a perfect testing ground for key narratives, taglines and imagery, because responses come back nearly in real time. You'll soon learn to distinguish between perpetual haters and people airing legit concerns. You'll spot gaps in your messaging, which are an opportunity to explain better what the product can and cannot do. If people repeatedly ask what sounds like a dumb question, it is probably because you've made the answer too hard to find.

Considering the expense and effort it takes to get this far, it can be worth running focus groups or beta testing any campaign that risks pushing boundaries too far, or messaging that might have even a wee chance of misleading some buyers.

Be bold, but know we all have a limited line of vision to the responses we may elicit. Test ideas with care, and allow yourself a cooling-off period before pushing out content that may be a little edgy for your brand. The same applies to responding to customer complaints or ad comment take-overs. You will be tested — and expect anything you post online to be captured in a screen shot.

NAVIGATING ETHICAL GRAY AREAS

IN ALL THE EXCITEMENT of innovation and with the immediacy of publishing digital content, it's never been easier to overlook potential ethical concerns. Consider whether your images, video and text content might inadvertently exploit vulnerable emotions, injure sensitive individuals, or lead to unexpected dependencies.

Your goal has probably always been to create a product that genuinely improves users' lives without ever causing harm or taking advantage of anyone's weaknesses.

Have objective friends or level-headed colleagues routinely sanity-check your campaign ideas with this in mind. Even catastrophic blind spots are often embarrassingly obvious in hindsight, once irreversible damage is done.

There's a reason these lurking dangers are called blind spots — they are completely invisible to you at a particular moment in time. And like that motorcycle you can't quite detect on the freeway, they're still very real. So are the consequences of driving into them.

I have often found it helpful to have an impromptu content workshop whenever important messaging needs to be created quickly. When a blowup is happening on one of your ads or posts, it's worth making sure your colleagues at various levels, with different perspectives, take part in crafting a response. Responses that combine humor, humility and respect usually work best. Such moments are the proving ground of your brand's true spirit.

Sometimes sensitivities are not glaringly obvious, or are barely predictable at all. I have seen combative discussions explode on social media out of what initially appeared to be a completely benign image of something that ought not have been controversial at all. But we live in a divided and highly polarized world.

Previously gray areas can suddenly be seen as binary in someone's context. Their comments become your business. Providing a forum for hate and ugly words can damage your brand in the eyes of everyone watching.

UNDERSTANDING VULNERABLE CONSUMERS

SOME CONSUMERS MIGHT be especially vulnerable to persuasive marketing, or might have unique needs that are in essence exploited by reaching directly to them. Take care to avoid (intentionally or not) targeting demographics like children, the elderly, or individuals with addiction or mental health challenges. Recognize that even if they are unanticipated in your audience targeting, some vulnerable people are sure to come across your messaging. Be sure your product serves their needs without manipulation, and build easy off-ramps.

Make canceling an order before it has shipped quick and painfree. Thoughtfully craft a return policy that leaves people who bought by mistake a clear, easy, face-saving way out. Be sure vulnerable consumers never feel stuck with a purchase they didn't fully understand, and ensure that they won't be afraid or embarrassed, or out-of-pocket to return it. Support them with care and ample respect when they do.

AVOIDING MANIPULATIVE PRACTICES

ETHICAL PRODUCT MARKETING deliberately shuns manipulative practices that can coerce or mislead people into making decisions they might later regret.

Steer miles clear of dark patterns like false urgency, false scarcity, or misleading phrasing that might deceive some readers — or create buyer's remorse through purchases that in fairness ought never have been made. If your goal is to delight every single customer, you get it. Don't panic when things aren't going as you'd hoped and lose sight of that. Be mindful in executing novel approaches not to wander off-course with tactics that morph into questionable territory.

TRANSPARENCY AND HONESTY

HONESTY AND TRANSPARENCY are the bedrock of every great product brand's communication. Be clear about the limitations and any potential risks consumers may face in using your product. Avoid overstating its capabilities or downplaying any potential drawbacks or negative consequences.

Holding back the hype can be counterintuitive, but let customers be the ones who rave about how amazing your product is — testimonials and reviews are more effective than anything a brand can say about itself anyway.

If you sense you're crossing a line, you probably are. Dial back to a place where you can be confident no one will be disappointed if they buy based entirely on your claims.

HONORING CONSUMER WELL-BEING

IN BEING CONSISTENT with your goals from the beginning, your product should by default enhance consumers' lives and never hinder them. That means steadfastly putting customer well-being above short-term profits — even if you're having a lousy quarter or find yourself under intense pressure to convert new customers, and fast.

If any aspect of your product enables excessive use or contributes to addictive behavior, consider design modifications or implementations that minimize or eliminate the chance of overuse.

While this is especially relevant in gaming apps and products containing addictive substances, it can apply to any other product that has habit-forming attributes — even some in diet, fitness or wellness spaces. We all know someone who has gone overboard with an activity or product generally considered healthy, to the eventual detriment of their own well-being. What could happen if a customer went seriously over-the-top with your product?

And then there is misuse. A lot of products that are necessary and normally helpful to consumers can be harmful or even deadly if used the wrong way. Vehicles, hunting rifles, knives, perfumes, electronic devices, cookware, athletic equipment and even some toys can cause serious harm, whether intentionally or by accident. As the person behind the product, you have a legal and moral responsibility to minimize potential risks for everyone who comes into contact with it. Even silly, stupid people.

Each of these ethical considerations could be the subject of an entire book, and I won't try or pretend to be comprehensive in this one fairly short, relatively preachy chapter. As a product maker and a leader, it's your responsibility to decide how far to go in investing your probably ever-shrinking resources into research and consultants.

If your gut is wrenching as you read this, now is the time to open your mind to your beliefs and true feelings about the impacts your product might have.

ETHICAL DECISION-MAKING FRAMEWORKS

ETHICAL DILEMMAS CAN often pop up during the product development process. When they do, think about using ethical decision-making frameworks, such as the "Golden Rule" or "Utilitarianism" to guide your choices.

The Golden Rule (sometimes called the ethic of reciprocity) essentially states that we should only treat others as we would like to be treated. "Do unto others," and all that. It emphasizes empathy and perspective-taking, promoting fairness, respect and compassion in every decision you make. If you're an ethical person, you probably already think this way.

INNOVATION INTERLUDE:
FAIRPHONE AND ETHICAL PRODUCT DEVELOPMENT

Fairphone demonstrates how a company can develop products with a strong focus on ethical considerations and social responsibility.

Fairphone's approach to ethical product development includes:

Functional Benefit: A fully functional smartphone

Emotional Benefit: Guilt-free tech consumption

Transformative Benefit: Supporting fair labor practices and sustainability

Coveted Condition: Being a socially responsible tech consumer

Key elements of Fairphone's ethical strategy are:

Conflict-free minerals: Sourcing materials from conflict-free zones and promoting fair mining practices.[3]

Modular design: Creating phones that are easy to repair and upgrade, reducing e-waste.[4]

Worker welfare: Ensuring fair wages and good working conditions in their supply chain.[5]

Longevity: Designing phones to last longer than the industry standard, with long-term software support.[6]

This ethical approach has allowed Fairphone to carve out a niche in the competitive smartphone market. By 2024, the company had sold over 550,000 phones.[7]

Fairphone showed how it's possible to develop consumer electronics with a strong emphasis on ethics and sustainability. By prioritizing fair labor practices, sustainable materials, and product longevity, Fairphone has created a unique value proposition that resonates with socially conscious consumers.

Utilitarianism is an ethical theory that suggests the best action is the one that maximizes overall happiness or utility, and minimizes suffering for the greatest number of people. It focuses on the consequences of actions, and seeks to achieve the maximum positive impact.

Understand and reference these frameworks, extracting and creating your own strong and practical guidelines to ensure that your decisions consider both your customers and society as a whole.

It's easy and worthwhile to ask the following questions when weighing alternate actions:

1. **Would I be happy having any of the possible consequences of this decision happen to me as the consumer, or to have a friend or loved one affected?**
2. **Does this choice help maximize the happiness of all the people it affects?**
3. **Are we achieving the greatest possible positive impact by choosing this direction?**

The purpose is to establish your ethical True North, and create frames of reference that will be helpful and relevant whenever you are challenged with hard decisions. Place your core values at the heart of the framework you will use, to arrive at outcomes that consistently and reliably benefit your buyers and others reached by the far-reaching ripples you create. Think about the legacy you are building, and the many human lives your product will touch.

LONG-TERM CONSEQUENCES

EVERY PRODUCT THAT gets used on a recurring basis has long-term consequences. Have you anticipated all such potential impacts of adopting yours? Will it lead to a purely positive impact on individuals and society, or might it inadvertently contribute to some negative outcomes, even in rare instances?

Think about conducting a thorough ethical impact assessment, to predict and assess any unintended side effects from bringing your product into the world.

Negative long-term consequences or even short-term ones are more than an ethical consideration. If your product becomes very successful, count on people finding ways to misuse it. The bigger you become, the higher the risk. Even if you aren't remotely negligent in any way, you can still find yourself staring down a costly class-action lawsuit.

Deep diligence in assessing wide-ranging impacts forces you to remove the blinders and will lead to a kinder and safer product — while potentially shielding you from devastating legal woes. Talk to a knowledgeable product liability lawyer to flush out any potential concerns specific to your product. (That's my disclaimer and my only advice when it comes to anything involving legal matters: talk to a good lawyer!)

ETHICS TAG-TEAMING

TRULY ETHICAL PRODUCTS begin grounding their values from the earliest days. This means incorporating ethical reviews directly into your product development process. You can seek early input from a wide range of perspectives, including ethicists, psychologists and representatives from potential user groups. Tag-teaming ethical dilemmas through collaborative reviews can shed light on murky spots and make you better connected to every customer. The information you gather will anchor your messaging and become central to your content marketing. And the wider your eyes are open, the more your entire process becomes a series of conduits to responsible product design.

Collaborative ethical reviews don't need to be formal or complicated. Document what you learn and continuously go back to the important points. You don't have to act on every recommendation: even the ones that are not quite realistic or appropriate to your product will make you wiser and better at developing need-centric products with maximum positive impact.

It's a smart and liberating way of thinking. And it helps counteract the head-in-the-sand approach you can easily fall into when overwhelmed by all the complexity that arises from putting unique new products out to the world.

SAFEGUARDING USER DATA AND PRIVACY

THE THINGS A BAD ACTOR (or criminal organization) could do with your user data are terrifying. And the augmenting power of AI in the wrong hands is increasing the risks and potential impacts exponentially. Every piece of information you have about a kind, trusting customer could potentially be used to harm that person.

With data-driven products and valuable customer databases, protecting user data and privacy is one of your most critical responsibilities. Ensure that your online store and marketing efforts collect only necessary and low-sensitivity data and implement robust security measures to prevent data breaches. Even if you collect minimal customer information and have a narrow audience, stay aware of changes to regional privacy regulations wherever your customers live, and stay on top of cybersecurity best practices and implementations, always taking abundant precautions.

For ages, privacy policies and actions taken for customer data protection were largely seen as set-it-and-forget-it items on a checklist. That has changed forever, and ongoing scheduled reviews are essential. Your customers not only deserve maximum protection, they need it to stay happy and whole.

THE BIGGER PICTURE: SOCIAL RESPONSIBILITY

IT'S SO EASY TO GET distracted by exciting opportunities, endless metrics and myriad sales activities, and forget that your product is part of a living, feeling human ecosystem. Staying committed to being a positive contributor to society, as the leader you are, means you continuously take on big issues like environmental impact, diversity and inclusion, accessibility and societal well-being. Whether you like it or not, each of these is connected to your core values.

They will impact how your brand and product are known — and remembered.

It's a lot of work that's often not visibly linked to ROI (especially in early days), but the human outcomes might yield what is most meaningful to you and everyone your product touches in our need-driven world.

KEY INSIGHTS FROM CHAPTER 21

- Navigate ethical gray areas and avoid exploiting vulnerabilities.
- Prioritize transparency, honesty and user well-being.
- Explore and use ethical decision-making frameworks to guide choices.
- Anticipate long-term consequences of your product's adoption.
- Recognize that being ethically responsible is connected to safeguarding your business from legal liability.
- Incorporate collaborative ethical reviews into your process.
- Safeguard user data and prioritize privacy.
- Develop habits for contributing positively to societal issues through your products.

—

As you work to strike a balance between innovation and ethical responsibility, you can create products that not only fit genuine needs but also contribute positively to individuals, society and the world at large.

Ethical product development aligns with need-centric product development and ensures your innovations have a lasting, satisfying and meaningful impact without compromising integrity or well-being.

DO THESE NOW FOR QUICK WINS:

REVIEW MARKETING STRATEGIES

Over the next 15 minutes, take a critical look at your current or planned marketing tactics, assets and content. Do they align with your ethical standards and avoid exploiting vulnerabilities or manipulating emotions?

What could go wrong if vulnerable people were enticed, and how would you respond? Make necessary adjustments to messaging and imagery to prioritize consumer well-being and transparency.

QUICK SOCIAL MEDIA CONTENT AUDIT

Evaluate your social media content for any potential ethical concerns, such as inadvertently exploiting vulnerabilities or promoting harmful behaviors. Remove or revise any posts that could be perceived as insensitive or manipulative, and ensure future content aligns with ethical guidelines.

UPDATE PRIVACY POLICIES AND SECURITY MEASURES

Review and update your privacy policies to make sure they reflect current data protection regulations and best practices. Implement additional security measures, if necessary, to safeguard user data and protect against potential breaches. Regularly monitor and update security protocols to stay ahead of emerging threats.

INTEGRATE ETHICAL REVIEWS INTO PRODUCT DEVELOPMENT

Incorporate ethical reviews into your product development process by seeking input from diverse perspectives, including ethicists, psychologists, and potential user groups. Document key insights and recommendations to inform decision-making and messaging throughout the development lifecycle.

ASSESS LONG-TERM CONSEQUENCES

Take 10 minutes to reflect on the potential long-term impacts of your product on individuals and society. Consider conducting a thorough ethical impact assessment to identify any potential negative consequences and explore strategies to mitigate them. Consult with legal experts to address any concerns related to product liability and risk management.

IMPLEMENT CUSTOMER FEEDBACK MECHANISM

Set up a system for collecting and addressing customer feedback regarding ethical considerations. This could include a feedback form on your website or a dedicated email address for ethical inquiries.

Invite feedback on social media and actively engage with people who post comments to demonstrate your commitment to responsible product development.

EDUCATE TEAM MEMBERS

You understand the importance of ethical product development and the potential implications of unethical practices. Now it's time to transfer these values and beliefs to your team. Encourage open dialogue and collaboration to ensure everyone understands their role in upholding ethical standards and prioritizing consumer well-being.

Talk about consequences to the business if things go wrong and invite all team members to share concerns and ideas. The more watchful eyes you can cultivate, the fewer blind spots will exist.

STAY INFORMED ON REGULATORY CHANGES

Stay current about changes to regional privacy regulations and emerging ethical considerations in your industry. Dedicate time to research and stay updated on relevant laws, guidelines, and best practices to ensure compliance and ethical integrity in your product development and marketing efforts.

PROMOTE DIVERSITY AND INCLUSION

Evaluate your company's diversity and inclusion initiatives and identify opportunities to promote inclusiveness within your teams and product offerings.

Consider ways to incorporate wide-ranging perspectives into your product development process and marketing strategies to ensure inclusivity and representation.

This will not only benefit the business by building deep and well-rounded teams, but will inevitably result in products that resonate with a wider range of buyers.

LEAD BY EXAMPLE

Be a true leader by consistently demonstrating ethical behavior and decision-making in your interactions with customers, employees, and stakeholders.

Foster a culture of integrity, transparency, and accountability within your organization to prioritize ethical considerations at every level.

CHAPTER 22

Into a Need-Driven Future

In This Chapter:

- *Embracing change as an opportunity*
- *How technology, cultural shifts, and lifestyle changes influence needs*
- *Adopting agile methodologies and user-centric design thinking*
- *Building collaborative networks and hedging bets to navigate uncertainty*
- *Seeking sustainable and scalable solutions for long-term relevance*

A SHORT TIME AGO, no one could have predicted the far-reaching impacts of a global pandemic, multiple early-twenty-first-century wars and the explosion of artificial intelligence.

Changes around us have radically transformed the way we buy and sell products, both on levels we can easily see and on many others we can't even imagine.

In many ways, our values, social connections, lifestyles and dreams for our own future have been wildly recalibrated from where they seemed to be heading just a few years back.

As the surrounding landscape continues to surprise us, so will the needs and desires of the people for whom we make products. Embracing change and anticipating future needs is crucial to staying relevant and successful in this Tasmanian devil of a world marketplace.

Predicting future needs is fairly impossible to do in detail with much accuracy, yet many innovators are working right now on products that will capitalize in remarkable ways on next year's top news stories.

Luck will be a factor, but luck alone is never enough. (Good thing, because except for a few repeat lottery winners and a fellow named Timothy Dexter — look him up — it's seldom highly reliable.)

So, what, then?

Well, there are a number of useful factors you can analyze, upon which future successes are most likely to be built: data, trends, marketplace gaps and technologies that are emerging (or finally maturing enough) to open doors for unprecedented solutions.

DATA

DATA IS CLOSER TO a rear-view mirror than a crystal ball. It only represents what has happened in the past, and its curation and reporting can be influenced by flaws or biases. Data that shows what has already worked is based only on what has been tried so far, under specific conditions — during a window of time that's gone forever. Patterns sometimes persist, but times continuously change, and so do human behaviors. Sometimes really quickly.

As we've seen, successful innovators don't waste much time watching what competitors are now doing. They often don't look specifically at what customers are asking for. Some of the greatest claim not to go looking for obvious marketplace gaps to fill. (Bear in mind that most of those famous visionaries have also found themselves rebuilding from scratch.)

Data is important and very helpful when combined with a sound understanding of its accuracy, limitations and weaknesses. Historic data helps shape our understanding of causation and enables us to build helpful predictive models. It tells us how people have behaved, what has previously worked — as well as what gave us what we've got right now. And data is perhaps at its most valuable when combined with innovative future-oriented thinking.

TRENDS, MARKETPLACE GAPS AND EMERGING TECHNOLOGIES

INSTEAD OF CONSTANTLY combing through analytics and sales data, visionary innovators think mostly about what is likely to happen next: what consumers are ready to adopt, where trends are heading and (perhaps most importantly) which desirable innovations technology and infrastructure are becoming mature enough to fully support very soon. The reason the Palm Treo and other early smartphones failed to become popular was not so much a dearth of consumer acceptance or desire as the lack of reliable, ubiquitous high-bandwidth wireless data. The iPhone came at exactly the right time, when massive 3G data networks were poised to change the wireless game. And Steve Jobs was even willing to risk cannibalizing his lucrative iPod market to be sure adoption was a slam-dunk. It was a combination of vision, timing and *cojones* that few brands would have dared to make.

Likewise, Tesla could not have possibly achieved its success a mere decade earlier. The battery and electric motor technology had to be ripe. The company had to figure out how to efficiently build two million cars a year and a substantial network of charging stations had to exist before the product, however good or affordable, could possibly be scaled to a mass market. And buyers had to be ready to change the way they bought cars, with the confidence to make online purchases with a vastly unprecedented price tag.

Think about all the behavioral evolution, technological empowerment and psychological shifts affecting your industry. What behavior patterns are changing now, and when will that trend reach a tipping point that enables new behaviors to become acceptable? What technologies might make adoption easier, more beneficial and more frictionless? What needs exist today on a larger scale than a few years ago — or even just last year?

UNDERSTAND THE EVOLVING LANDSCAPE

CONSUMER NEEDS EVOLVE all the time, influenced by all kinds of factors, including cultural shifts, seasonal interests, special occasions, life changes, technological advancements and global events. No matter how old you are or how you live, your needs are different than they were just five years ago. Think about what you were itching to buy then, and what you've fantasized about most recently. Not nearly the same, right?

As a product maker, looking at past success stories can help you understand how innovators have seized on similar opportunities to propel their own products' adoption. A product that is fulfilling a need perfectly today might not be sufficient tomorrow, especially if the need changes or a multitude of competing solutions pop up offering new features and superior user experiences.

And things just become obsolete. Thousands of products that were universally popular a decade or more ago have vanished entirely or become relegated to tiny niche markets. Calculators, flashlights, video recorders, cameras, alarm clocks, pagers, radios, landline phones, Rolodexes and daily planners have been entirely replaced by a singular device. Almost no one buys postcards or USB drives anymore. My old journalism school colleagues now wear a tall stack of hats as podcasters, bloggers, video game reviewers and social media influencers because newspapers have all but vanished, dragging away these people's former jobs.

Trends give, and trends take away. Behaviors change quite slowly — until the rate of change becomes blindingly fast. It's that tricky.

It's on you to stay attuned to emerging trends and evolving consumer expectations, and to detect when people are beginning to solve problems in new ways. While online search patterns are a trailing indicator, they are helpful in detecting and evaluating rising needs. (I love Google Trends as a way of exploring the popularity of concepts and validating hypotheses.)

Whenever something big happens in the world and people adjust their behaviors in response to the impacts, ask yourself what human needs are likely to rise, and which will fall, as a result. What technologies do you see reaching maturity that can now (or soon) reliably support completely new solutions?

How can you combine the two to create a product that seems to magically appear in the just the right place at exactly the right time?

TECHNOLOGY'S INFLUENCE ON NEEDS

GREAT TECH BREAKTHROUGHS tend to reshape the way we perceive needs. New innovations open doors for novel possibilities and generate demand for products that address previously unmet needs. Think of how advancements in technologies like AI, AR/VR, blockchain, predictive analytics and robotics might impact your product's relevance and ability to help customers achieve their goals.

Become an expert about the next wave of technology and plan how you can use it to make your product more amazing and successful than it could ever have been before.

What needs might that technological advancement itself cue up, and what completely new problems will it give you the opportunity to solve?

CULTURAL AND SOCIAL SHIFTS

CULTURAL NORMS AND societal values will never stop changing. By definition they represent a snapshot (or at most a short video clip) in time. A need-centric approach to product development requires sensitivity to these shifts. Every meaningful response to the ways people behave and think has its own ripple effects. Successful product makers tend to have keen observation skills and be finely attuned to their intuition.

A popular interest in eating fewer animal products drove the success of Beyond Meat. Docusign and Zoom capitalized on a boom in remote business models to achieve a critical network effect that would power their products to market domination. DoorDash made hay when people on pandemic lockdown couldn't go to restaurants, and the company leveraged the habits and desire for convenience that flourished in the context of forced behavior, to remain the market leader years later.[1]

Regardless of what you make, be tuned in to directional changes in attitudes toward widely held values like sustainability, inclusivity and social responsibility — and adapt your product planning accordingly. Clients of mine have built entire businesses on serving the next generation of customers, whose values, methods and priorities are vastly different from those of their predecessors.

Nearly every sector is being swept by huge changes now. Incumbents who stagnate can quickly go from feasting on wagyu beef to eating a crafty newcomer's dust.

ADAPT TO CHANGING LIFESTYLES

CONSUMER LIFESTYLES ARE also in a constant state of flux. Far-reaching factors like demographic shifts, changing work preferences and increased urbanization bring new needs, along with a wildly different set of human expectations. Smaller trends, shifting economics, and more slowly evolving priorities can have less visible, yet very significant downstream impacts on what people need in order to live their dream lifestyle — or possibly even a stripped-down version.

Flexibility in product development allows you to recalibrate, course-correct or fully pivot to address the next inevitable shift in lifestyle-related needs. It's possible the product has to be fundamentally rethought in order to succeed; sometimes it can be adapted.

It might even stay the same, while the use case is what changes, as a new round of customers discover ways for it to meet their own needs. That can mean revisiting positioning, messaging and buyer personas to embrace your new audiences.

There are many great examples of how that kind of repositioning has happened. One of my favorites is a product originally created in the early 1900s to clean coal furnace soot from wallpaper. While the inventor, a company called Kutol, was the world's largest manufacturer of wallpaper cleaner at the time, the product was headed for obsolescence with coal-burning furnaces being phased out.

But serendipitously, people had begun embracing a new use for Kutol. Recent magazine articles had given it a bizarre popularity with mothers and teachers, not as a cleaning product, but a modeling clay. Kutol was easy to sculpt, and could be dyed any color. Plus, it was non-toxic.

And since the day when Play-Doh was first marketed as a toy in 1956, more than three billion cans have been sold. You're not supposed to eat the stuff, but there's a good chance you remember that salty taste as distinctly as I do. One of the most ubiquitous toys in history, created by repositioning a wallpaper cleaner.[2]

The subject of wallpaper reminds me of a manufacturing technology that was first developed to make a textured wall covering. It didn't sell well for that purpose — or in the first repositioning attempt as insulation for greenhouses. But third time's a charm and the globalization of manufactured products made bubble wrap a multi-billion-dollar staple as a protective shipping material.[3]

Then there is Sildenafil, which started out as a medication to treat hypertension and angina. Clinical trials found it to have little effect on angina, but indicated other notable consequences — leading the manufacturer Pfizer to reposition the drug and brand it as Viagra.[4]

To make dough rise, my grandmothers (and *their* grandmothers) used sodium bicarbonate, also known as baking soda, as a leavening agent. When lifestyle trends more recently shifted towards eco-friendly and natural living, baking soda found a new role. It boomed as a versatile household cleaner and odor absorber: people use it to clean sinks, deodorize carpets and remove stains. Its gentle abrasive properties and ability to neutralize odors without harsh chemicals have made it an attractive option for eco-conscious consumers. The increase in demand has been tremendous: good old sodium bicarbonate saw its sales worldwide nearly triple between 2018 and 2024.[5]

Recently when I was trying to remove hardened grease from a range hood, the half-dozen or so chemical cleaners I scrubbed it with had almost no effect. With low expectations, I gave baking soda a shot — and it cut right through. Who knew?

Change can be electrifying when you're on the right end of it. How can lifestyle trends or evolving needs change the ways consumers might use or perceive your product? And how can you seize on that?

STAY AHEAD OF THE CURVE

THE KEY TO THRIVING in a need-driven future is to adopt a highly proactive mindset right now. That means rather than occasionally fretting about what complications and problems the future may bring, you are constantly imagining the possibilities — and how to capitalize on them.

Once you begin to think through the lens of a future world where you are harnessing new opportunities, it becomes easier and easier to pull ideas from a combination of recognizing behavior patterns, identifying emerging pains, and projecting the upside potential of each breakthrough. Instead of reacting to today's big thing (alongside a million other product makers), you get to be the innovator who anticipates coming needs — and reaches customers first.

This requires a combination of foresight, market research, causation awareness, perceptiveness and creativity that's within you to develop and hone. Every great visionary has begun by recognizing this potential, and turning it into a superpower.

FAIL YOUR WAY TO SUCCESS

INNOVATION IS THE ROCKET FUEL of adapting to future needs. Encourage a culture of enthusiastic experimentation within your organization. Think like Thomas Edison and create room for failure, knowing it's often through repeated failures that the most groundbreaking innovations emerge. Developing a process of rapid elimination can be as important as the ability to recognize what is actually working so that you persist only with productive efforts.

You have limited focus to pursue new opportunities. Every single challenge you accept costs valuable resources — particularly the one you can never make, borrow or buy more of: your time. Experiment and take careful notes while quickly letting go of failures.

DESIGN FROM THE OUTSIDE IN

USER-CENTRIC DESIGN THINKING becomes even more crucial when envisioning future possibilities. Regularly engage with and observe people who represent your ideal customer so that you can understand their evolving needs, pain points and heartfelt desires.

How are these things different today from the way they were five years ago?

Pay special attention to how younger people achieve the same things in new or different ways than a seasoned user does.

Are new tools, mindsets or technologies shaping these fresh approaches?

What might that lead to next, and how will the related expectations be different from what they have traditionally been?

INNOVATION INTERLUDE:
SONOS AND ANTICIPATING FUTURE NEEDS

Sonos exemplifies how a company can succeed by proactively anticipating future trends in home audio and smart technology.

Sonos' approach to meeting future needs includes:

Functional Benefit: High-quality, multi-room audio systems

Emotional Benefit: Seamless, personalized audio experiences

Coveted Condition: Being seen as tech-savvy and design-conscious

Key elements of Sonos' future-oriented strategy:

Early focus on wireless: Launching wireless speaker systems in 2005, well before smart homes became mainstream.[6]

Platform agnosticism: Developing a system compatible with various music services, anticipating the shift towards streaming.[7]

Voice assistant integration: Partnering with multiple voice assistants, foreseeing their growing importance in smart homes.[8]

Sustainability initiatives: Designing products for longevity and repairability, aligning with growing environmental concerns.[9]

This proactive approach has driven Sonos' growth. The company's revenue increased from $901 million in 2017 to $1.6 billion in 2023.[10]

Sonos' success illustrates how anticipating future trends can lead to market leadership. By recognizing early the potential for wireless, connected audio systems in smart homes, Sonos positioned itself at the forefront of a major shift in home entertainment.

This ongoing pattern of observation, analysis and projection helps you realign with changing expectations — and think in terms of very exciting possibilities.

ADAPT ON THE FLY

TRADITIONAL PRODUCT DEVELOPMENT cycles often cannot keep up with the rapid pace of change. The Agile software development methodology is a set of frameworks and practices created by the software industry to deal with changes that sometimes happen faster than code can be written. As the Agile Alliance describes this approach, "It's really about thinking through how you can understand what's going on in the environment that you're in today, identify what uncertainty you're facing and figure out how you can adapt to that as you go along."[11]

Learn from the software world and adopt development methodologies that allow you to iterate quickly and make rapid adjustments for evolving needs. These approaches can include iterative prototyping, feature sprints, user feedback loops and continuous improvement by planning future model releases.

The goal is to purpose-build your processes to not just respond to, but grab hold of change, never cementing the product to a fixed moment in time. Do it well and the Most Advanced Yet Acceptable alternative will always come from you — not a competitor.

HEDGE LIKE A FUTURIST

IN LANDSCAPING, A "HEDGE" is a fence of shrubbery along the boundary of your property, as a protective barrier to keep intruders out. And in gambling, the same term refers to a secondary bet you make to reduce your potential losses from the first one.

So, when someone is "hedging their bets," they are metaphorically creating a protective barrier around their initial wager by creating ways to benefit from different outcomes.

Being a product maker involves a fair bit of gambling. And a practical way to stay ahead of the curve is to build futurist thinking right into your product development strategy. If you had a crystal ball, you could use your lottery and horse race winnings to retire comfortably, or to build next year's big thing. But in all likelihood, you don't.

Neither do Jeff Bezos or Elon Musk. What real-life visionaries instead do is employ futurist thinking. And they hedge their bets.

This means envisioning a variety of potential futures and designing product directions that align with multiple scenarios, programming adaptability into your company's DNA. It means not fearing being wrong, because you've got the alternate outcomes covered.

You don't need to build out or even prototype each possible variant, but having different product pathways mapped out in advance will give you a mental head-start, no matter which adventure the world collectively chooses.

BUILD ADAPTABLE FOUNDATIONS

AS YOU'RE BECOMING increasingly attuned to how changes in the world will affect tomorrow's consumers, develop the habit of visualizing how your product will evolve, and how it'll scale with changing needs.

Scaling can be done with optional add-ons and accessories that bring new value to the core product, like adding lenses and a tripod to a smartphone or action camera. Think about ways consumers can enhance your product to make it more uniquely their own. Build in the capability to expand its functionality, extend its life, or add personalization to achieve deeper emotional attachment.

Building adaptable foundations is a way to ensure your product stays relevant as people and their lifestyles change.

ASSEMBLE COLLABORATIVE NETWORKS

COLLABORATION IS ANOTHER key to navigating the future. When we were preparing to launch the Parallel Pillow, giving back was central to the client's core values. In past lives within the sleep space, the founders had a lengthy history of donating and volunteering with charitable organizations. Strong relationships existed with national charities, through which we tapped into vast infrastructures that could enable the distribution of Parallel's donation pillows to places of greatest need throughout the United States, while achieving levels of credibility and trust seldom afforded to a startup. Supplying and replenishing fresh, sanitary pillows is a major expense to halfway houses, shelters and other initiatives that help people in transition, so Parallel's proposal was received with huge gratitude. That kind of alliance is a gratifying win-win.

Who are your obvious allies, partners and collaborators? Who else should be one? Forge partnerships with like-minded or complementary organizations, research institutions and trusted experts to gain insights and foresight that can inform your product development strategies.

What does your network look like if you begin to see others in even slightly related spaces as potential collaborators? How can your product help those allies to kick butt, and likewise boost your reach and utility to the people who need it most?

Think first of how you can add value to a prospective partner, ahead of what you stand to gain. Lead with that. Good ones will appreciate it, eagerly join forces — and reciprocate.

EMBRACE CHANGE AS AN ESSENTIAL OPPORTUNITY

IN THE NEED-DRIVEN FUTURE, change is an opportunity more than it's a threat. And it is essential.

Doors that are closed today often can't be opened under the same conditions that got them that way. But the closing of one additional door forces shifts in energy, flow and focus, enabling all kinds of new possibilities.

By leaning into change, training yourself to be attuned to evolving consumer needs and building flexibility (including for failure) into your product development processes, you get to position yourself as a legit innovation leader and progressively build a solid market presence.

As a product maker, your ability to navigate the labyrinth of consumer needs is possibly what will most determine your long-term viability. By continuously adapting, innovating and anticipating emerging needs (while hedging your bets), you become a leader in need-driven product development, contributing to consumer satisfaction, and maybe even guiding the direction in which the market itself evolves.

Innovating is a job for visionaries and risk-takers. I hope by reading this book you've come to understand how products succeed through becoming framed by our brains as "needed."

I hope you're better equipped to ensure your own products can overcome friction and bring enough value to buyers to be adopted and succeed — ideally before going to the cost and trouble of creating them.

I also hope you have a better understanding of how you can anticipate future needs, and use that knowledge to build ethical products that will delight current and future generations of consumers.

And when your product is on the market, my greatest hope is that you can trigger fantasies of a Coveted Condition™ in the people who will value it the most: the ones who truly need it — and who, by succeeding in their own lives, will make your product a massive success.

KEY INSIGHTS FROM CHAPTER 22

- Change is the only constant. Stay nimble, adapt quickly, and keep your finger on the pulse of emerging trends. You're navigating a turbulent sea: stay flexible and ride the waves.
- While historical data offers valuable insights, it's a rear-view mirror. Combine data with forward-thinking vision and intuition for what's next. It's like driving with a GPS and a sense of adventure — you need both to reach your destination and enjoy the journey.
- Consumer needs are influenced by a myriad of factors, from social media trends to global events. Tune into the cultural zeitgeist, and tailor your product to meet evolving desires.
- Technology is rewriting the rules. Stay ahead of the curve by leveraging emerging tech to enhance your product's appeal.
- Embrace an agile mindset, iterate quickly, and pivot when necessary. Avoid locking your product into a fixed moment in time.
- Your customers are your biggest advocates and critics. They're your greatest resource. Listen to their feedback, engage with their needs, and let them inform your product's evolution. But be discerning and don't mistake trolls for customers.
- Building a product is like a 3D chess game — you need to think several moves ahead, on more than one level. Hedge your bets by mapping out multiple product pathways.
- Plan for scalability, add value with complementary features, and ensure your product can grow alongside your customers.
- Assemble an extended dream team in which each member brings unique strengths, propelling your product forward as you help them attain their own goals.
- Change enables opportunity. Embrace uncertainty, adapt to new challenges, and turn boulders in your path into stepping stones.

DO THESE NOW FOR QUICK WINS:

ANTICIPATE FUTURE NEEDS

Develop a simple worksheet to brainstorm potential future needs based on emerging trends, tech advancements and cultural shifts.

Set aside dedicated time to fill out the worksheet individually or as a team, focusing on identifying at least three potential future needs relevant to your product or industry.

CHANGE-FOCUSED USER FEEDBACK SESSIONS

Schedule a user feedback session within the next week to gather insights into evolving consumer needs and pain points. Target things that are changing most.

Prepare a list of open-ended questions about relevant changes you've noticed to guide the discussion, and encourage participants to freely share their experiences and insights.

Seek to learn how they see change affecting your product, and explore opportunities they see. Get excited about the potential change can bring.

COLLABORATION OUTREACH

Reach out now to one potential collaborator or partner within your network to explore opportunities for collaboration or knowledge sharing.

Schedule a brief intro meeting or call to discuss areas of synergy and how you might be able to work together in the future.

Keep it going. Use your learnings to plan the next meeting. Schedule it before the first one ends and make it even more productive. Imagine the progress if you continue this monthly, or even weekly.

AGILE EXPERIMENTATION

Identify one aspect of your product development process that's suited to experiment with using Agile methodologies, such as iterative prototyping or rapid iteration cycles.

Set a specific goal for the experiment and allocate resources and time to implement it within the next sprint or development cycle.

RISK ASSESSMENT BLITZ

Take 30 minutes to conduct a quick risk assessment for your product, identifying potential obstacles or challenges that could impact its success. Become a pessimist, just briefly.

Prioritize your top three highest risks and brainstorm strategies or contingency plans to mitigate their impact and ensure business continuity if they materialize.

TECH SCAN

Spend 15 minutes researching emerging technologies relevant to your industry or product.

What is leading today's tech news? How could that impact you?

Make a list of two to three new technologies that show promise for addressing unmet needs or enhancing your product's capabilities, and note how you might incorporate them into your roadmap.

EXPERIMENT DOCUMENTATION

Document one recent experiment or trial conducted within your team, including the hypothesis, methodology, results, and key learnings. Keep it simple but meaningful.

Share this documentation with colleagues and encourage them to provide feedback on the experiment's effectiveness and implications for future projects.

Acknowledgments

WRITING HAS ALWAYS been a gigantic part of my life. Fresh out of college with a journalism diploma, I co-founded a magazine publishing startup, where part of my job was designing ads. That gave me a taste of marketing and inspired to hang my agency shingle at the age of 24. I've since penned novels, screenplays, award-winning business columns, websites, and hundreds of blog posts. Most of it has been ghostwriting, which is fine. I don't mind the anonymity, and it's the process that I love most. But I've had a yearning to do something else.

This book incubated inside of me for a long time, and I'm glad to have finally got it into your hands. Many thanks are due.

First, my incredible wife, Tia, who deserves a medal of honor for how she's expertly managed our busy life around a multitude of projects. Thanks for putting up with my late-night creation frenzies, random bursts of inspiration when I ought to have been doing other things, and the occasional "I need to rewrite everything" meltdown. You're the real MVP here, and have all my gratitude.

Jennifer McIntyre, my editor *extraordinaire* — you're a whiz with words and structure. Your suggestions and encouragement have been the special ingredient that got this book from "meh" to "yeah!" Thank you for bringing so much fun and wisdom.

To my awesome team at Graphos Product — you all rock! Many of your brilliant ideas, passionate discussions, and our shared beliefs have found their way into this book in one form or another. Thanks for being the finest collaborators anyone could ask for.

And to all my clients over the last three decades — thank you for entrusting me with your products, your challenges, and your dreams. You've enabled me to make a living doing what I love. Every success, every stumble, and every "aha!" moment with you has helped to shape the ideas in this book. You're the bold heroes who take the big risks and pressure-test ideas and marketing theories in the real world.

To Alan Klement, Rob Fitzpatrack, Ian Chamandy, Patrick Renvoisé, Justin Jackson, and everyone I've interviewed, whether specifically for this book or for the *Product Knowledge* podcast, thank you for your time and insights.

Huge thanks to Alexander von Ness, for creating a book cover that so beautifully represents all the excitement and promise of a winning product.

Finally, and most essentially, to *you*, treasured reader — thanks for taking a chance on this book!

Whether you're a seasoned product leader, a startup maverick, or just someone curious about why we buy what we do, I hope you find many things here that spark your imagination and maybe even change the trajectory and impact of your work.

This book has been a passion project, fueled by curiosity, exercise endorphins, and my belief that any of us can create products that truly matter to people.

Thanks for being part of this enlightening, exciting journey.

If you enjoyed this book, please post a review or share it with fellow innovators. I hugely appreciate it!

Glossary

Addressable Market: The specific portion of a total market that a company can realistically target and serve with its products or services, considering factors such as geography, customer characteristics, and the company's capabilities.

Agile: A methodology in product development and project management that emphasizes flexibility, iterative progress, and rapid response to change. It involves breaking projects into small pieces and collaborating with customers to continually improve the product.

B2B (Business-to-Business)**:** Transactions or relationships between businesses, as opposed to between businesses and consumers (B2C). B2B often involves more complex decision-making processes and longer sales cycles.

CLIMB (Customer Life-Improving Mechanisms and Benefits)**:** A framework for mapping, scoring, and prioritizing product attributes that make it desirable and needed by buyers. It categorizes benefits into four ascending levels: functional, emotional, transformative, and transcendent.

Conversion rate: The percentage of visitors to a website or viewers of an advertisement who take a desired action, such as making a purchase, signing up for a newsletter, or downloading a resource. It's a key metric in measuring marketing effectiveness.

Coveted Condition: The desired long-term future state that a product helps a customer achieve, going beyond immediate functional benefits. It represents the aspirational outcome that motivates customers to buy and use a product.

Customer Jobs Theory: The idea that customers "hire" products to do specific jobs in their lives. This concept helps in understanding why customers make purchase decisions and how products can be designed to better fulfill these jobs.

Diffusion of Innovation: A theory that explains how, why, and at what rate new ideas and technology spread through cultures. It categorizes adopters into groups like innovators, early adopters, early majority, late majority, and laggards.

Dog brain: A metaphor for the limbic system of the brain, responsible for emotions, memory retrieval, and quick decision-making. In marketing, it refers to the part of the brain that makes impulsive, emotion-driven decisions.

Duration Neglect: A cognitive bias where people's judgments of experiences disregard the total duration of the experience, focusing instead on peak moments and the ending. This has implications for how products and experiences are designed and marketed.

Early Adopters: The second segment of customers to embrace a new product after Innovators. They are often opinion leaders willing to try new things and can be crucial in establishing a product's initial success.

Escape velocity: The point at which a product gains enough momentum to sustain its growth without constant marketing efforts. It's when organic growth and word-of-mouth become significant drivers of adoption.

Friction: Barriers or resistance that prevent or slow down a customer's decision to purchase or use a product. This can include complexity, high costs, or inconvenience in the buying or usage process.

Industry vertical: A specific sector or niche within a broader industry, used for targeted marketing. It allows companies to focus on customers with similar characteristics and needs within a particular field.

JTBD (Jobs to Be Done)**:** A framework for understanding customer behavior by focusing on the underlying job a customer is trying to accomplish. It helps in designing products that fulfill specific customer needs or "jobs."

Lock-in: A situation where customers become dependent on a vendor's products or services, making it difficult or costly to switch to a competitor. This can be due to high switching costs, proprietary technology, or the inconvenience of changing established habits or systems. Lock-in can create a barrier to adopting new products, even if they offer significant improvements.

MAYA (Most Advanced Yet Acceptable)**:** A theory suggesting that successful products balance novelty with familiarity to appeal to mass markets. It posits that products should be innovative enough to be exciting but familiar enough to be comfortable.

Mere-Exposure Effect: The tendency for people to develop a preference for things merely because they are familiar with them. This psychological principle is often used in marketing to build brand recognition and preference.

Natural mapping: A design principle where controls logically correspond to their intended outcomes, making products more intuitive to use. It relies on physical analogies and cultural standards to create interfaces that users can understand instinctively.

Need Neutralizers: Factors that diminish or negate the perceived need for a product, such as high costs, inconveniences, or design flaws. These can significantly impact a product's adoption and success.

No-Go List: A list of showstopper beliefs or characteristics that would make a prospect refuse to buy or be unqualified for a product. It helps in refining target audiences and avoiding wasted marketing efforts.

Peak-End Rule: A psychological principle stating that people's overall memory of an experience is disproportionately influenced by its most intense point (peak) and its ending, rather than the average of every moment of the experience. This has implications for product design and customer experience management.

Planning fallacy: The tendency to underestimate the time, costs, and risks of future actions and overestimate the benefits of the same actions. This cognitive bias can lead to overly optimistic product development plans and market predictions.

Segmentation: The process of dividing a market into distinct groups of buyers with different needs, characteristics, or behaviors. It allows for more targeted and effective marketing strategies.

Social proof: The psychological phenomenon where people follow the actions of others in an attempt to reflect correct behavior in a given situation. In marketing, it's often used through testimonials, reviews, and user statistics to influence potential customers.

Tank brain: A metaphor for the neocortex of the brain, responsible for rational thinking, analysis, and slower, more deliberate decision-making. In marketing, it refers to the part of the brain that makes logical, considered decisions.

The three selves: A concept describing three aspects of human consciousness — the remembering self (past experiences), the experiencing self (present moment), and the third self (hopes, dreams, and future aspirations). Understanding these can help in creating more effective marketing messages and product experiences.

Total Addressable Market (TAM)**:** The total market demand for a product or service, usually expressed as the revenue opportunity available. It represents the maximum potential market size if a company could serve all possible customers.

UGC (User-Generated Content)**:** Content created by users or customers of a product or service, often used in marketing to provide authenticity and social proof. This can include reviews, social media posts, photos, and videos.

UX (User Experience)**:** The overall experience of a person using a product, especially in terms of how easy or pleasing it is to use. It encompasses all aspects of the end-user's interaction with the company, its services, and its products.

Voice of Customer (VOC)**:** A research technique used to capture customers' preferences, expectations, and aversions regarding a product or service. It involves collecting and analyzing customer feedback to inform product development and marketing strategies.

Notes

Chapter 1: Decoding Consumer Needs

1 Emmer, Marc. "95 Percent of New Products Fail. Here Are 6 Steps to Make Sure Yours Don't." *Inc. Magazine*, 6 July 2018, https://www.inc.com/marc-emmer/95-percent-of-new-products-fail-here-are-6-steps-to-make-sure-yours-dont.html/.

Chapter 2: Birth of a Product Enthusiast

1 Hoffman, Reid. "How to Turn Skeptics into Fans: John Foley, Founder & CEO of Peloton", https://mastersofscale.com/john-foley/.

2 MakerBot Industries, LLC. "Fast Pedalling to Market: Peloton Used MakerBot to Prototype New Commercial Bike." MakerBot, ND, https://www.makerbot.com/stories/design/peloton-case-study/.

3 Carson, Biz. "Peloton CEO John Foley Faces the Skeptics Again: This Time, Buyers in Its $8 Billion IPO." *Forbes*, 26 September 2019, https://www.forbes.com/sites/bizcarson/2019/09/26/peloton-ceo-john-foley-faces-the-skeptics-again-this-time-buyers-in-its-8-billion-ipo/?sh=4103db3a4349/.

4 "Masters of Scale." Created by Reid Hoffman, episode 65, 25 August 2020. How to Turn Skeptics into Fans: Peloton's John Foley, https://mastersofscale.com/john-foley/.

5 Griffith, Erin. "Peloton is a Phenomenon. Can it Last?" *The New York Times*, 28 August 2019, https://www.nytimes.com/2019/08/28/technology/peloton-ipo.html/.

Chapter 3: Why "Want" Isn't Good Enough

1 Gourville, John T. "Eager Sellers and Stony Buyers: Understanding the Psychology of New-Product Adoption." *Harvard Business Review*, 1 June 2006, https://hbr.org/2006/06/eager-sellers-and-stony-buyers-understanding-the-psychology-of-new-product-adoption/.

Chapter 4: The Most Powerful Word in Marketing

1 Michel, et al. "Quantitative Analysis of Culture Using Millions of Digitized Books." Google Books, https://books.google.com/ngrams/.

2 Trentmann, Frank. *Empire of Things: How We Became a World of Consumers, from the Fifteenth Century to the Twenty-First.* Harper, 2016.

3 Johnson, Samuel. *A Dictionary of the English Language.* 6th Edition, 1785.

4 Trentmann, Frank. *Empire of Things: How We Became a World of Consumers, from the Fifteenth Century to the Twenty-First.* Harper, 2016.

5 Stearns, Peter N. *Consumerism in World History: The Global Transformation of Desire.* Routledge, 2001.

Chapter 5: The Psychology of Needs

1 McLeod, Saul. "Maslow's Hierarchy of Needs." *Simply Psychology*, 20 March 2020, https://www.simplypsychology.org/maslow.html/.

2 Gull, Nicole. "The Ultra-Viral Rise of Prime, the Internet's Favorite Sports Drink." *Wired UK*, 13 July 2023, https://www.wired.co.uk/article/congo-prime-sports-drink/.

3 Van der Stigchel, Stefan. "Daydreaming and Concentration: What the Science Says." *The MIT Press Reader*, 19 August 2022, https://thereader.mitpress.mit.edu/daydreaming-and-concentration-what-the-science-says/.

4 Gipson, Johnell. "Tom Hanks Says He 'Went Crazy' While Filming 'Cast Away' — 'When Wilson Was Born, I Had Dialogue with Him.'" *Showbiz Cheat Sheet*, 21 October 2020, https://www.cheatsheet.com/entertainment/tom-hanks-says-he-went-crazy-while-filming-cast-away-when-wilson-was-born-i-had-dialogue-with-him.html/.

5 McSween, Pierre-Yves. *Do You Really Need It?* Toronto, Random House Canada, 2018. p. 26.

6 Mecking, Olga. "Summary of *This is Marketing* by Seth Godin." Quartz, 4 February 2019, https://qz.com/1538408/this-is-marketing-by-seth-godin/.

7 Morse, Gardiner. "Decisions and Desire." *Harvard Business Review*, January 2006, https://hbr.org/2006/01/decisions-and-desire/.

8 Quartz, Steven, and Asp, Anette. *Cool: How the Brain's Hidden Quest for Cool Drives our Economy and Shapes Our World.* New York, Farrar, Straus and Giroux, 2015. Pp. 70-72.

9 Cross, Tim. "Did Gillette's 'The Best Men Can Be' Campaign Succeed? Here's What the Data Said…". *Video Ad News,* 17 January 2017, https://videoadnews.com/2019/01/17/did-gillettes-the-best-men-can-be-campaign-succeed-heres-what-the-data-said/.

10 Potkewitz, Hilary. "Headspace vs. Calm: The Meditation Battle That's Anything but Zen." *The Wall Street Journal,* 15 December 2018, https://www.wsj.com/articles/headspace-vs-calm-the-meditation-battle-thats-anything-but-zen-11544889606/.

11 Hofstede, Geert. "The Cultural Relativity of the Quality of Life Concept." *Academy of Management Review,* Academy of Management, 6 January 1984, https://doi.org/10.5465/amr.1984.4279653/.

12 Tay, L., and E. Diener. "Needs and Subjective Well-Being Around the World." *Journal of Personality and Social Psychology,* vol. 101, no. 2, 2011, pp. 354–365. American Psychological Association.

13 Ryan, R.M., and Deci, E.L. "Self-Determination Theory and the Facilitation of Intrinsic Motivation, Social Development, and Well-Being." *American Psychologist,* vol. 55, no. 1, 2000, pp. 68-78. American Psychological Association, https://psycnet.apa.org/doiLanding?doi=10.1037%2F0003-066X.55.1.68/.

14 Anderfer, Clayton P. "An Empirical Test of a New Theory of Human Needs." *Organizational Behaviour and Human Performance,* vol. 4, no. 4, 1969, pp. 142-175. ScienceDirect, https://www.sciencedirect.com/science/article/abs/pii/003050736990004X?via%3Dihub/.

15 Bump, Pamela. "Millennials vs. Gen Z: Why Marketers Need to Know the Difference." *Hubspot,* 11 December 2019, https://blog.hubspot.com/marketing/millennials-vs-gen-z/.

Chapter 6: How Our Brain Recognizes Need

1 Shell, Ellen Ruppel. *Cheap: The High Cost of Discount Culture.* New York, Penguin Group, 2009. Pp. 59-60.

2 Shell, Ellen Ruppel. *Cheap: The High Cost of Discount Culture.* New York, Penguin Group, 2009. Pp. 72-75.

3 Gill, Karen, and Kubala, Jillian. "Teen Brain Development: Timeline, Effects, Factors." *Healthline,* 18 April 2023, https://www.healthline.com/health/teen-brain-development/.

4 Renvoisé, Patrick, and Morin, Christophe. *Neuromarketing: Understanding the "Buy Buttons" in Your Customer's Brain*—Rev. & Updated. Nashville, HarperCollins Leadership, 2007. Pp. 5-8

5 Arminjon, Mathieu. "The four postulates of Freudian unconscious neurocognitive convergences." *Frontiers in Psychology*, 20 June 2011, https://www.frontiersin.org/articles/10.3389/fpsyg.2011.00125/full#h5/.

6 Morse, Gardiner. "Decisions and Desire." *Harvard Business Review*, January 2006, https://hbr.org/2006/01/decisions-and-desire/.

7 Berger, Jonah. *Contagious: Why Things Catch On.* Simon & Schuster, 2016. Pp. 108-113.

8 LaMorte, Wayne W. "Behavioral Change Models—Diffusion of Innovation Theory." Boston University School of Public Health, 2019, https://sphweb.bumc.bu.edu/otlt/mph-modules/sb/behavioralchangetheories/behavioralchangetheories4.html/.

9 Fadell, Tony. *Build: An Unorthodox Guide to Making Things Worth Making.* HarperCollins Publishers, 2022. Pp. 152-154

10 3 Iqbal, Mansoor. "Duolingo Revenue and Usage Statistics (2023)." *Business of Apps*, 17 January 2023, https://www.businessofapps.com/data/duolingo-statistics/.

11 Santanachote, Perry. "The Most Influential Products of the Past Decade." *Consumer Reports*, 26 December 2019, https://www.consumerreports.org/emerging-technology/most-influential-products-of-the-past-decade/.

12 Gauntlett, David. *Making is Connecting.* New York, John Wiley & Sons, 2018. P. 12.

Chapter 7: We Don't Need Another Apple

1 Holst, Arne. "Number of employees of Apple from 2005 to 2022." *Statista*, 4 January 2023, https://www.statista.com/statistics/273439/number-of-employees-of-apple-since-2005/.

2 Thangavelu, Poonkulali. "How Patagonia's Marketing Strategy Makes Sustainability Cool." *Investopedia*, 25 June 2021, https://www.investopedia.com/articles/personal-finance/070715/how-patagonias-marketing-strategy-makes-sustainability-cool.asp/.

Chapter 8: The Elements of Product Need

1 Hiskey, Daven. "The Accidental Invention of the Post-It Note." *Today I Found Out*, 9 April 2011, http://www.todayifoundout.com/index.php/2011/11/the-accidental-invention-of-the-post-it-note/.

2 Matheson, Rob. "'Personal thermostat' startup heats up for commercialization" *MIT News*, 27 September 2017, https://news.mit.edu/2017/personal-thermostat-startup-heats-commercialization-0927/.

3 Composto, Jordana, et al. "Thermal Comfort Intervention for Hot-flash Related Insomnia Symptoms in Perimenopausal and Postmenopausal-aged Women: An Exploratory Study." *Taylor & Francis Online*, vol. 19, 2021, no. 1, 2019, pp. 38-47, https://www.tandfonline.com/doi/full/10.1080/15402002.2019.1699100/.

4 Kim, Anna. "How Toms Went From a $625 Million Company to Being in Massive Debt." *Business Insider*, 27 December 2020, https://www.businessinsider.com/rise-and-fall-of-toms-shoes-blake-mycoskie-bain-capital-2020-3/.

Chapter 9: A Buyer in Need has a Job Indeed

1 Christensen, Clayton M., et al. "Know Your Customers' 'Jobs to Be Done.'" *Harvard Business Review*, https://hbr.org/2016/09/know-your-customers-jobs-to-be-done/.

2 Fadell, Tony. *Build: An Unorthodox Guide to Making Things Worth Making*. HarperCollins Publishers, 2022. Pp. 270-280.

3 Klement, Alan. *When Coffee and Kale Compete: Become Great at Making Products People Will Buy*. CreateSpace Independent Publishing Platform, 2018. Pp. 97-103.

Chapter 10: A Step Farther: The Coveted Condition

1 Roof, Katie. "MasterClass Raises $225 Million, Valued at $2.75 Billion." *The Wall Street Journal,* 13 May 2021, https://www.wsj.com/articles/masterclass-raises-225-million-valued-at-2-75-billion-11620905400/.

Chapter 11: The "Third Self" and Need

1 Kahneman, Daniel. *Thinking, Fast and Slow*. Toronto, Anchor Canada, 2011. P. 380

2 Perez, Sarah. "Meditation app Calm hits $2B valuation with fresh funding." *TechCrunch*, 8 December 2020, https://techcrunch.com/2020/12/08/meditation-app-calm-raises-75-million-hits-2-billion-valuation/.

Chapter 12: The Intersection of Goals and Beliefs

1 Shieber, Jonathan. "Impossible Foods confirms $500 million fundraising, has raised $1.3 billion in total." *TechCrunch*, 16 March 2020, https://techcrunch.com/2020/03/16/impossible-foods-confirms-500-million-fundraising-has-raised-1-3-billion-in-total/.

Chapter 13: Why Do I Need *This* Thing?

1 Mandin, Laurier. "Why Should I Choose Your Product? with Author Ian Chamandy." *The Product Knowledge Podcast,* Graphos Inc., 24 March 2020, https://graphosproduct.com/why-should-i-choose-your-product-with-author-ian-chamandy/.

2 Thaler, Richard H., and Sunstein, Cass R. *Nudge: Improving Decisions About Health, Wealth and Happiness.* New Haven, Yale University Press, 2008. P. 62.

3 Cialdini, Robert B. *Influence, New and Expanded: The Psychology of Persuasion.* New York, HarperCollins Publishers, 2021. P. 131

Chapter 14: Suddenly, You Need Bacon

1 Olson, Alexandra. "Oatly, the oat milk company, to go public." AP News, 23 February 2021, https://apnews.com/article/oatly-oat-milk-company-go-public-7bdf21f1e7f660b93700530e05e55b8b/.

Chapter 15: The Need for a Better Product

1 Dyson. "2020 Global Results." Dyson Newsroom, 25 March 2021, https://newsroom.dyson.com/news/2021/03/25/2020-global-results/.

Chapter 16: What's So Bad About the Status Quo?

1 "The status quo is very good…." *Seth's Blog,* Seth Godin, 19 August 2023, https://seths.blog/2023/08/the-status-quo-is-very-good.

Chapter 17: What the World *Doesn't* Need Now

1 Wakabayashi, Daisuke and Bowles, Nellie. "Juicero, Start-Up With a $700 Juicer and Top Investors, Shuts Down." *The New York Times,* 1 September 2017, https://www.nytimes.com/2017/09/01/technology/juicero-start-up-shuts-down.html/.

Chapter 18: What the World *Doesn't* Need Now

1 Aaker, David. "Why Did Segway Fail to Meet Expectations?" *Prophet,* https://www.prophet.com/2011/04/30-why-did-segway-fail-or-did-it/.

2 Hartung, Adam. "The Reason Why Google Glass, Amazon Fire Phone and Segway All Failed." *Forbes*, 12 February 2015 https://www.forbes.com/sites/adamhartung/2015/02/12/the-reason-why-google-glass-amazon-firephone-and-segway-all-failed/.

3 Golson, Jordan. "Well, That Didn't Work: The Segway Is a Technological Marvel. Too Bad It Doesn't Make Any Sense." *WIRED,* 16 January 2015, https://www.wired.com/2015/01/well-didnt-work-segway-technological-marvel-bad-doesnt-make-sense/.

4 Brooke, Chris. "Millionaire Segway tycoon dies in cliff plunge on one of his own scooters." *Daily Mail,* 27 September 2010, https://www.dailymail.co.uk/news/article-1315518/Segway-tycoon-Jimi-Heselden-dies-cliff-plunge-scooters.html/.

5 Cialdini, Robert B. *Influence, New and Expanded: The Psychology of Persuasion.* New York, HarperCollins Publishers, 2021. P. 247

6 Kahneman, Daniel. *Thinking, Fast and Slow.* Toronto, Anchor Canada, 2011. P. 252.

7 Mandin, Laurier. "Finding the (Real) Truth in Product Validation with Rob Fitzpatrick." *The Product Knowledge Podcast,* Graphos Inc., 11 December 2019, https://graphosproduct.com/finding-the-real-truth-in-product-validation-with-author-rob-fitzpatrick/.

Chapter 19: Needs vs. Resistance

1 Thompson, Derek. *Hit Makers: The Science of Popularity in an Age of Distraction.* New York, Penguin Press, 2017. Pp. 47-52.

2 Zajonc, Robert B. "Mere Exposure: A Gateway to the Subliminal." Current Directions in Psychological Science, vol. 10, no. 6, 2001, pp. 224-227.

3 Cialdini, Robert B. *Influence, New and Expanded: The Psychology of Persuasion.* New York, HarperCollins Publishers, 2021. P. 86.

4 Sherwin, Katie. "Natural Mappings and Stimulus-Response Compatibility in User Interface Design." Nielsen-Norman Group, 14 October 2018, https://www.nngroup.com/articles/natural-mappings/.

Chapter 20: Scaling For Needs

1 Netflix. "Netflix Investors: Quarterly Earnings." Netflix Investor Relations, 19 January 2023, https://ir.netflix.net/financials/quarterly-earnings/default.aspx/.

2 Brennan, Louis, and Garnsey, Elizabeth. "Netflix: A Case of Transformation for the Digital Future." *The European Business Review,* 17 September 2020, https://www.europeanbusinessreview.com/netflix-a-case-of-transformation-for-the-digital-future/.

Chapter 21: Compel Responsibly

1 Boone, Brian, and Cochran, Samantha. "What Really Happened to the McDonaldland Characters?" *The Daily Meal,* 11 September 2023, https://www.thedailymeal.com/1118167/what-really-happened-to-the-mcdonaldland-characters/.

2 Goldblatt, Mark. "6. Marketing Ethics: Selling Controversial Products – Good Corporation, Bad Corporation: Corporate Social Responsibility in the Global Economy." Milne Publishing, https://milnepublishing.geneseo.edu/good-corporation-bad-corporation/chapter/6-marketing-ethics-selling-controversial-products/.

3 Fairphone. "Fairphone's Impact." Fairphone, 2023, https://www.fairphone.com/en/impact/.

4 Fairphone. "Modular Design." Fairphone, 2023, https://www.fairphone.com/en/story/modular-design/.

5 Fairphone. "Social Impact." Fairphone, 2023, https://www.fairphone.com/en/impact/social-impact/

6 Fairphone. "Longevity." Fairphone, 2023, https://www.fairphone.com/en/impact/longevity/.

7 Abnett, Kate. "The 'ethical' Smartphone Maker That Takes Aim at the Industry's Shortcomings." Reuters, 14 March 2022, https://www.reuters.com/technology/ethical-smartphone-maker-that-takes-aim-industrys-shortcomings-2022-03-14/.

Chapter 22: Into a Need-Driven Future

1 Kaczmarski, Michal. "Which Company is Winning the Restaurant Food Delivery War? — Bloomberg Second Measure." *Second Measure,* 8 January 2024, https://secondmeasure.com/datapoints/food-delivery-services-grubhub-uber-eats-doordash-postmates/.

2 Bellis, Mary. "Inventing Play-Doh" ThoughtCo, 20 January 2020, https://www.thoughtco.com/who-invented-play-doh-1992323.

3 Hiskey, Daven. "Bubble Wrap Was Originally Supposed to be Wallpaper." *Mental Floss,* 16 November 2012, https://www.mentalfloss.com/article/13092/bubble-wrap-was-originally-supposed-be-wallpaper/.

4 Anderson, Leigh Ann. "Viagra: How a Little Blue Pill Changed the World." Drugs.com, 4 October 2023, https://www.drugs.com/article/viagra-little-blue-pill.html/.

5 "Sodium Bicarbonate Market Size, Share & Growth | Report, 2032." *Market Research Future,* https://www.marketresearchfuture.com/reports/sodium-bicarbonate-market-2632/.

6 Griffith, Erin. "How Sonos Is Building the Audio Internet." *Fortune,* 23 October 2018, https://fortune.com/longform/sonos-speaker-audio-internet/.

7 Pierce, David. "Sonos Doesn't Need to Be Amazon — Or Apple." *Wired*, 23 April 2017, https://www.wired.com/2017/04/sonos-platform-agnostic/.

8 Goode, Lauren. "Sonos' IPO Filing Shows Risks of Relying on Amazon, Apple and Google." *The Verge,* 6 July 2018, https://www.theverge.com/2018/7/6/17542168/sonos-ipo-filing-risks-amazon-apple-google-alexa/.

9 Pino, Nick. "Sonos Promises to Make Future Speakers More Repairable and Energy Efficient." *TechRadar,* 20 September 2022, https://www.techradar.com/news/sonos-promises-to-make-future-speakers-more-repairable-and-energy-efficient/.

10 Sonos, Inc. "Sonos Reports Record Fourth Quarter and Fiscal 2023 Results." *BusinessWire*, 8 February 2023, https://www.businesswire.com/news/home/20230208005624/en/Sonos-Reports-First-Quarter-Fiscal-2023-Results/.

11 "What is Agile? Agile 101." Agile Alliance, https://www.agilealliance.org/agile101/.

Index

V

W

Z

About the Author

LAURIER MANDIN is a product marketing expert with over 30 years of experience helping innovators create and sell products people truly need.

As the founder of Graphos Product, he's guided numerous startups and established brands to market success through need-centric product development and compelling marketing strategies.

With a deep understanding of consumer psychology and behavioral economics, Laurier brings a unique perspective to product creation and marketing. His insights have helped transform struggling products into market leaders and have launched many innovative products to commercial success.

Learn more, and advance your product every single day by subscribing to Laurier's daily emails at **lmandin.com**.

Printed in Great Britain
by Amazon

d72e84bf-665e-40eb-b94e-8a663e1f2cb2R01